'Kate Adams has been quietly crafting an wordlessness of traumatic experience. Her grasp of the workings of wounded minds an͟ ͟ ͟ ͟ ͟ ͟ ͟ ͟ ͟ ͟ ͟ ͟ ͟ ͟ ͟ ͟ ͟ Adams has a unique, fresh approach that is indeed attuned to how hurt gets so big that it can neither be consciously felt nor known, for example, her exploration of "dead thoughts." It's not too often that I read chapter after chapter with anticipation of learning something new. She has been incubating the work of many skilled clinicians, and the child who has emerged is playful, astute, broad-minded, self-effacing, and compassionate. Her language is highly accessible, and she puts on no airs, quite the contrary in a totally down-to-earth cultivated garden of organizing themes. I'm delighted with her gifts and you will be, too. When I encouraged her to write a book, I knew she had much to say, but honestly I had no idea how much my patients and I would benefit from her effort. Get a copy of her book, and say hello to the brilliance and humanity of Kate Adams.'

Richard A. Chefetz *is the author of* Intensive Psychotherapy for Persistent Dissociative Processes: The Fear of Feeling Real *(W. W. Norton, 2015).*

'Kathleen Adams has given us a remarkable compendium, integrating neurobiology, attachment theory, contemporary psychoanalysis and theories of group psychotherapy. The staggering breadth and depth of theoretical integration is impressive and necessary to grasp the subtle and profoundly complex ideas and patients Dr. Adams addresses. This book should be read widely and outlines important paradigm shifts in the way we think about trauma and shock.'

Paul LePhuoc *is a Clinical Assistant Professor in the Department of Psychiatry and Behavioral Sciences at Baylor College of Medicine.*

'Dr. Adams has an impressive art of weaving the early effects of trauma from the incubator to day-to-day life. She reviews case examples of the many clients/patients who seem to fall through the cracks of normal psychology and brings them to life through treatment and expressive story. I only wish that I would have had this resource available to me when I began my career of focus on Developmental Trauma. I not only see this as an excellent resource for post-graduates but also as a required text in both psychology and counseling programs. Dr. Adams' work again reinforces that we should not base our patient/client evaluations on first appearances.'

Stephen J. Terrell *is the founder of the Austin Attachment and Counseling Center and co-author of* Nurturing Resilience *(North Atlantic Books, 2018).*

'In this groundbreaking text, Dr. Adams describes the all-too-often unrecognized and unexplored internal experiences of individuals who struggle with developmental trauma. With clarity and sensitivity, she offers us a deeper understanding of the numerous and complex ways these clients suffer, despite appearing to function quite well in the world. Dr. Adams thoroughly synthesizes and illuminates concepts of neurobiology, trauma research, attachment theory, dissociation, and shame with many rich and moving case histories. She brings the theoretical to life on the page and leaves us hopeful for richer, more courageous conversations with our clients. She shows us what our clients need from us if they are to begin living more authentic and gratifying lives. This book is now on my list of must-reads for new clinicians—graduate students and supervisees—and study group participants.'

Allyson Jervey *is an LCSW-supervisor and former Adjunct Professor at the Steve Hicks School of Social Work, University of Texas. She is also the Director of Jervey and Associates Psychotherapy in Georgetown, Texas.*

Attuned Treatment of Developmental Trauma

This book takes a painstaking look at developmental trauma as it manifests in group, individual, and combined psychotherapies, tracking the growth of non-abused individuals who have courageously addressed overwhelming childhood experiences to make sense of the chaos in their lives.

The cumulative impact of repetitive stress, fear, and shame in childhood wreaks havoc on the developing brain, resulting in a life-long vulnerability to anxiety, despair, and dissociative moments that are often described as developmental trauma. Adverse childhood experiences are often overlooked by therapists. This book focuses specifically on the profound suffering of high-functioning private-practice patients who manifest developmental trauma from chronic shock, shame, and neglect. Adams offers a synthesis of diverse theoretical worlds in her study of adaptations to cumulative trauma, namely, relational psychoanalysis, the British school of object relations, trauma theory, neuroscience and interpersonal neurobiology, developmental psychopathology, and attachment theory.

Using richly detailed clinical material, this book provides invaluably clear examples to illustrate the effects of disorganized states in infancy, making it essential reading for psychoanalysts, psychotherapists and clinical psychologists working with traumatized patients.

Kathleen Adams has specialized in primitive states, dissociation, and developmental trauma since 1977. Extensive experience in inpatient settings complements her long-term outpatient psychotherapy practice with children, adolescents, and adults.

Psychoanalysis in a New Key Book Series
Donnel Stern
Series Editor

When music is played in a new key, the melody does not change, but the notes that make up the composition do: change in the context of continuity, continuity that perseveres through change. Psychoanalysis in a New Key publishes books that share the aims psychoanalysts have always had, but that approach them differently. The books in the series are not expected to advance any particular theoretical agenda, although to this date most have been written by analysts from the Interpersonal and Relational orientations.

The most important contribution of a psychoanalytic book is the communication of something that nudges the reader's grasp of clinical theory and practice in an unexpected direction. Psychoanalysis in a New Key creates a deliberate focus on innovative and unsettling clinical thinking. Because that kind of thinking is encouraged by exploration of the, sometimes surprising, contributions to psychoanalysis of ideas and findings from other fields, Psychoanalysis in a New Key particularly encourages interdisciplinary studies. Books in the series have married psychoanalysis with dissociation, trauma theory, sociology, and criminology. The series is open to the consideration of studies examining the relationship between psychoanalysis and any other field—for instance, biology, literary and art criticism, philosophy, systems theory, anthropology, and political theory.

But innovation also takes place within the boundaries of psychoanalysis, and Psychoanalysis in a New Key therefore also presents work that reformulates thought and practice without leaving the precincts of the field. Books in the series focus, for example, on the significance of personal values in psychoanalytic practice, on the complex interrelationship between the analyst's clinical work and personal life, on the consequences for the clinical situation when patient and analyst are from different cultures, and on the need for psychoanalysts to accept the degree to which they knowingly satisfy their own wishes during treatment hours, often to the patient's detriment. A full list of all titles in this series is available at:

www.routledge.com/Psychoanalysis-in-a-New-Key-Book-Series/book-series/
LEAPNKBS

Attuned Treatment of Developmental Trauma

Non-abused, High-functioning People Living Outside of Time

Kathleen Adams

LONDON AND NEW YORK

Cover image: sharply_done; gettyimages

First published 2023
by Routledge
4 Park Square, Milton Park, Abingdon, Oxon OX14 4RN

and by Routledge
605 Third Avenue, New York, NY 10158

Routledge is an imprint of the Taylor & Francis Group, an informa business

British Library Cataloguing-in-Publication Data
A catalogue record for this book is available from the British Library

Library of Congress Cataloging-in-Publication Data
Names: Adams, Kathleen (Kathleen Ann), author.
Title: Attuned treatment of developmental trauma : non-abused,
high-functioning people living outside of time / Kathleen Adams.
Description: Abingdon, Oxon ; New York, NY : Routledge, 2023. |
Includes bibliographical references and index. |
Identifiers: LCCN 2022007436 (print) | LCCN 2022007437 (ebook) |
ISBN 9781032201283 (hardback) | ISBN 9781032201306 (paperback) |
ISBN 9781003262367 (ebook)
Subjects: MESH: Psychological Trauma–therapy | Trauma and Stressor Related Disorders–therapy |
Adverse Childhood Experiences–psychology | Psychoanalytic Therapy–methods
Classification: LCC RC552.T7 (print) | LCC RC552.T7 (ebook) |
NLM WM 172.5 | DDC 616.85/21–dc23/eng/20220609
LC record available at https://lccn.loc.gov/2022007436
LC ebook record available at https://lccn.loc.gov/2022007437

ISBN: 9781032201283 (hbk)
ISBN: 9781032201306 (pbk)
ISBN: 9781003262367 (ebk)

DOI: 10.4324/9781003262367

Typeset in Times New Roman
by Newgen Publishing UK

Contents

Acknowledgments

To Les, for inspiring me to write
To Tod, for drenching me in love, security and blueberries
To Allyson, Gerry and Jan, for their steadfast support
To John, for being the captain of my ship
To Faith, for being the most patient editor in the world
To Rich, for all the ways you have of being you

Credits List

The author also gratefully acknowledges the permission provided to republish the following materials:

Kathleen A. Adams (2006). Falling forever: The price of chronic shock. *International Journal of Group Psychotherapy,* 56(2), 127–72. Copyright © the American Group Psychotherapy Association. Reprinted by permission of Taylor & Francis Ltd, www.tandfonline.com, on behalf of the American Group Psychotherapy Association.

Kathleen A. Adams (2011). The abject self: Self-states of relentless despair. *International Journal of Group Psychotherapy,* 61(3), 332–64. Copyright © the American Group Psychotherapy Association. Reprinted by permission of Taylor & Francis Ltd, www.tandfonline.com, on behalf of the American Group Psychotherapy Association.

Introduction

In this book we will share in the healing journeys of many brave souls who emerged from challenging beginnings. All the patient material is drawn from high-functioning, mildly dissociative individuals in my private practice, and has been altered to preserve their anonymity.

Theoretical material drawn from the accumulated clinical wisdom of relational psychoanalysis, traumatology, interpersonal neurobiology, and attachment theory illuminates their journeys. Throughout over 40 years of clinical practice, I have wandered through dark nights of the soul with many mentors: *In person* with Thomas Moore, Christopher Bollas, Philip Bromberg, Rich Chefetz, Thomas Ogden, Michael Eigen, Heinz Kohut, Bessel van der Kolk, Allan Schore, Dan Siegel, Lawrence Hedges, Diana Fosha and Otto Kernberg. *Self study* with John Bolby, D. W. Winnicot, Mary Main, Harold Searles, J. Grotstein, Julia Kristeva, Frances Tustin, Judith Mitrani, Peter Levine, and many more. (I will be referring to these clinical masters and their works throughout the book.) I sought to integrate the wisdom of disparate clinical voices across child and adult psychoanalysis, interpersonal neurobiology, child development, traumatology, systems of group psychotherapy, and affective neuroscience. Their teachings shone with brilliance, illuminating aspects of the black hole that I had not noticed before. Yet I was troubled by the politics of psychotherapy and the seemingly inevitable dogmatization that haunts every new breakthrough. Each is well grounded in partial truths, mirroring the parable of the blind men who struggle to

DOI: 10.4324/9781003262367-1

conceptualize the essence of an elephant via touch. Like the blind men with the elephant, every powerful clinician articulates profound truths about the fractured and shattered souls who appear in our office. The differences among these clinical geniuses melt away when understood through the lens of attachment disorganization and dissociative processes.

Many books address the understanding of severe dissociative disorders and profound abuse or the treatment of severe shock, but they do not explore the cumulative trauma of overwhelming experience that emerges from non-abusive environments. In this book I hope to touch your hearts and tune your "third ear" so that you will be empowered as a healer with these challenging but mostly invisible populations. Some of the clinical material you encounter may unexpectedly slip under your defenses and traumatize you a bit. Even though we aren't dealing with profound abuse in this book, clinical encounters with developmental trauma may be just as overwhelming to us as the suffering of those who were abused. Perhaps even more so. It is often harder to preserve distance from the pain in the clinical material when you don't know ahead of time exactly what to protect yourself against.

When I was chief psychologist at a children's psychiatric hospital, we received a little girl who was a refugee from Vietnam. She hid, shaking and terrified, beneath the covers and generally rebuffed all our efforts to reassure her; indeed, she bit and scratched us if we came too near. It took days to find a translator who could speak her dialect (at least five different variants of Vietnamese exist; hers, Cham, was the rarest). As the translator arrived her face lit up with joy as she exclaimed in Cham, "Finally someone who can understand me!" She threw herself upon the translator's lap and sobbed in relief. Within the week she was fortunately reunited with her family. I have heard the same refrain many times from patients who had seen three or four therapists before discovering me, or from individuals around the world who had never felt properly understood before reading my articles online: "Finally, someone who speaks my language!" This book is the culmination of my life's work. I hope you find it inspiring and thought-provoking.

Part I

Emerging from the Fog: Navigating the Wilderness of Developmental Trauma

Chapter 1

Our Pain Knows No Time

We begin by encountering the timelessness of pain from early childhood and examine the politics, art, and poetry that abound when early traumatic stress is front and center. This chapter bluntly challenges the denial and resistance of the psychotherapy professions to embracing the relevance of early trauma. For generations the cultural zeitgeist denied even the existence of child abuse. Although we have come a long way from those days, many clinicians are still oblivious to the relevance of other kinds of early childhood traumatization.

We examine the clinical struggles of high-functioning patients with developmental trauma and the difficulties they encounter, feeling misunderstood in many therapies. Helplessness, dread, terror, and chaos: these feelings inhabit the body "now" as implicit memories of infantile annihilation anxiety. The patients described in these chapters are not neurotic, character-disordered, or self-disordered. Developmental trauma disorder in non-abused patients can be viewed as some variant of dissociative disorder not otherwise specified (DDNOS) and/or complex post-traumatic stress disorder (complex PTSD). Patients who don't fit into traditional theoretical schema often fall between the cracks or land in impasse. The politics and Balkanization of psychotherapy contribute to this difficulty: One tends to "see" and "hear" only that which one is expecting. I examine truths and myths about resilience. I explore the incubation and sharing of horror by well-known artists, writers, and filmmakers, with a clinical nod to the utility of poetry and metaphor in capturing the essence of preverbal trauma.

Chapter 1 ends on a spiritual note. No one treads the path of the dark night unscathed. Although spirituality is a controversial notion in many psychotherapy circles, anyone who works in the field of trauma finds themselves eventually grappling with existential and spiritual questions, conundrums, agonies, and Gordian knots. Facing disintegration, breakdown, shattering, jolting, and shocking experiences takes courage: how much easier it might be to build a fortress to keep out the monsters. Yet the processing of unbearable early experience offers both destructive and creative opportunities for adult psychotherapy patients in their foray into the meaning of life. To borrow Eigen's metaphor, we step through disintegration threats like children stepping between cracks in the sidewalk to ward off horror and avoid fault lines in the personality (1998). What enlivens or deadens the self who encounters a true soulmate on this journey into the dark night? Answering that question is our calling, if we are up to the challenge.

Chapter 2

Our Pain Is the Crack in the Shell that Encloses Our Understanding

This chapter reviews what we know about attachment, cumulative trauma, neglect, and the Adverse Childhood Experiences study. Theoretical and research-based groundwork illuminate the depth of early traumatization in non-abused patients, paving the way for future chapters that are more clinical in focus. I start by touching upon the ubiquity of shock, panic, dread, and randomness.

Next, I examine the research about cumulative trauma from early overwhelming experience, attachment trauma, and other toxic stressors that disrupt our ability to discern safety and danger. This chapter explores rather thoroughly the literature on fear conditioning and disorganized attachment. Limbic resonance is emphasized as a necessary ingredient in working with early traumatization.

As the chapter moves into the experience of shock, especially attachment shock (Adams, 2006), neurobiology melds with psycho-analytic theory. While this literature is dense and relatively unfamiliar to most clinicians, it is essential to understanding the manifestations of early traumatization that are so frequently overlooked by therapists. I introduce the concept of attachment shock and explore various clinical manifestations linking attachment shock to second skin defenses, the broken container, and black hole phenomena.

Chapter 3

Retreat from the Body: Birth and Beyond

Detailed clinical vignettes illustrate the poignancy of developmental trauma from challenging beginnings. These challenges interfere with the hard wiring of vitality affects. Brain development skews toward surviving instead of toward thriving and exploring the world. I look first at birth trauma, prematurity, and adoption—everyday occurrences to be sure, but devastating to the survivors who rarely know enough to inform their therapist of their difficult beginnings in life. It really *does* affect ongoing development if one spends several months in a neonatal intensive care unit, for example. If a child was given up for adoption, that process creates lifelong ripples of abandonment no matter how hard we pretend that children are just resilient. Medical traumatization during childhood is the next focus, as I look into the psychotherapy of individuals who endured restraints, repeated surgeries, and traumatic accidents during their childhood.

Illness in the family takes a toll on the developing self as well. It is as if all the air were sucked into caring for the sick family member and the child is left in a vacuum, starving for air. Detailed case examples illustrate the coping mechanisms children use to survive a dying parent, a dying sibling, and a psychotic sibling.

This chapter closes with a review of the art and music of Joni Mitchell, an icon of brilliance in the music world. Her art and music contain shadows of polio, despair, and other challenges—hallmarks of subtle developmental trauma.

Chapter 4

No Safe Harbor: Children of Perdition

Here we delve into difficult subjects of dread, formlessness, and the structure of evil. This chapter explores the dark underbelly of chronic shock. I routinely ask new patients if they wish they could "wake up dead," and they greet this question with nervous relief until I explain the difference between wishing oneself were dead and making plans to die. "I was afraid you would think I was crazy, or hospitalize me" is the frequent reaction. Dead thoughts are qualitatively different from suicidal ideation. Dead thoughts speak to the sense of life as a perpetual nightmare that one cannot awaken from.

The chapter shifts to encompass five faces of shock, illustrated with detailed clinical examples. Shock is a somatic experience that is rarely recognized as part and parcel of the therapeutic process. The five faces of shock are:

- *Cephalic shock* (Lewis, 1981, 1983/2004, 2006). This shock is a kind of falling anxiety, a chronic state of disequilibrium due to insecure holding during infancy. Lewis, a body therapist, noted that individuals whose parents did not know how to hold them safely tend to develop lifelong patterns of tension in the neck and shoulders from trying to use these muscles prematurely to hold themselves against gravity.
- *Abandonment shock: The shock of being unseen, overlooked, or forgotten.* This kind of shock is the frozen form of attachment disorganization and separation anxiety, neurologically described as dorsal shutdown. "Ghosting" is a current, culturally sanctioned form of abandonment that is deeply distressing.
- *Shattershock: Disorganized torture, black holes, and the fractured container.* This refers to the explosive form of attachment shock endemic to disorganized attachment. The psyche shatters like glass in a windshield when a rock glances off it. Shattershock is the breaking of the mind under conditions of fright with no solution. The zone of shattershock is the legacy of parents who were never themselves parented in a secure fashion; they may be frightened by, oblivious to, or uncomfortable with, their childrens' intensity.
- *Soulshock: Horror and the structure of evil.* Soulshock is the terror of fear, the horror of nightmares coming true. This section touches upon issues of evil and dehumanization even in highly successful, non-abused patients. Two complex clinical examples of this structure of evil are presented. These examples illustrate the vulnerability of those with developmental trauma from neglect to predation and cruelty at the hands of others.
- *Potential shock: Dread.* The final section of this chapter deals with various forms of dread. Dread collapses the space between past,

present, and future and also the space between reality and fantasy. Detailed clinical examples illustrate the ubiquity and complexity of dread.

Chapter 5

Sometimes It Takes a Village: Treating Developmental Trauma in Combined Therapy

This chapter illustrates the use of combined therapies to help patients with developmental trauma. Group, individual, and art therapy have contributed to the healing of many patients. The combination of family illness and severe neglect is a major point of focus. I relate the therapy of two men raised in affluent families. One man raised primarily by nannies due to his parents' illnesses used the metaphor of being a "hamster in a cage." His story began in Chapter 4 to reveal how his background set him up for exploitation by others. The second man grew up with a mother addicted to tranquilizers and never developed any sense of self. Under the sway of "relentless hope" he sabotaged his present, his future, and ultimately his life. Neither of them had a reliable way of discerning safety or danger, and both suffered devastating life consequences from this deficit. We learn about the "dead mother" and come to understand the disorganizing effects of maternal despair on the development of children with severe illness in the family. We explore the interface of deprivation, neglect, and familial illness.

Part II
Group Therapy with Developmental Stress and Trauma

Chapter 6

Falling Forever: The Price of Chronic Shock

This chapter chronicles a year in the life of a therapy group with high-functioning patients who secretly felt disorganized and chaotic. An apparently resistant patient who grew up with unavailable parents used dreamwork to reveal the extent of her neglect and encapsulated dissociative states. A key point in this group occurred when I, as the therapist, made a serious error and apologized to the group. The impact of my apology reverberated in the group for months: no one had ever experienced repair before. This group marked my first recognition of dissociative features in non-abused patients.

Chapter 7

The Abject Self: Self-states of Relentless Despair

This chapter, adapted from Adams (2011), examines vertical splits and abject worthlessness, with clinical descriptions of deadness as a theme in dreamwork and life metaphor. The mechanisms by which attachment-oriented group psychotherapy can help instill hope, and counter deadness, chronic shame, and despair are illustrated in detailed clinical examples of patients with developmental trauma working in group to effect change and growth.

References

Adams, K. (2006). Falling forever: The price of chronic shock. *International Journal of Group Psychotherapy,* 56(2), 127–72.

Adams, K. (2011). The abject self: Self-states of relentless despair. *International Journal of Group Psychotherapy,* 61(3), 333–64.

Eigen, M. (1998). *The psychoanalytic mystic.* ESF Publishers.

Lewis, R. A. (1981). A psychosomatic basis of premature ego development. *Comprehensive Psychotherapy,* 3, 91–102.

Lewis, R. A. (1983/2004). Cephalic shock as a somatic link to the false self personality. Available at: www.yumpu.com/en/document/read/11428826/cephalic-shock-as-a-somatic-link-to-the-false-self-personality.

Lewis, R. A. (2006). Frozen transference: Early traumatization and the body-psychotherapeutic relationship. *USA Body Psychotherapy Journal,* 5(2), 18–25.

Part I

Emerging from the Fog

Navigating the Wilderness of
Developmental Trauma

Chapter 1

Our Pain Knows No Time

And He makes suffering his school of love
The memory of past anguish haunts our sleep
And drop by drop into the heart sinks deep.
Thus wisdom comes to man without man's will.

Aeschylus

This is a book about something many—even most—therapists have
little training in, and that is developmental trauma. In the fields of
psychoanalysis, somatic experience, and affective neuroscience, developmental trauma is becoming understood as being at the root of the
dysregulation, low self-esteem, anxiety, despair, dreaded relationship
problems, and other forms of suffering that drive people to seek us
out for psychotherapy. Why do your non-abused, high-functioning
patients say their lives are a mess? They describe growing up in relatively functional families, yet can't escape the uneasy sense that something is terribly wrong or is about to go terribly wrong. These are the
people who have experienced overwhelming stress from any number
of sources early in life and didn't get soothed during these stressful
periods. In this book we will examine all sorts of causes of intense distress in your patients that don't fit into our usual nomenclature: neurosis, personality disorder, or victim of abuse. Developmental trauma
is often described as "different" than shock trauma, which is generally presumed to occur after a major overwhelming experience (Isobel
et al., 2017). However, little has been written about the overlap
between cumulative relational trauma and the cumulative trauma of
chronic shock (Adams, 2006). In this book the term developmental

DOI: 10.4324/9781003262367-3

trauma focuses on the interface of cumulative stressors from both physical and relational sources, including interpersonal and chronic shock trauma.

Developmental trauma is the inevitable aftermath of unsoothed distress in the first few years of life. When high-functioning patients with undetected developmental trauma walk into their first therapy appointment, they invariably introduce themselves with haunting perplexity: "I had an ok childhood, no abuse or anything, my parents are great people, so why am I (such a mess, this unhappy, unable to commit)?" In this book I introduce a listening perspective that will help you work more deeply with the overwhelming affects and bewildering struggles of your private-practice patients, especially those that are difficult and confusing yet report no abuse in their backgrounds. In the course of depth therapy, these patients often reveal covert primitive ego states existing in parallel with sophisticated, mature functioning; puzzling somatic symptoms; daunting relationship dysfunction; and/ or a disconcerting lack of body awareness.

Why do so many high-functioning patients, without overt abuse history or significant character pathology, develop dissociative traits, transitory paranoid states, autistic enclaves, and vulnerability to disintegration? Why do these patients live in the chill of chronic apprehension, to the detriment of their ability to truly relax into peacefulness and play? These are not the self-disordered patients that Kohut worked with, although his patients had similar vulnerability to disintegration. These patients do not establish narcissistic transference relationships with their therapists, nor are they usually neurotic or character-disordered. These are patients with developmental trauma from unattuned parenting, depressed and anxious parenting, medical traumatization early in life, and other adverse events resulting in cumulative trauma.

Over my lifetime of work, about 30 per cent of my non-abused private-practice patients presented with the "hidden trauma" (Lyons-Ruth et al., 2006) of unbearable, unsoothed early experience. And from my years of consultation, it seems that this percentage holds steady in other therapists' practices as well. Yet therapists in general are unprepared to do the deep work required with these patients without excellent supervision in primitive states and dissociative processes.

Bromberg (2006) notes that early unsoothed developmental trauma derails lifelong stability and safety. "The reason that developmental trauma is of such significance is that it shapes the attachment patterns that establish what is to become a stable or unstable core self" (p. 6). In his foreword to Bromberg's next book (2011), Schore notes that the consequence of chronic developmental trauma is "…a progressive impairment of the ability to adjust, take defensive action or act on one's own behalf, and a blocking of the capacity to register affect and pain, all critical to survival" (Schore, 2011, p. xxiv).

Attachment researchers and psychoanalysts have come to the conclusions that, awful as chronic abuse is, under-responsiveness of the environment to early suffering is also devastating. Bromberg (2011) asserts that unhealed developmental trauma, the "shadow of the tsunami" from early life, is what both drives our private-practice patients to come see us and impedes their progress unless therapists are sophisticated in their understanding of dissociative structures, autistic enclaves, and clues about early developmental trauma.

The goal of this book is to heighten your awareness of unhealed developmental trauma and the pathways to subtle dissociative structures that developmental trauma engenders in your private-practice patients. Detailed clinical examples will hopefully enliven the theoretical material for you. Most therapists miss the subtle signs of developmental trauma and consequently do adequate—but not life-altering—therapy with this population because they don't realize what they don't know about their patients.

One of my favorite authors in 1994 (Chessick) wrote about complacency in therapists who feel that they have "arrived" at a level of competence. In his article "On Corruption" he chides especially midlife therapists for being complacent and stagnant, content with what they already know. They feel like "good enough" therapists and feel little need to keep up with new developments in their field. The "field" of psychotherapy is exploding with new information about adverse child experiences, traumatic experience, and developmental trauma. There have been many books written about working with abuse survivors but few about working through developmental trauma from the early years.

My expertise with recognizing and treating developmental trauma and subtle dissociative structures was influenced by four intersecting currents: (1) my many years working intensely with hundreds of children carrying the shadows of developmental trauma, both inpatient and outpatient; (2) 20 years of training in dissociation resulting from severe abuse and trauma that exposed clues about unspoken, unknown early trauma; (3) 40 years of working in psychoanalytic group therapy focusing on attachment and other developmental trauma; and (4) 7 years of studying developmental trauma specifically with international experts.

One of the foremost experts in both psychoanalysis and developmental trauma was Philip Bromberg, who died in 2020. Let's see what he has to say about all this.

> If we accept that developmental trauma is a core phenomenon in the shaping of personality then we also accept that it exists for everyone and is always a matter of degree. If that is so, then the stability achieved by even secure attachment is also a matter of degree. That is to say, everyone is vulnerable to the experience of having to face something that is more than his mind can deal with, and the differences between people in how much is unbearable is what we work with in the large grey area we call "developmental trauma" or "relational trauma."
>
> (Bromberg, 2011, p. 14)

> When a child suffers consistent nonrecognition and disconfirmation of her self-experience—the cumulative nonrecognition of entire aspects of self as existing—what happens is that developmental trauma and vulnerability to massive trauma become interwoven. In adulthood, the capacity to then live a life that is creative, spontaneous, stable and relationally authentic requires an extraordinary natural endowment, and probably a healing relationship…[offering] the restoration of felt legitimacy in the right to exist as more than an object in the mind of another, and release from torment by the illegitimatized "not-me" parts of self that haunt the corridors of the mind as a dissociated affective tsunami and take possession of life. *Wherever a developmental tsunami has hit, if left unhealed it has left a shadow. One lives with the shadow and, to one degree or another, it follows the person along the path to adulthood* (emphasis mine). Sometimes it accompanies the person

throughout life, held as part of a dissociative mental structure. The price paid for the protection afforded by a dissociative mental structure—the brain's proactive effort to foreclose the potential return of affect dysregulation associated with the residue of the relationally unprocessed trauma—is huge.

(Bromberg, 2011, pp. 4–5)

Pain from a stressful childhood exists outside of a temporal structure. When we "remember" something painful, the memory is usually unanchored in time. Since children do not establish a sense of time during their first few years of life, both emotional and physical pain endured in early childhood may well be endless as well as timeless. When such memories surface in later life they are not usually sensed as "from the past" but, rather, as explosive intrusions into the here and now. Hence the volatility of couples' fights, transference enactments, and the inexplicable power of body memories to sweep one away from oneself on a roller coaster into confusing chaos.

Implicit Memory

In memory research, the initial impact of an experience on the brain is called an "engram" (Schacter, 1982). Engrams include multiple layers of experience. For an adult, these include factual (knowledge); autobiographical (one's sense of self and one's memory in time); somatic (what one's body felt like at the time); perceptual (what things looked like, how things smelled); emotional (one's mood at the time); and behavioral (what one's skeletal muscles and viscera did at the time). Explicit memory concerns the first two layers of the engram—the factual and autobiographical; the next four layers are implicit memory. For an infant or very young child, all that is available is implicit memory, that which involves parts of the brain that do not require conscious processing during encoding or retrieval (Squire et al., 1993). Research has shown that infants are perfectly able to react to a previously fearful stimulus with distress, even though they do not have the ability to think, "Oh yes, I remember that was scary before."

Body memories, sometimes described as flashbacks, are specifically somatic and emotional. They are experienced as happening in the present. We do not have the sensation or cognitive awareness of "memories" when we experience these "memories in feelings," but they are deeply physiological states connected to our arousal states and nervous system. Implicit memories formed during toxic stress play a key role in our stress responses and sense of safety. Kohut (1971) described a key form of combined implicit/explicit memory which he called a "telescoping" memory. It is particularly useful to understand this kind of memory as a psychotherapist because you will encounter this phenomenon often. Imagine a collapsing pill cup, the kind you might buy in a drugstore. When a patient reports a "strong" memory from middle childhood, odds are good that they had several similar experiences earlier in life that elude memory entirely but were life defining. Like the rings of the pill cup, they echo across a lifetime.

For example, I have two strong memories from ages 4 and 12. Each involves being highly excited about something and having the excitement quashed in a moment. The first memory involved making up a song and dancing in excitement as I performed it for my mother. Unable to experience or resonate with delight, she barked at me to quiet down and go outside: "Stop that racket!" The second, telescoping memory occurred as I returned in sixth grade from a newcomers party for my new school. I had immediately been accepted by my peers and I was elated. Dropped off by a friend's mother, I rushed into the house eager to share the good news and was treated as if I were being completely insensitive and inappropriate. I was remonstrated about a lack of caring and rudeness and sent to my room in confused shame. As it turned out, my grandfather had suddenly died a few hours before and everyone was in shock and grief.

It was important in my own analysis to understand that these two memories, so strong in intensity, had rings of shadows going backwards and forwards throughout my life. Of course, I later married someone who had little tolerance for delight. On our honeymoon, after traveling for 14 hours to reach our island resort, we found the restaurant wouldn't open for 15 minutes. We hung out outside the restaurant door on a bench in paradise, with music playing loudly around us. When my favorite all-time song, "Under the Boardwalk" came over the loudspeaker, I started humming and dancing. We were alone in this outdoor lobby, and I danced "for" my new husband in a trance of ecstasy while the song played, entreating him to join me. He caustically told me to sit down because I was embarrassing him. This was a "telescoping" memory that captured a lifetime of disappointment.

Does Preverbal Trauma Exist?

Our profession's openness to the examination of early childhood experience is inexorable, inevitable, and necessary in light of the prevalence of trauma in world culture (van der Kolk, 2015). Breakthroughs in the study of right brain affective neuroscience and its applications to therapy (Schore, 2019a, 2019b) emphasize the role of early development in shaping our nervous system and identity. We need to embrace the recognition and treatment of the childhood trauma that resides in the hearts, brains, and viscera of our patients. Fifty percent of my practice steadily comprises high-functioning individuals with a profound early (but non-abusive) trauma background, who have completed several psychotherapies with an essential part of their "self" unacknowledged, unseen, unchanged, untouched, and unmoved by any previous therapy. They come to me from varying backgrounds but sing a common refrain: "I feel like my therapist was very helpful, but never really 'got' what I'm about, what my life is like, what I struggle with." They describe leaving therapy feeling slightly pathologized in inaccurate ways, although helped significantly to live better lives. At core, however, they all express a lifelong lack of recognition by their therapists of the crazy blend of strengths and vulnerabilities they contend with on a daily basis. The patients you will journey with in this volume all suffered from complex challenges early in life that were overwhelming, if not impossible.

> When we think of damaged bonds, we think of ties to one another, parent-baby bonding, links to self, other, universe. No one escapes damage to these bonds.... We make the best of damaged selves with a mixture of pushing past, ignoring, transcending, and trying to heal our sense of injury.
>
> (Eigen, 2002, p. 1)

Eigen continues, with a reference to Bion:

> At times one might say: "In the beginning there was catastrophe" (Bion 1967a)…writings give voice to the traumatized self. If Walt Whitman sings the body electric and catalogues joys of self, Bion details what it is like for self to be electrocuted and to continue as the remains.
>
> (Eigen, 2002, p. 29)

Theories have always held a blunt as well as a cutting edge for us in our profession: theoretical certainty crushes the life out of psychotherapy as quickly as it facilitates compliance in our patients. Tunnel vision of any dimension constricts the intuition and contracts the heart of the listener/analyst. Our patients come to us already stuck, stagnant, and boxed in by their own fears, structures, and templates; should we not meet them with open arms ready to come to know them in all the dimensions they bring with them and then learn to open precisely the doors to new freedoms that they spontaneously move toward?

My first analytic supervisors told me "Listen carefully, and your patient will tell you who he thinks he is and what he thinks he needs. But if you really listen with your eyes and your heart, your patient will teach you who he is, who you are to him, and what he needs from you in particular" (Robert Prall (1982), and Bernie Spector (1983), personal communications). Bion (1967a) asked us to encounter our patients unclouded by yesterday's visions, to listen with innocent ears, to let go of our theories that secure us firmly in our own identities so that we can stand on the edge of the unknown with our patients and discover possibility together. Unfortunately, all too many therapists prefer to stay experience-distant instead of experience-near, and nowhere is that truer than in dealing with complex developmental trauma patients with mild dissociative features.

Many therapists don't even think of their patients as "trauma patients" despite clinical histories of early neglect, separations, divorce, loss, adoption, hospitalizations, and/or dysfunctional families without enough love to go around. In 2017, I was invited to give a presentation on preverbal trauma issues to a gathering of very seasoned group clinicians. It used to be believed that early experiences can never be recovered or explored in psychotherapy, but many therapists have found this belief to be inaccurate. The reconstruction of preverbal experience was explored at length by Blum (1980) and Anthi (1983). At the time their work was considered controversial in analytic circles. Today, clinicians influenced by the confluence of interpersonal neurobiology (Schore, Damasio, Siegel), somatic practitioners (Kelleman, Kain and Terrell, Levine), relational psychoanalysis (Ogden, Bromberg), and trauma (Goodwin and Attias, the ACE Study, van der Kolk), and many others understand that early experience is definitely recoverable with a therapist who is paying attention.

Yet in that workshop of experienced clinicians, only one out of the 50 present believed they had a single patient with early, preverbal trauma in their practices. Instead, they diagnosed them in the fashion most familiar to them and inserted them into their groups, undertaking defense analysis, tackling characterological issues, and exploring underlying conflicts and fantasies. They knew very little about their patients, really. Their questions about "how would I handle this or that crisis in the group?" were frustrated over and over as I asked, "What do you know about this patient's early experiences? It all depends on context."

That workshop focused on group clinicians, but I encounter the same knowledge gaps in individual therapy practitioners—both psychodynamic and somatic. Somatic practitioners understand shock trauma and work from the bottom up to help patients live fully in the present, but sometimes overlook crucial aspects of their patients' early childhoods that would illuminate and clarify their self-understanding. Few psychodynamic clinicians today have a thorough grounding in child development and trauma theory and prefer to focus on the "adult in their patient," brushing aside annoying childlike self-states. One patient (who ended up in my office later after being fired for being resistant) annoyed her therapist (whom she adored) when she would become agitated by mis-attunement and needed to get up and pace while trying to communicate the chaos swirling inside her. Rigid protocols fail to permit our patients to unfold and reveal who they really are unless we broaden our scope and *ask* about early experience, *listen* for vertical splits such as subtle "me" and "not-me" states (Chefetz & Bromberg, 2004), and *look* underneath their surface presentation for the depth within.

Case Example

A seasoned therapist was presenting a difficult patient in study group for peer consultation. The patient had severely injured his back several years before in an accident and was on massive amounts of pain killers which failed to neutralize his pain sufficiently to enable him to live a satisfying life. His psychiatrist wondered if his pain was psychosomatic and referred him to therapy; painkiller prescriptions became contingent upon participation in psychotherapy. The patient attended therapy regularly, which took enormous physical effort and psychological stamina. His therapist reported that this patient seemed unwilling to participate in a satisfactory therapeutic alliance. He seemed constantly preoccupied with his pain and did not produce free associations. He expressed frequent suicidal ideation but said he would not act on his impulses until his mother, who lived in a distant town, had died because his suicide would grieve her terribly. Nonetheless he talked openly of suicidal fantasies, which the therapist felt anxious about. The patient said he enjoyed the therapy because it allowed him some human contact, the only contact he had during the week outside of work.

If the therapist questioned him about aspects of his life before the accident, the patient cooperated with exploration but returned to his pain at the beginning of the next session. The therapist felt the therapy was not "getting anywhere" and felt de-skilled by this patient's "resistance" to self-exploration and obsessive focus on his pain. The study group pointed out that this patient was dealing with physical and psychological trauma. In chronic pain patient's lives, the broader focus of "life itself" narrows to an hour-by-hour valuation of what can be managed. I asked whether the therapist had explored with the patient what response he was hoping for when he said "my back really hurts today," and the therapist replied, "no," that he saw the patient's single-minded preoccupation with his pain as a significant resistance that needed to be overcome, rather than an opening for deepening around issues of helplessness, absolute dependence upon the psychiatrist for pain relief and terror of its withdrawal, shame about his change in life station and diminished competence, and existential issues of fate, spirituality, locus of control, and what can be tolerated.

The therapist himself happened to injure his back, and during the next session the patient observed the therapist's wincing and asked him about it. The therapist joined with his patient around a brief exploration of the coincidence that both of them had hurt backs and wondered if their backs could talk to each other and what they might say. From that point forward, the therapy began to deepen. The therapist admitted it had never occurred to him to think of his back patient as a trauma patient before he discussed him in his study group and that this new conceptualization shifted his countertransference disappointment, inadequacy, and irritation with this patient markedly. Soon thereafter he learned that his patient had been hospitalized for weeks as a 4-year-old with a life-threatening case of chicken pox. In those days, parents were not allowed to room in. When asked directly about his experience, the patient was able to describe many horrors: the unbearable pain of his chicken pox, the discomfort of repeated IV insertions, the forlorn loneliness and feverish confusion of being on his own with strangers bustling about him, the screams of other children on the pediatric floor, and the frantic worry he could sense in his parents when they were allowed to visit. Had he not been asked about this experience, his panic about his pain would have been dismissed as hypochondriacal or simply mysterious.

Our Profession Cannot Face the Extent of Childhood Terror

We step over the bodies of the collapsed and dead children in our consulting rooms much like the hardened denizens of the big city step around the drunks and ignore the screams in the brownstone next door. We keep our work tidy and address the adults in our patients, the ones who can size up our predilections and match their dreams to our comfort zones. Therapists, even well-analyzed ones, flinch from the rawness of childhood terror, shock, and desperation. I have dear friends and colleagues who regularly shred the souls of their traumatized patients and in frustration send them to me to "clean up" the mess they have made of their patients' sense of self, their hopes, their dignity, and their dreams.

Trauma Is Not Simply Abuse or Catastrophe

The "big-T trauma patients" that are familiar to us, such as political refugees, disaster survivors, rape and assault victims, and even child-onset sexual assault victims don't fit well into our methodology, mess up our psychodynamic therapy groups, don't free associate well, don't particularly take well to "working in the transference," and generally make us feel incompetent and vaguely annoyed at their intransigence and resistance to doing "real" therapeutic work. Bollas (1989) courageously revealed that he gets depressed and disappointed when a patient finally summons the courage to reveal a sexual molestation.

When I am in such a situation, I usually think, "Oh, no! Not that," or "Well, that's the end of an interesting prospect," or some such response.... I know I always feel a depression when I hear this news, and this mood is not, I confess, an act of empathy. It is not because I feel sorrow for the victim. Instead, I am disappointed over the (apparent) ending of the analytic.... Just as the patient's heavy declaration ends my right to imagine my patient in many ways, to reflect on many issues, to get lost on tangents of speculation, to play with representations. No! I must stick to the fact: the actual event. It is to dominate, control, and centre the analysis.

(pp. 179–80)

However, when patients approach us with stories of early deprivation, neglect, and chaos, we often interpret "upward," focusing on conflict and character, and then go home to our full lives and families without a clue that we are missing the point. The point, as you shall see, is that we are working with people who are falling into an abyss, and we are making polite conversation about their defenses and fantasies while they continue to fall, shatter, and shake. Meanwhile our patients with subtle early trauma experience are so desperate for a secure attachment experience that they collude with our roadmaps, willingly fantasize, earnestly explore conflicts, and stolidly work on their character flaws.

Developmental trauma patients certainly can present with conflict and characterological issues, but it is important to note that a fair percentage of these patients have dissociative symptoms, suicidal ideation, and the like and yet have very little core character pathology. Their defensive structure is different than the preoedipal patients addressed by Spotnitz (1976) whose core themes in therapy center around self-hatred and resistance analysis. Nor are they self-disorders, establishing a narcissistic transference like Kohut's patients. Rather, their core issues are body-centered: terror, attachment security, dissociative mechanisms, vertical splits (side-by-side self-states), and vulnerability. Being able to stand being alive, tolerating indescribable dysregulation, shame about needs for attachment, and confusion about why relationships are so difficult end up being the central themes they wrestle with.

Their life stories are sometimes underwhelming or confusing at first, which is why many therapists miss the subtle signs of developmental trauma. They may not be able to present a coherent narrative about how they manage such high functioning in some areas of their lives but not others.

> Because developmental trauma, by its very nature, occurs when we are experiencing more nonverbal stages of development, the underlying narrative of that essential story is often hidden and intertwined with later experiences that make the foundational impact of the events of our early lives.... The narrative of developmental trauma is inextricably interwoven with our physiology, our experience of safety or lack of safety, and our experience of connectedness or isolation....
>
> (Kain & Terrell, 2018, p. 153)

These patients often start out therapy with readily apparent vertical splits (side-by-side self-states instead of repressed) and a unique combination of high work achievement and capacity to develop a strong therapeutic alliance alongside an unusual vulnerability and lack of a rigidified defensive structure. Their self-esteem is visibly fragile, and they shatter easily when misunderstood. Their key struggles center on existence, safety, annihilation anxieties, existential and spiritual concerns, and bottomless despair paired with incredible resilience and capacity for hope. Relational *needs* rather than *desires* for gratification are at stake.

> What may be most crucial is neither gratification nor frustration, but the process of negotiation itself, in which the analyst finds his own particular way to confirm and participate in the patient's subjective experience yet slowly, over time, establishes his own presence and perspective in a way that the patient can find enriching rather than demolishing.
>
> (Mitchell, 1993, p. 196)

These patients are exquisitely sensitive to characterological countertransference enactments by their therapists such as arrogance, evasiveness, false-self presentations, hostility, condescension, a need to distance through intellectualization, and especially disingenuity. They tend to work deeply, bravely, and honestly with a therapist who meets them with equal emotional depth, authenticity, courage, and honesty.

Politics and Science

I continue to be troubled by the politics of psychotherapy and the seemingly inevitable dogmatization that accompanies each new break-through. Throughout time, wisdom becomes corrupted by ego and politics, and, as in Antoine de Saint-Exupéry's *The Little Prince*, a new genius author becomes the new "king." 'Tis the nature of science to advance cyclically, with much human protest, and to retreat amidst new developments. Innovations in science, especially with the breakthroughs in information technology, are now facilitated by invisible and informal networks, with the more formal networks of science defining research priorities and controversies (Brown et al., 1998; Crane, 1972).

> An innovation is typically a recent publication or group of publications concerning a particular question that captures the interest of a diverse group of [theorists] across institutions and sometimes across disciplines…so that an informal research group begins to coalesce around the idea.
>
> (Brown et al., 1998, p. 433)

Paradigm shifts shake up the order of things, turn known frontiers upside down, and evacuate containers into the void once again. Psychohistorians might say we tend to lose our balance only to recover it again a year or a decade later as, for some individuals, the new knowledge or ideas rapidly become assimilated into the old body of wisdom. Polarization divides the rest of the scientific community, and bitter feuds develop over therapeutic certainties.

Rutan (1992) likens our fierce adherence to one or another scientific faith/belief system to the social systems of churches:

> …as we select one of the various "churches" within which to practice and become learned in the mystical writings and secret languages of our chosen faith, we then become schooled in the particular rituals of that system. In our field we refer to these as the techniques of psychotherapy. Technique always follows and is rooted in theory. This is the same mentality as religious sects,

distrusting those from different camps, especially the unsaved who begin from very different assumptions than ours.

(p. 12)

A good example of this sect-like mentality is the fact that developmental trauma disorder has yet to be recognized as a diagnostic category. Since 2009, trauma specialists (van der Kolk and d'Andrea, 2010) have used "developmental trauma disorder" to describe complex trauma in childhood that interacts adversely with attachment trauma. Unresolved traumatization interacts with developmental stress and chronic adaptations to serial trauma. This leaves little time for recovery, and later developmental periods are compromised. Van der Kolk and others have been researching "disorders of extreme stress" in children for decades. Together with the National Child Traumatic Stress Network, they have proposed that Developmental Trauma Disorder be officially included in diagnostic manuals, only to be met with spurious claims of insignificant research, despite multiple available studies.

The politics of science and big Pharma may be involved in the resistance to such an obviously useful diagnostic categorization. It is curious indeed why even the profoundly abused and neglected children that comprise van der Kolk's target population fail to be taken seriously as a community health problem. Instead, these children are diagnosed with attention deficit hyperactivity disorder (ADHD), reactive attachment disorder, bipolar disorder, oppositional defiant disorder, and other medicalized diagnoses.

> It is ironic that people with complex trauma histories probably make up the bulk of patients seen in mental health centers, yet they remain nameless and diagnostically homeless....The clinical wisdom that results from intimate exposure to chronically traumatized people continues to be largely anecdotal and transmitted in supervision sessions, small conferences, and informal discussions among colleagues. Because dissociation is of little interest to mainstream psychology and psychiatry, it is not being systematically studied....
>
> (Lanius et al., 2010, p. 65)

If we are honest with ourselves and not corrupted by complacence, no matter how well read we are, we are still using up formidable amounts of intellectual and emotional energy trying to comprehend and cope with unbearable experience. In the face of *the impossible* we are led kicking and screaming into the architecture of our own private abyss. It is not possible to emerge unscathed and unshaken by such experience unless we either dissociate from our patients (by falling back on our favorite explanatory theory or feeling sorry for them), or fall back on the clinical gymnastics and pyrotechnics of trying too hard to "help" them. Door number ONE more often than not leads to rupture in the therapeutic alliance or stagnant psychotherapy; door number TWO nearly always ends up in a disastrous mess.

Truths and Myths about Childhood Resilience

As we shall see in Chapter 2, adverse childhood experience can be mitigated somewhat by both internal and external sources of resilience. However, as Terr (1990) discovered in her long-term work with kidnapped children, adult clinicians are likely to write off children's apparent well-being after traumatic experience with the aphorism: "kids are resilient," unaware that dissociative defenses and fortresses of terror and despair lie underneath. This phenomenon was explored in a 2020 PBS documentary "The Windemere Children: In Their Own Words" (Arthur et al., 2020, Directors), which followed the lives of 300 traumatized Jewish child refugees who had been orphaned during the Holocaust and brought to an English estate for art therapy and healing. Siegel (1999a) notes,

> If the capacity of the mind to adapt remains into adulthood, then the emotional relationships we have throughout life may be seen as the medium in which further development can be fostered. These attachment relationships and other forms of close, emotionally involving interpersonal connections may serve to allow synaptic connections to continue to be altered, even into adulthood.
>
> (p. 86)

Higgins (1994) asked 30 seasoned clinicians to find 40 highly resilient people from their lifelong practices for her to study in depth. These adults had all had brutal childhoods, yet had managed to create successful lives of hope and happiness. After elaborate interviewing and study, several theoretical constructs emerged about resilience:

(1) Growth is an active process of constructing and organizing meaning throughout the life span. "The resilient demonstrate robustly the human capacity for stubborn, determined expansion of the self" (p. 68).

(2) Understand the resilient individual on the basis of his highest level of functioning: "Like an extensive set of Ukrainian nesting dolls, we are a collection of selves, simultaneously encompassing all of our previous versions yet understood by the most recent 'us' through the assumptive lens of our current developmental complexity" (p. 70).

(3) We all need holding environments in the spirit of Winnicott's astute observation that there is no baby without a mother; there is no adult without a "holding environment" of culture, friendship, community, workplace, and social structure to foster his growth. Clearly one factor that helps fortify resilience is having had some figure available to one early on: a neighbor, a preschool teacher, a grandmother, even loving pets, who brought consistent light and hope into an otherwise bleak life.

When Higgins interviewed the resilient individuals about what else enabled them to survive the hellholes of their childhoods with hope intact, several factors stood out:

(1) Their ability to recruit surrogate families or surrogate parents and to be "adopted" throughout later childhood and adolescence by neighbors, friends' families, and other adults who could see their uniqueness as young individuals and took the heart, time, and energy to invest in them.

(2) Presence of peer groups, ever increasingly today replacing the traditional family structure in fractured families where love is on a strict ration. Such groups often exert a powerful socializing and healing influence on youngsters scapegoated or neglected by their families.

(3) Influence of books, movies, and television shows that mobilize the imagination, talk about feelings, and become a personal, immediate,

and sustaining relationship matrix. Clusters of adolescents watch "TV du jour" together and analyze the characters and their own reactions to the programs, learning a bit about themselves in the process. Adolescent programs these days are geared toward group and family dynamics. Feelings are discussed openly, the unsayable is said, unlike the milieu in their families of origin where nothing "real" might be said unless Dad is drunk.

(4) Using their imagination to develop a "faith system" that prizes human relationships, personal growth, humane relationships, spiritual influence of some form, and personal responsibility.

(5) Activism of some kind seems to be a root value around which their evolving faith system can crystallize. "What does not kill you, makes you stronger." These individuals have a deeply felt code of honor, ethics, and interdependence.

6) Possession of a strong vision of the future, with realistic hopes, dreams, and plans to move closer to bringing parts of the vision into reality.

The Incubation and Sharing of Horror: Art and Storytelling

Although life's blessings can mend some of the rifts and tears in the "psychic skin" (Anzieu, 1990) of early childhood, childhood traumatic experiences involving panic, disorientation, terror, and horror leave indelible fingerprints on the psyche that neither time nor experience can erase. Traumatic terror, shock, confusion, dizzying disorientation about real/not real—these are feelings that Alfred Hitchcock, Edgar Allan Poe, Stephen King, and various artists have invited their audiences to "taste" and master vicariously (Terr, 1990). Nowhere is this more readily apparent to us than in art, film, and creative writings of genius.

Artists

Sometimes, art seduces, soothes, loves with abandon, and calms, as in a Monet watercolor. Other art does not lull, it alarms. Traumatic art doesn't pass time quietly, it rages, erupts, disconcerts, gnashes its teeth, shakes, and breaks us. Horror is contagious.

Freida Kahlo had a physically traumatic life. In early childhood she had polio: nothing is so horrifying as the iron lungs children were placed in, usually without much consistent parental presence. In 1925, Kahlo was injured so seriously in a bus accident that she had to undergo 30 medical operations in her lifetime. Brilliantly gifted, she created harrowing works of art.

Edvard Munch's most famous painting is "The Scream." He wrote that sickness, madness, and death were the black angels that guarded his crib. His work is often characterized by despair and anguish. Goya was tormented by fears of death and madness. He and his wife suffered multiple miscarriages, but we know little of his early life. His series of "Black Paintings" was morbid and full of despair. Van Gogh, who committed suicide by gunshot at age 37, was given the name of his stillborn brother who had died a year before Vincent's birth. He was unhappy as a child when he was sent away to a series of boarding schools. In letters to his family, he described his youth as austere, cold, and sterile. After struggling with mental illness and difficulties in self-care, he spent time in and out of asylums. His last words were "The sadness will last forever."

Terr (1990) writes about the life and art of the Belgian painter Rene Magritte, who was 14 years old when his desperately depressed mother committed suicide. The sons of the family were "in charge" of keeping an eye on her in the middle of the night lest she slip away and do herself in—an impossible burden. One night she drowned herself, and the impact of seeing her body is memorialized in Magritte's life works of art: the river, the nightgown, the coffin, and her awful face, mutilated, swollen, and ugly. What Magritte does, Terr explains,

> ...is to establish the emotional tone of trauma. He remembers his own trauma—behaviorally, at least. He then hands it to his viewer. A horror, sudden and unexpected, is infected into the most serene of [his] landscapes, the most perfectly drawn and realistic of settings. The juxtaposition of real and horrible tends to jar the onlooker. Inside the viewer's mind, a small aliquot of psychic trauma sneaks in. The trauma lasts for just an instant. But the viewer may be sorry that he stopped to look. One cannot get rid of the Magrittes simply by leaving the museum.
>
> (Terr, 1990. p. 188)

Writers and Filmmakers

Terr (1990) also studied the writings of Stephen King and the films of Alfred Hitchcock to understand the facile manner in which they infuse their audience with post-traumatic contagion. Terr, who has spent a lifetime studying the long-term effects of childhood trauma, believes that since horror is contagious, writers such as Hitchcock and King must "release their own childhood horrors back into the external world from whence they originally came" (1990, p. 49). These creative acts of imagination combine both defenses of passive into active and projective identification. Hitchcock was locked into a prison at age 5 to "teach him a lesson" and his films are haunted and hounded by images of wrongful imprisonment and horror. About King, Terr says:

> Stephen King, a traumatized child, closely mimics the sensations of psychic trauma in his writing. Abandoned by his father at age 2, he reportedly witnessed a friend die by being hit by a train but was never able to remember the incident. He gives the reader the sensations of trauma and then leaves the reader dangling alone with these sensations.... In general, King's techniques appear unconsciously set up to mimic the sensations of "everyday routine" in the reader's mind. He forces the reader to identify with the about-to-be-traumatized characters, then King winds up...and blasts his reader out of his seat with something that wasn't supposed to happen—something unexpected, shocking and overwhelming.
>
> (p. 331)

Stories convey powerful truths, often with great subtlety. One patient, seizing eagerly upon a throwaway remark I made about the idea of something called "a second skin," rushed to recount his favorite childhood chapter-book story about a lobster who had to shed his shell. The lobster felt horridly vulnerable, you see, but none of his friends understood his anguish or terror. They did not need shells to survive, as he did. As my patient did. We spoke about that lobster for the next 6 months.

It is in metaphors like the lobster story that preverbal material resonates most deeply. When *Fantasia 2000* was released, a number of patients spent large parts of their sessions talking about three pieces on the DVD edition. One involved mothering, merging, vitality affects, and separation anxiety; one involved catastrophic destruction and a strong father presence; one involved loss and the afterlife. All three pieces were deeply spiritual without being the least religious.

Poets

Metaphor and poetry allow us to open to subtle realms of transformational archetypes, dream language, and the synthesis of the spiritual that mere verbal discourse can never approximate. Like Ogden and other analysts, I have turned to poetry to convey somewhat the paradoxical and complex nature of this subtle realm I am inviting you to explore with me. Ogden wrote:

> In my own efforts to become an analyst—a struggle I face in every analytic session—I look not only to the work of other analysts but increasingly to the work of poets...in an effort to bring to the senses through the use of words all that is human.
>
> (2001, p. 294)

Like poetry, psychotherapy work with developmental trauma relies upon metaphor to capture a depth of human experience that mere "discussion" can only simulate. Without the spirit and soul of metaphor and the transcendence of emotional presence, preverbal work on the intellectual level is like the Möbius strip: no matter how far one explores, one is still on the surface. Psychotherapy moves through developmental levels like weather moves through the coastal mountains: dropping some rain here, uprooting some trees there, leaving trunks charred by lightning strike elsewhere, with snow at the altitudes. Like the figure–ground illusion of the lady and the vase, the analytic eye moves back and forth between unfolding layerings of vision, nuance, and meaning. At its essence, psychotherapy with developmental trauma becomes a gradual unfolding of authenticity, realness, and groundedness: a graceful dance of exit from a time warp or wormhole of past horrors.

Charles Simic, a Yugoslavian poet who was sensitized at a very young age to the cruelty of man and the randomness of fate, writes evocative poetry that conveys the theater of the absurd and a sensitivity to terror.

Simic's poetry conjures the unbearable nature of preverbal and developmental trauma: echoes of chaos in the lived felt sense. Like all great authors, Simic wrote about what he knew best. At age 3 he was hurled from his bed by an exploding German bomb, and then subjected to the vagaries of war trauma. He and his family were forced to evacuate their home several times to escape bombings.

In interviews, this Poet Laureate explains that he envisions poetry as a visceral time machine, a portal to early experience that eludes narrative and linearity. He says that growing up as a child in war-torn Europe shaped much of his world view. Being one among millions of displaced persons made an impression on him that he could never shake off. The vileness and stupidity that he witnessed in his life imbues the heart of his poetry. He has won many prizes for his poetry collections, including the Pulitzer in 1990, the Wallace Stevens award in 2007, and the Frost Medal in 2011. His poetry is stunning, a doorway into Twilight Zones of the heart.

> Nearest Nameless
> So damn familiar
> Most of the time,
> I don't even know you are here.
> My life,
> My portion of eternity.
>
> A little shiver,
> As if the chill of the grave
> Is already
> Catching up with me–
> No matter.
> Descartes smelled
> Witches burning
> While he sat thinking
> Of a truth so obvious
> We keep failing to see it.
>
> I never knew it either
> Till today.

When I hear a bird shriek:
The cat is coming,
And I felt myself tremble.

> "Nearest Nameless," p. 157 from *The Voice at 3:00 AM*
> by Charles Simic. Copyright © 2003 by Charles Simic.
> Reprinted by permission of Mariner Books,
> an imprint of HarperCollins Publishers.

Trauma and the Shaman

The compelling aspect of current day understandings about interpersonal neurobiology, affective neuroscience, and post-traumatic growth may be subtle invitations to follow the shamanic tradition with its richness; mystery; vastly tangled complexity; intermingling of past, present, and future; and interplay among heart, body, mind, and spirit. Masud Khan captured somewhat the physicality and viscerality of shamanic work in his chapter "To Hear with Eyes" (1974), asking of us that we work with all our senses and be open to the impossible, the unusual, and the unexpected. This journey is a demanding one, not for the faint of heart. The work itself is draining, at times terrifying, and always unnerving. One cannot accompany a patient on a spiritual path through despair and horror into uncertainty and the abyss without being touched, shaken to the core oneself. So how does one sit with the shattered souls of individuals with developmental trauma? Patiently, for within pain of dreamtime sits still. You must summon the tender strength that comes from openness to your own deepest wounding. You must have conviction that by invoking the courage to face it down, even those with the deepest wounds will emerge stronger than before (adapted from Steele, 1989). Without therapeutic attention to the spiritual realm, the psychoanalytic tapestry woven in psychotherapy with people who are haunted by childhood traumatization will come unraveled again and again. Mitrani (1996) cautions:

> Hamilton (1990) reserves the word trauma "for responses to events which arouse in most of us intense feelings of horror, a sense of outrage and very often a feeling of revulsion and turning away. We would rather not know and hear" (p. 74)...as therapists we

might often rather turn away in order to insulate ourselves from such trauma, as have our patients who suffered the insult of catastrophic events at those moments in time…when they were ill-prepared to do otherwise. We must always be aware of our own as well as our patients' limitations, the threshold of our intolerance of the horrific, the outrageous, and the revolting, especially our own tendency to turn away from or perhaps to "abjectify," to hurl away, or to cut off our patients' communications prematurely when these threaten to debride our old wounds, long ago scarred over and forgotten.

(p. 202)

What we struggle to intercept is the perpetuation of an intergenerational trauma spiral so familiar to all of us, from our patients to their children, down to their children's children. The nascent infant brain struggles to make meaning out of malevolent, accidental, or even random parental discharge events. Trauma researchers are finding that it is not easy even for adults to process traumatic events as integrated experiences:

The normally integrated components of experience for adults include both somatic and mental elements—affects and sensations from the body, thoughts, images and cognitive mechanisms in the mind, as well as a mysterious "meaning" dimension, which has to do with whether something can be integrated as a part of one's personal identity and narrative and narrative history. Related to this dimension of meaning, and rarely discussed by clinicians, is that animating spirit at the center of all healthy living. This spirit, which we have described as the transcendent essence of the self, seems to be compromised in severe trauma. It is never annihilated completely because, presumably, this would be the literal death of the person. But it may be "killed"…in the sense that it cannot continue living in the embodied ego.

(Kalsched, 1996, p. 37)

In his case studies of abused and neglected patients, Sheingold (1989) aptly called this "soul murder." Levine (1997) speaks movingly of the need for rituals to call back the dissipated fractured pieces of the human spirit from the etheric universe after a traumatic shattering.

Van der Kolk and his colleagues have learned how important it is for traumatized individuals to master their helplessness and sense of vulnerability by trying to make meaning out of their experiences. In conversation with Bessel van der Kolk, Turner (2017) argues that psychotherapy of trauma also must address the spiritual and philosophical beliefs that are central to individual identity and motivation.

"Throughout history, gifted humans have transformed the negative effects of trauma...shamans are chosen by their communities precisely because they stared down suffering or death and returned from the trauma stronger and able to guide and heal others" (Korn, 1997, p. 7). Trauma is frequently understood to be uncontrolled, terrifying, and overwhelming life events, for which disorganized attachment experience is a poster child. Dissociative processes, dizzying shifts in affect, and vertical splits are common in patients with severe early childhood trauma and/or privation, and the number of such patients is legion. The therapist/patient dyads struggling with disorganized attachment pockets, issues, enclaves, unmentalized experiences, and concomitant inexplicable physical symptoms are often fatigued, confused, uneasy, on edge, overwhelmed, hypervigilant, and pressured. A metaphor of being lost at sea with a broken radio in the middle of a big storm with a modest sailboat (and no crew) seems apt.

Our challenge is finding a way to keep our hearts open to our patients throughout this struggle, without losing our way in the maelstrom. The challenge for our patients is to follow the trail of breadcrumbs we leave on the pathway which leads to the House of Hope. I tell many of my child patients a fairy tale that incorporates the elements of their own life story and various heroic opportunities to invest their life with meaning, for the search for meaning is a critical aspect of traumatized people's efforts to master helplessness and vulnerability. Visualization imagery to reclaim the lost aspects of their soul, self, and heart (Stratton, 1997) can be a healing self-affirmation. Who knows what meanings children's minds accrue from the daggers and glass shards of a traumatized parental mind? Certainly not least is a conviction that the world is not safe. Becker (1973) writes,

> ...those extra sensitive types who have filled the roles of shaman, prophet, saint, poet, and artist [therapist?]. What is unique about their perception of reality is that it is alive to the panic inherent in

creation: Sylvia Plath somewhere named God "King Panic."...I think that taking life seriously means something such as this: that whatever man does on this planet has to be done in the lived truth of the terror...He cannot flee from dread.

(pp. 282–3)

Many of us experience a strong visual/visceral connection when touching into the magical side of childhood: melodies of the lullaby variety, gazing at sunbeams, holding a wriggling puppy, shrieking in joy, opening presents, turning a somersault, cuddling, being read to, learning to write one's alphabet. The darker symphonies are the ones where we listen to the darker melodies:

> Brought to my knees, my overly defended heart broken open, I learned that suffering could indeed be the proximate cause of faith. I watched as the masks I had used to hide my pain fell, and the boundaries of isolation that kept me from more full connection to others and to the wholeness of life crumbled. Faith is about opening up and making room for even the most painful experiences, the ones where we "take apart the chord" of our suffering to find notes of horror, desolation and piercing fear. If I could be willing to make room for an aching numbness, and the river of grief it covered, allowing it, even trusting it, I would be acting in faith. Perhaps this is how suffering leads to faith. In times of great struggle, when there is nothing else to rely on and nowhere else to go, maybe it is the return to the moment that is the act of faith. From that point, openness to possibility can arise, willingness to see what will happen, patience, endeavor, strength, courage. Moment by moment, we can find our way through.
>
> (Salzberg, 2003, pp. 118–22)

Moore (1992) points out that, whereas the psychotherapy arts are at least essentially scientifically informed, care of the soul is a sacred art. "In the modern world we separate...spiritual practice and therapy. There is considerable interest in healing this split, but if it is going to be bridged, our very idea of what we are doing has to be radically re-imagined" (p. xv). Although spirituality is a controversial notion in many psychotherapy circles, anyone who works in the field of trauma finds themselves eventually grappling with existential and spiritual questions, conundrums, agonies, and Gordian knots. Frightening pre-verbal experience is the quintessence of traumatic experience and by its nature, inarticulate.

Both spiritual concerns and intensely felt emotions are well within the scope of profound, deep human experience. Trauma is an overwhelming, uncontrollable human experience, and there is no more overwhelming or less controllable era in personal history than infancy. Buddhist teachers have long held that trauma is one of the four portals to transformation, the others being meditation, sexual ecstasy, and death. Shamans are about the business of emotional presence, healing traumas, and sharing wisdom about love and self-discipline as conduits to enlightenment. Shamans are frequently defined as those who mediate between the physical and spiritual realms and who are said to have particular powers, such as prophecy and healing. As therapists, we are the modern-day cultural equivalents of the shamanic healers of yesteryear, the ones people come to in search of inner healing, the acquisition of wisdom, surcease from a sense of pervasive guilt and unworthiness, a guidebook for how to love just the right amount, and relief from inner terror and torment.

The depth and profundity of psychotherapy is the fire in the belly that comes from walking on the coals of one's own nightmares; steady rhythms of attachment, and, yes, love that comes from reawakening the light in the eyes of our patients so that they can turn toward, as nature intended, instead of turning away or against (Horney, 1991). We brace to endure the steady rhythm of enactments, abandonments, and near misses, hoping that dawn will come soon enough to avert a catastrophe. We catch our breath when our patients start to believe in a possibility bigger than themselves, perhaps to hope, to dream of a destiny instead of doom or fate (Bollas, 1989).

References

Adams, K. (2006). Falling forever: The price of chronic shock. *International Journal of Group Psychotherapy, 56*(2), 127–72.

Aeschylus. (1895). Translations from Homer and Aeschylus, J. Anster (Trans.). In *Hermathena, 9*(21), 265, Trinity College.

Anthi, R. C. (1983). The reconstruction of preverbal experience. *American Journal of Psychoanalysis, 31*(1), 33–58.

Anzieu, D. (1990). *Psychic envelopes.* Karnac.

Arthur, G., Welch, F., & Burley, F. (Directors). (2020). *The Windemere children: In their own words* [film]. PBS.

Becker, E. (1973). *The denial of death.* The Free Press.

Bion, W. R. (1967a). *Second thoughts.* Heinemann.

Blum, H. P. (1980). The value of reconstruction in adult analysis. *International Journal of Psychoanalysis,* 61, 39–52.

Bollas, C. (1989). *Forces of destiny: Psychoanalysis and the human idiom.* Free Association Books.

Bromberg, P. M. (2006). *Awakening the dreamer: Clinical journeys.* Routledge.

Bromberg, P. M. (2011). *The shadow of the tsunami.* Routledge Press.

Brown, D., Hammond, D. C., & Scheflin, A. W. (1998). *Memory, trauma, treatment, and the law.* W. W. Norton & Co.

Chefetz. R. A., & Bromberg, P. M. (2004). Talking with "me" and "not-me": A dialog. *Contemporary Psychoanalysis,* 40(3), 409–64.

Chessick, R. D. (1994). On corruption. *Journal of the American Academy of Psychoanalysis,* 22(3), 377–98.

Crane, D. (1972). *Invisible colleges: Diffusion of knowledge in scientific communities.* University of Chicago Press.

de Saint-Exupery, A. (1943). *The little prince.* Harcourt.

Eigen, M. (2002). *Damaged bonds.* H. Karnac Books Ltd.

Hamilton, V. (1990). Reflections on 23 years of learning and friendship with John Bowlby. *The Tavistock Gazette,* 29, 20–3.

Higgins, G. O. (1994). *Resilient adults.* Jossey-Bass.

Horney, K. (1991). *Neurosis and human growth: The struggle toward self-realization.* W. W. Norton & Co.

Isobel, S., Goodyear, M., & Foster, K. (2017). Psychological trauma in the context of familial relationships: A concept analysis. *Trauma, Violence, & Abuse,* 38(3), 482–95.

Kain, K., & Terrell, S. (2018). *Nurturing resilience: Helping clients move forward from developmental trauma—an integrative somatic approach.* North Atlantic Books.

Kalsched, D. (1996). *The inner world of trauma.* Routledge.

Khan, M. (1974). To hear with eyes. In M. Khan (Ed.), *The privacy of the self: Papers on psychoanalytic theory and technique* (pp. 234–50). International Universities Press.

Kohut, H. (1971). *Analysis of the self.* International Universities Press.

Korn, L. (1997). *Community trauma and development* [paper]. World Conference on Violence and Human Co-Existence, August, Dublin, Ireland.

Lanius, R., Vermetten, E., & Pain, C. (2010). *The impact of early life trauma on health and disease.* Cambridge University Press.

Levine, P. A. (1997). *Waking the tiger.* North Atlantic Books.

Lyons-Ruth, K., Dutra, L., Schuder, M., & Bianchi, I. (2006). From infant attachment disorganization to adult dissociation: Relational adaptations or traumatic experiences? *Psychiatric Clinic of North America, 29*(1), 63–86.

Mitchell, S. (1993). *Hope and dread in psychoanalysis.* Basic Books.

Mitrani, J. L. (1996). *A framework for the imaginary.* Jason Aronson.

Moore, T. (1992). *Care of the soul.* HarperCollins.

Ogden, T. H. (2001). An elegy, a love song and a lullaby. *Psychoanalytic Dialogues, 11*(2), 293–311.

Rutan, J. S. (1992). *Psychotherapy for the 1990s.* Guilford Press.

Salzberg, S. (2002). *Faith.* Riverhead Books.

Schacter, D. L. (1982). *Stranger behind the engram: Theories of memory and the psychology of science.* Erlbaum.

Schore, A. N. (2011). Foreword. In P. M. Bromberg. *The shadow of the tsunami.* Routledge Press.

Schore, A. N. (2019a). *Right brain psychotherapy.* Norton Series on Interpersonal Neurobiology.

Schore, A. N. (2019b). *The development of the unconscious.* Norton Series on Interpersonal Neurobiology.

Sheingold, L. (1989). *Soul maker: The effects of childhood abuse & deprivation.* Yale University Press.

Siegel, D. J. (1999a). Toward an interpersonal neurobiology of the developing mind: Attachment relationships, "mindsight," and neural integration. *Infant Mental Health Journal, 22*(1–2), 67–94.

Simic, C. (2003). Nearest nameless. In *The voice at 3:00 a.m.* Harcourt Brace & Company.

Spotnitz, H. (1976). *Psychotherapy of the preoedipal conditions.* Jason Aronson, Inc.

Squire, L. R., Knowlton, B., & Musen, G. (1993). The structure and organization of memory. *Annual Review of Psychology, 44*, 453–95.

Steele, K. (1989). Sitting with the shattered soul. *Pilgrimage: Journal of Psychotherapy and Personal Exploration, 15*(6), 18–25.

Stratton, E. K. (1997). *Seeds of light.* Simon & Schuster.

Terr, L. (1990). *Too scared to cry.* Harper & Row.

Turner, C. (2017). Numinous physiology: A theological reflection on angels, trauma and spirituality. *Practical Theology, 10*(4), 337–50.

van der Kolk, B. A. (2015). *The body keeps the score: Brain, body, and mind in the healing of trauma.* Penguin Publishing Group.

van der Kolk, B. A., & d'Andrea, W. (2010). Towards a developmental trauma disorder diagnosis for childhood interpersonal trauma. In R. A. Lanius, *The impact of early life trauma on health and diseases: The hidden epidemic* (pp. 57–68). Cambridge University Press.

Chapter 2

Our Pain is the Crack in the Shell that Encloses Our Understanding (following Gibran)

Shock: An Offering to the Gods—Dread, Panic, and Random

Three brothers Dread, Panic, and Random are sitting at the gaming table grumbling about the general sorry state of mankind. Panic snorts: "We need a new diversion. Earth has gone to hell since being divided up by war god Mars and speedy messenger Mercury. These humans worship at the very altars of religious strife and the information age, thanks to those two. The only people who aren't completely besotted with war and the information age are the little children and the poets. Children actually see us: they have always known we are the monsters under their beds. The poets? They are only just beginning to take us seriously. They sense us, fear us, and even worship us secretly. But children rapidly forget and poets, well, poets may as well be speaking a foreign language for all the attention their words command. Our godhood is literally disappearing, I tell you." Random listened intently, contemplating whether or not he wanted to give away his ace in the hole. "Panic is right," he said. "We should take notice lest we become unnecessary." "Speak for yourself," Dread bragged, yawning languorously. "I am present before every birth and every death, at every doctor visit…in every war, and at every glitch in these so-called information machines…you should hear how people fuss every time something goes a tiny bit wrong, and they fear it will get worse…. We are being made irrelevant, and better have a sit down with the Fates to decide what comes next." Silently, Random chuckled. These jokers had no idea he, Random, was behind every happenstance, every disaster, every trauma, all wars, most births, half the deaths, most marriages, and almost all of the tragedies that these humans suffered. And the fun he had been having playing with children's expectations…Oh! Another birth in New York City to an already overburdened family…he was going to play a hunch that he could have more fun there than at cards. "I fold," he said.

It is my hope that the brothers will be somewhat mollified by their central role in this chapter. No one pays much attention to what children

DOI: 10.4324/9781003262367-4

have to say about the monsters under their beds, nor to the collective voices of poets and their sibs, the singer songwriters who are the canaries in our culture's coal mines. Yet these voices rise to an eerie clamor in our consultation offices, demanding that we know, that we see, that we listen. More likely than not, we choose to look away from the monster under our bed and pretend he is not there. My job is to remind us about him. His name is Shock. He has no friends. No one wants him around. As he wanders the world, he has the experience of being massively shunned and disowned. It's as if none of us ever had long conversations with him once upon a time long ago when the world as we knew it was terribly confusing and hard. Now that we're all grown up and everything, we snub him every time he comes around, even when he sneaks into one of our patient's pockets to visit us again on our own turf.

That's it exactly, you see; on our home turf we are relatively invincible to the shocks of the unexpected: we've seen it all. Trauma is "in" our patients, not in us. We can control the rise of horror in our souls so much more easily when we can place it definitively outside of ourselves. In order to be allowed into the therapy office, Shock has to take formal obedience training so that he can behave acceptably in our offices, heeding our fierce demands that he stays where he belongs. "Stay," we command, pointing to the inside of our patients. "Heel" we command, as our patient exits the side doorway. If Shock creeps into our dreams at night, we give him stern lectures about boundaries and countertransference.

Outside of mass tragedies like 9/11 or school shootings where there is community grieving, we don't easily share experiences of being shocked to the core, shocked to death, shocked out of our wits, shaken up by shock, falling into the endless abyss of shock. After a bad car wreck, we share the disgust at the repair bill ("Can you believe it?") but not the horror of the shock experience which haunts our every breath for weeks.

Oh, we might share the moment of horror ("I couldn't control the wheel and saw the oncoming traffic slow to a dead crawl as I prepared to die"), but not the tedium of not being able to fall asleep because the bed keeps sliding out from under us; not the confounded movie reel in our head faithfully ticking off each precious second of life as it ebbs away on the highway; certainly not the invisible geyser that lurches in our chest every time a car passes us on the freeway.

This is why I use poetry freely throughout this book.[1] I have found that the condensed visual shock of metaphor opens a portal into another dimension that many of us only visit perchance in our dreams and nightmares. To call this dimension "primary process" robs it of vitality, "kick," punch, and essence and establishes a "too comfortable" distance from this uncomfortable topic of trauma. You may well find yourself squirming away from shock in this book, especially from the shock in the poetry. If you find yourself "confused" by a poem and "not getting it," you might consider reading it aloud and imagining what it could possibly have to do with shock. Walter Benjamin (1969) has thought long and deeply about how shock and poetry intertwine. Shock is intimately linked to the visual, and, according to Benjamin, the shock motif is always image-based. How curious and wonderful that the profundity of a philosopher and world-class literary critic so closely corresponds to the conclusions drawn by our gifted psychoanalytic scholars. Preverbal experience has, by definition, not yet been *thought* about but only lived in the body of the person experiencing it. It follows therefore that shock will be hard to *write about, to describe, to make sense of.* Where shock and wonder are close at hand, so is poetic thinking, because the poetic is suspended somewhere between the past and the future. Poets build bridges for us to cross over into the unexplored, unnamed, unmapped wilderness then turn back again to the safe, the familiar. I frequently turn, then, to the poets to open the portal for us to walk through together.

The Unthought Known

In a moment of serendipity, I came across Judith Mitrani's books *The Framework for the Imaginary* (1996) and *Ordinary People, Extraordinary Expectations* (2001), and with Theodore Mitrani, *Encounters with Autistic States* (1997), as well as Peter Levine's many books on shock trauma. These authors opened my eyes to an underground world of abject experience and subtle dissociation that I had quietly inhabited since infancy without ever having quite *thought about* it, despite years of traditional analysis and years of study with dissociative disorders experts. I sought out additional work with an analyst who was familiar with trauma and shock. He told me that, even absent abuse, my childhood had resembled life in a concentration camp.

I hope to offer the reader a guided tour, gentler than the journey I myself had, through the work of some of the greatest thinkers about preverbal and developmental trauma. You may find, as I did, that you already knew some of what you are about to read, but never said it out loud to yourself before. Bollas (1987) aptly calls this "the unthought known." Poetry does this, comes at us sideways and slips in through the cracks in our soul that we weren't watching, waking up sleeping guardians of memory. Psychoanalytic writers are harder to wade through, somehow, than poetry, although the heart of the meat is just as rich. Perhaps it is merely that there are so many more words involved. I hope to distill the essence of authors writing about early childhood trauma sufficiently to whet your appetite for more of them, without losing their spirit, vitality, or zeitgeist in the process.

What Is the Role of Early Experience?

In this millennium, psychoanalytic theory no longer has the luxury of ignoring the role of body, spirit, trauma, and dissociation in its conceptualizations. Analysts had long argued that people continually re-create the patterns of their past in their present. Early beliefs persist not *despite* subsequent life experiences but *because* of them; patterns keep getting formed in a way that stays consistent throughout the years. Yet it behooves us to listen to what neuroscientists have to say on the subject of the relative importance and indelibility of early experience. Neuroscience—with information on strange attractors, chaos theory, and Hebbian learning applied to child and adult development—is now on the cutting edge of understanding about how people construct their later experience to conform to earlier experience. Our patients, who encountered unbearable affects early in life, need us to be able to recognize and resonate with the body and affect states they wordlessly struggle with. As you read through this whirlwind tour of neuroscience research, bring the material alive by thinking about how this information illuminates your understanding of a patient or two you have been mired in impasse with.

Cumulative Trauma from Toxic Stress: Adverse Childhood Experiences (ACEs) and Epigenetics

Masud Khan (1963), a British psychoanalyst, first noted that psycho-physical events that traumatize infants and toddlers can have lifelong consequences far beyond what might be readily apparent. He coined the term "cumulative trauma" to describe the layers of shockwaves that ripple throughout the psyches and (we now know) nervous systems of children who miss out on the natural protective shield of good mothering. In 1985, the Centers for Disease Control (CDC) and Kaiser Permanente launched a longitudinal study of the medical and psychiatric consequences of early exposure to verbal, physical, or sexual abuse; physical violence; psychiatric illness in the family; neglect; or loss of a family member due to suicide or incarcerations in prison: Adverse Childhood Experiences (ACEs) (CDC & Kaiser Permanente, 1998). The list of ACEs grew to include prematurity, neonatal intensive care unit (NICU) hospitalizations, separation from a parent, complex divorces, medical traumatization, hospitalizations, and surgeries—and potentially some adoptions. The higher a person's ACE score, the greater the likelihood that the person will experience chronic diseases, addictions, autoimmune dysfunction, suicide, and early death. This study had staggering implications for the long-term effects of early trauma, and the list of possible long-term effects continues to grow (Harris, 2018). Putnam added lifelong dysregulation and identity states to the list:

> Children subjected to repeated ACEs will grow up to become adults with painful, shameful and disowned identity states that shape a disorganized, fragmented, and conflicted sense of self. When confronted with traumatic reminders, their emotions are likely to swing rapidly, their reasoning may derail, and their behavior can swing out of control. They will have trouble learning from experience and forming healthy relationships.... They dislike—even hate—and distrust themselves."
>
> (Putnam, 2016, p. 226)

Kain and Terrell (2018) note that "adverse childhood experiences disrupt neurodevelopment in its very early stages, and those disruptions then continue, evolve, and deepen through the maturation process with continued negative impacts, including a higher risk for early death" (p. 195). Fortunately, protective factors also exist, as displayed in the Resilience Questionnaire, proposed in 2006 and updated in 2013, by Rains and McClinn. Kain and Terrell believe these "resilience factors" instill a sense of safety and belonging in children who experience ACE trauma, thereby increasing their emotional and physical sturdiness and decreasing their vulnerability to "survivor" physiology.

Moreover, there is increasing consensus that the intergenerational transmission of trauma occurs frequently. The work of Vivian Rakoff (1967) was considered controversial when he declared about the children of his patients who were Holocaust survivors: "The parents are not broken conspicuously, yet their children, all of whom were born after the Holocaust, display severe psychiatric symptomatology. It would almost be easier to believe that they, rather than their parents, had suffered the corrupting, searing hell" (cited in Yehuda & Lehrner, 2018, p. 245). The fact of intergenerational transmission of trauma is now well accepted and supported by animal studies, studies of Holocaust survivors, prisoners of war studies, terror attack survivor studies, and the like.

> There is now converging evidence supporting the idea that off-spring are affected by parental trauma exposures occurring before their birth, and possibly even prior to their conception. On the simplest level, the concept of intergenerational trauma acknowledges that exposure to extremely adverse events impacts individuals to such a great extent that their offspring find themselves grappling with their parents' post-traumatic state. A more recent and provocative claim is that the experience of trauma—or more accurately the effect of that experience—is "passed" somehow from one generation to the next through non-genomic, possibly epigenetic mechanisms affecting DNA function or gene transcription. At the current time, the idea that epigenetic mechanisms underlie clinical observations in offspring of trauma survivors represents a hypothesis to be tested.
>
> (Yehuda & Lehrner, 2018, p. 243)

Neglect Is as Devastating, and Far More Prevalent, than Abuse

Controversy still abounds about the methodology of transmission of trauma, but there is general agreement that neglect and early toxic stress are critical factors in childhood adversity. Geneticists are studying the stress pathways that ACE events, especially neglect, create: "The childhood trauma faced by an individual causes epigenetic changes that can impact adult life. Children who face traumatic situations like neglect, parental loss, divorce, and socioeconomic failures witness an effect in their behavioral and physiological features in the later stages of adulthood" (Megala et al., 2021, p. 1).

Groundbreaking research by Harry Harlow in 1958 explored the impact of deprivation on the development of young monkeys. Imagine a tiny, newborn monkey, taken away from its mother, placed in one of many stark environments. Behind Door #1 are three different empty cages into which the infants are placed. The wire-cage babies die within 5 days; if a wire mesh cone is introduced, the babies do better. If the cone is covered with a cloth, the babies survive and appear to be healthy, although not normal; they have contact comfort at least. Behind Door #2 are Wire and Cloth Monkey Mothers, perfectly proportioned with one breast. The Wire Mother is simply a wire frame shaped to support nursing, with radiant heat provided. The Cloth Mother is the same wire-covered frame, heated, with foam rubber and a changeable terry cloth cover on top. Both mother surrogates have faces; the Cloth Mother face is more lifelike, with bigger eyes. Pictures sprinkled throughout Harlow's paper show tiny infants huddling desperately against this Cloth Mother, which they vastly preferred over the Wire Mother. The baby monkeys used the mother surrogates much like they would use real mothers, as a secure base of operations. When frightened, the youngsters would vocalize and rush to cling onto their Cloth Mother's torso. If the surrogate mother was temporarily removed from the room, the baby monkeys became inconsolably agitated. One heartbreaking picture shows a disconsolate baby huddled at what would be the feet of the surrogate Cloth Mother, collapsed into a tiny ball. Monkeys who were raised without any surrogate mother for their first 250 days were initially alarmed when a Cloth Mother was introduced, but rapidly began relating to her as a source of security and reassurance, like the monkeys who were raised with her from the start. Pictures show these juvenile monkeys desperately clutching their new Cloth Mother, lying across her torso. If you can bear to check out these pictures, the website is: http://psychclassics. yorku.ca/Harlow/love.htm. The website search words are wire monkey + Harlow+ Nature of Love.

Although Harlow's research was ethically controversial (and would not be allowed today), it demonstrates the power of early neglect and deprivation to wreak havoc on future emotional functioning. Harlow's studies on young primates demonstrate the primacy of the parent–child attachment relationship and the importance of contact soothing and maternal touch in infant development. Without at least a cloth surrogate mother, the infants were paralyzed with fear, huddled in a ball, and failed to develop social skills. Harlow designed his research to highlight the importance of attachment, comfort, and love to psycholoanalysts who saw infants' internal life as being determined by fantasy rather than real life events.

Lyons-Ruth et al. (2006) propose that neglect and caregiver unavailability are a "hidden trauma" that creates pathways to attachment disorganization and dissociation later in life in non-abusive families:

> The dimensions of the parent-infant dialog most relevant to the later development of dissociation appear to be the contradictory communications, failures to respond, withdrawing behaviors, disoriented behaviors, and role-confused behaviors that override the infant's attachment cues but are not, in and of themselves, explicitly hostile or intrusive. In such instances, the caregiver behaves in ways that have the effect of "shutting out" the child from the process of dialogue. This shutting out of the child's contributions to the regulatory process eventually leaves the child without an internalized form of relational dialogue, or internal working model, that can produce a sense of safety and reliable comfort in times of distress.
>
> (p. 80)

In my experience, many clinicians still overlook or underestimate the importance of exploring these early experiences. I have been told, "I don't work with trauma," meaning "I don't work with populations who were physically or sexually abused." These therapists didn't realize that "trauma" was a much larger category of adverse experience. To Lyons-Ruth et al. (2006) the term hidden trauma describes early traumatization that does not involve violence, or physical or sexual abuse but nonetheless creates a pathway toward dissociative processes. "Therefore, the 'quieter' caregiving deviations such as withdrawing from emotional contact, being unresponsive to the child's overtures, or displaying contradictory, role-reversed or disoriented responses when the infant's attachment needs are heightened appear to be the maternal responses most implicated" (p. 69) in pathways to moderate or even subtle dissociation.

Attachment between mother and offspring is crucial, since mammals depend upon maternal care for survival. Attachment involves proximity-seeking, distress upon separation and comfort upon reunion, and attunement to a variety of infant biological states as well as affect states (Hofer, 1996; Schore, 2019). "Attachment involves a delicate feedback loop in which mother and infant regulate each other" (Pally, 2000, p. 92). The distress cry upon separation is universal to mammals (Hofer, 1996). Abrupt separations from the mother during critical phases of toddler and childhood development also yield catastrophic results for future brain development. "When the mother is absent, an infant loses all his organizing channels at once. Like a marionette with its strings cut, his physiology collapses into the huddled heap of despair" (Pally, 2000, p. 83).

Van der Kolk (2015) reports that the protest/despair response to separation is seen in all primates, human and nonhuman. Vulnerability to both depression and abuse of offspring is intimately related to early experiences.

> Later experiences only partially offset the effects of early social deprivation. An adequate support network may attenuate the devastating effects of early deprivation, but altered cognitive functioning, incapacity to deal with autonomic arousal and the loss of ability to fantasize and sublimate may continue to render a person vulnerable to loss of self-esteem, substance abuse, and problems in coping with aggression. Thus, early deprivation enhances vulnerability to later traumatic life events....
>
> (p. 39)

Lewis et al. (2000) report an ingenious experiment in which healthy monkeys were turned into poor mothers by being in an unpredictable environment that eroded their emotional availability. The distracted, apprehensive mothering endowed their offspring

> with emotional vulnerabilities and altered neurochemistries. The monkeys so raised showed magnified despair and anxiety reactions, and their brains revealed changes in the neurotransmitters that control these emotional states. Full grown, the brains of these animals evidence permanent alterations in neurochemistry…[with] lifelong changes in levels of neurotransmitters like serotonin and dopamine.
>
> (p. 90)

Despite the questionable ethics of such experiments, it is fascinating to see a working demonstration of ambivalent and disorganized attachment *in situ*.

Van der Kolk (1987) and others have demonstrated that disruptions of attachment during infancy can lead to lasting neurobiological changes inasmuch as unmitigated separation distress results in hyperactivity or underactivity of neurotransmitter systems. Protest and despair are the child's response to separation distress and a lack of mother/infant synchrony. Prolonged protest and despair experiences in childhood result in lasting psychobiological changes. Van der Kolk asserts that:

> In humans, damage related to protest may lead to panic attacks in adulthood, while excessive exposure to despair in infancy may give rise to cyclical depressions in adults…. The developmental stage at which the disruption occurs as well as its severity and duration probably all affect the degree and reversibility of the resulting psychobiological damage.
>
> (Van der Kolk, 1987, p. 51)

Basic Attachment Theory

Bowlby (1969/1982, 1973, 1980) was interested in establishing a link between adult psychopathology (especially intense anxiety, self-blame, dissociated mental states, compulsive caregiving, and over-reliance on the self) and early disruptions in the attachment system due to prolonged separation from the mother or loss of the mother. He conceived of basic attachment as a system of attachment-seeking behaviors that, under certain conditions of stress, lead the child to seek and be satisfied with nothing less than close proximity to, and contact with, the attachment figure. After extensive study of children who became somewhat distressed after experiencing major separations from or deaths of their attachment figures, Bowlby believed that children develop "internal working models" of how attachment works based on their experiences. These models of self and other relate to appraisal of self and attachment strategies based on whether children experienced themselves as being "loved and worthy" or "unwanted and rejected." Bowlby proposed that when attachment behaviors such as searching, crying, and calling persistently fail to gain a soothing response, children have to function defensively to separate attachment information from consciousness, that is, to dissociate. He hypothesized that, not only were separation and loss key circumstances in which "segregated attachment systems" were likely to develop, but also that being mocked or punished for displaying attachment behaviors and feelings could lead to a similar outcome.

Ainsworth and her colleagues (1978) further developed attachment theory by introducing a laboratory experiment called The Strange Situation. The setting is comfortable but unfamiliar to the child. Mother and baby are joined by a stranger, after which the mother twice leaves the baby for three minutes. A key coding element in The Strange Situation study was how infants responded when their mothers returned after the three minutes. Ainsworth and her colleagues first identified three groups of infants with qualitatively different attachment strategies for dealing with the fear generated by being left alone: secure, avoidant, and ambivalent; presumably, the three groups had differing expectations of how their mothers would respond to them. A fourth group of infants, called disorganized/disoriented, was eventually identified by Main and Solomon (1990). These infants seemed at a loss for a coherent attachment strategy, at least for a moment. Some just froze in place, or twirled; others displayed fear of their parent, contradictory behavior, and/or dissociative behavior when their mothers returned.

These researchers and others in the field have noted that parental responsiveness to infant emotional communications is a key determinant of secure attachment. Early attachment has been found to set the stage for lifelong patterns of personal relationships. Attachment experts observe that secure attachment is facilitated by both parental attunement and the ability to take infantile distress and protest in stride without retaliation or undue anxiety. Securely attached children can accept separations from their mother, protest, and make up, and continue on with their lives.

When the environment is less than optimal, infants are at risk of developing an insecure attachment style. We can surmise that early anxious attachment arises from a number of possible causes, ranging from overwhelmed, under-supported immature parents who do not have the time or peace of mind to be sensitive and consistently available with each of their children; ignorance, which might lead parents to let their babies cry for prolonged periods or to leave them repeatedly or for too long a time; faulty role modeling ("Don't you spoil that child!"); unhappy events or psychiatric illness in the parents' lives that might create emotional problems leading to preoccupation and distraction; alcoholism or substance abuse leading to parental emotional unavailability; marital discord and disharmony; illness or physical injury in the child or parent requiring prolonged hospitalization, restricted touch and/or physical separation; or frightening behaviors (Main & Hesse, 1990) such as looming, invasive touch, dissociation, or exaggerated startle reactions. Since the frightening parent is also the one the child must turn to for soothing and protection, it stands to reason that when the parent is repeatedly the source of danger as well as comfort, the child's attachment behavior would become hesitant and ultimately disorganized.

Let's describe the three insecure attachment styles in children more fully:

(1) *insecure-avoidant* children who protest little upon separation, but who, upon reunion with the parent, hover nervously nearby, and over the years grow up to be a bit lonely, withdrawn, and a bit closed down. Parents of children who show the avoidant pattern tend to be somewhat brusque and functional in their handling (Holmes, 1996). Insecure-avoidant children may grow up to be somewhat characterologically armored individuals, counter-dependent, overly self-reliant, and afraid to open their hearts to

fully experience their vitality, life force and vulnerability. When they have their own children, they dismiss their anxiety about how well they will do as parents. When interviewed, adults categorized as "dismissing of attachment" seem unable or unwilling to let their guard down enough to take attachment issues seriously. They frequently have trouble remembering their childhoods, answer questions about themselves guardedly and without elaboration, and dislike and distrust looking inward.

(2) *insecure-ambivalent* children (also called *resistant* children) protest furiously upon separation but dissolve into agitation upon parental return, burying themselves in their mothers' laps and clinging frantically to her. The ambivalent child has grown up in a home of inconsistency and/or chaos. Parents of children who show the ambivalent reaction tend to be less in sync with their children, ignoring them when they are obviously distressed, and intruding upon them when they are playing happily (Holmes, 1996). Ambivalent children may grow up to be adults who drive others away with their angry neediness, desperate clinginess, and inconsolability.

(3) *insecure-disorganized/disoriented* children are typically from distressed families in which a pervasive sense of anxiety and fearfulness was communicated to them as babies. Many of these children had been abused (Crittenden, 1988); their mothers had often been abused or had suffered tragic early losses that they had never had the opportunity to fully mourn (Firestone, 2021; Main & Hesse, 1990; Main & Solomon, 1990). Mothers of disorganized infants tend to proffer less emotional support and initiate fewer verbal communications than other mothers (Lyons-Ruth et al., 1987). In disorganized attachments, a child may have experienced abrupt shifts in state on the part of the parent that can result in fear and disorientation in the child's mind. These parents are too anxious or disconnected from their child's experience to soothe the child's arousal level (Carlson, 1998; Main & Morgan, 1996; Ogawa et al., 1997; Siegel, 2020). Mothers of disorganized-disoriented infants and preschoolers exhibit low involvement, teaching skill, positive parent–child mutuality, and conversational skill (Solomon & George, 1999). The children show no coherent pattern of response; they "freeze" or collapse to the ground or

lean vacantly against a wall upon reunion with their mothers. They may grow up to have dissociative symptoms, to have difficulty trusting others, and to be the most vulnerable to substance abuse problems because of the chaotic nature of their affect storms. They are less likely than the ambivalently attached to turn toward people for soothing and more likely to turn inward. "The minds of these patients are hypersensitively vulnerable to the detection of randomness and meaninglessness..." (Grotstein, 1990a, p. 265). Although Grotstein was writing about severely ill adults in psychoanalysis and attachment researchers were studying a group of compromised children in a difficult relationship environment, I believe they were observing and describing the same emotional sensitivities: a pattern that has come to be known as attachment disorganization or disorganized attachment.

Further Advances in Understanding Disorganized Attachment

Solomon and George (1999) discovered that the behaviors of young children following prolonged separation reflect actual disorganization of attachment strategies rather than defensive strategies such as avoidance or ambivalence. They also note that mothers of disorganized children exacerbate the child's attachment-related anxieties by rejecting, scolding, or frightening their children instead of soothing them. They conclude that these children are prevented from developing an organized attachment strategy by extreme states of destabilizing fear stimulated by the very caregiver they need reassurance from. Thus, disorganized attachment behaviors represent a profound failure to integrate attachment-related behavior, feelings, and thoughts. Lyons-Ruth et al. (2006) propose that potential dissociative pathways are the result.

Chronic exposure to shame and humiliation are beginning to be recognized as significant stressors contributing to attachment disorganization (Epstein, 2022; Herman, 2018). Herman argues that "where the attachment figure is a source of unremitting shame...the child is torn between need for emotional attunement and fear of rejection or ridicule.... She forms an internal working model of relationship in which her basic needs are inherently shameful" (2018, p. 158). Epstein's edited volume, entirely dedicated to clinical perspectives on shame traumatization, explores the self-generated "irresolvable" shame of abandoned children who "explain" to themselves that their abandonment is due to their inherent unlovability; it discusses the defensive value of shame in protecting against even more painful realizations of helplessness and vulnerability; and it examines "primary shame" (2022, p. 48), akin to Balint's basic fault—feeling defective because of unmet and unrepaired needs and longing for safety and connection.

In the preschool years, disorganized children have been shown to reorganize their attachment into one of two forms of controlling behavior toward the parent: *controlling-caregiving* children attempt to entertain, direct, organize, or reassure the parent, while *controlling-punitive* children attempt to coerce, attack, or humiliate the parent. Lyons-Ruth et al. (1999) identified two distinct organizations of parent–child behavior with disorganized infants: "helpless-fearful" and "hostile." In the helpless-fearful subgroup, parents combine fearfulness and withdrawal with nonhostile behavior toward the child. In the hostile subgroup, mothers displayed hostile and/or rejecting behavior. The authors speculate that both parental stances reflect alternative expressions of helplessness, perhaps related to difficulties in the parent's own attachment history. Solomon and George (1999) further suggest that it is the helplessness of the mother, being out of control of herself, the child, and/or the situation ("abdicated care,") that leaves the infant or child in states of terrifyingly unprotected abandonment. The child's basic survival instincts alert him on such occasions to a sense of dire peril: what Grotstein (1990a, 1990b) would term "predator-prey anxiety."

Moss et al. (1999) demonstrate that the role reversal and lack of emotional attunement characteristic of school age disorganized children and their caregivers contributes to dysfunctional relationships outside the family. They found that the mothers of disorganized children described ego-syntonic frightening, rejecting, and abandoning behavior toward their children. Not only did these mothers not describe reparative behavior toward their distressed children, they sometimes also described conscious decisions not to repair the situation. Solomon and George (1999) concluded that the failure to repair the relationship was a critical variable in the pathway to disorganized attachment.

Emotional Regulation

Our ability to appropriately evaluate danger/non-danger situations, recover from stress, soothe ourselves, and regain our emotional equilibrium after losing our emotional balance are all measures of our ability to self-regulate, an ability we had to learn at the cradle through the sharing and *amplification* of positive states with an attuned caregiver, and then by the sharing and *reduction* of negative states. Inevitable disruptions and successful repair efforts then taught us that we could rely upon the minds of those in our caretaking environment to know and respond to our needs; eventually, this knowledge would evolve into a higher order ability to self-soothe.

Pally (2000) reports a variety of studies that reveal that some infants are born with the ability to self-soothe and be soothed by others when emotionally distressed. Others who are harder to soothe and who cannot soothe themselves as readily, may be predisposed to dysregulated emotion. Two groups of babies have been identified that are impaired from birth in normal self-regulatory mechanisms; both groups seem relatively impervious to the usual "distract and reconnect" intervention that is a godsend in most families with an upset infant. "Infants with emotional dysregulation can show such lifelong consequences as attentional problems and learning difficulties" (Pally, 2000, p. 91). More recently, researchers have been investigating the possibility that genetic factors contribute a vulnerability for disorganized attachment. Findings to date have been inconclusive, with some studies suggesting a gene-environment (epigenetic) or bio-behavioral interaction (Bakermans-Kranenburg & van Ijzendoorn, 2007).

Limbic irritability is one consequence of early childhood stress according to Teicher (2002). Chronic exposure to stress hormones causes limbic electrical irritability that can produce emotional lability including exasperation, anxiety, and aggression. Teicher reports that he and colleagues also found reduced development of the left hemisphere cortices in subjects who had been mistreated compared with cortices of subjects who had not, and they found less integration between the right and left hemispheres in the former group. Given that the left hemisphere is associated with language understanding and expression and the right hemisphere with memories—especially negative memories—the individuals whose brains are the most likely to be over-excitable by past mistreatment are the least likely to be able to talk themselves down. More recently, a landmark paper by Lebois et al. (2020) demonstrated that trauma actually leaves visible "fingerprints" on brain architecture.

Jared is a good example of this kind of overexcitability. He was adopted at about age 2 from an orphanage in Guatemala. He has always been triggered into raging violence by harsh tones of voice and criticism. He spent 3 years in three rehabilitation centers from ages 12 to 15 working on his anger issues. Unfortunately, he was sexually abused at his first treatment center so had to spend extra time working that through. He was reluctant to engage in individual therapy with me until I explained that it wasn't going to be like it was in rehab. He was proud of the work he did in rehab but was intrigued that we could work on things other than the mistakes he had made the previous week. He is a gifted athlete and musician, and we spend much of our session time talking about these things. He also makes strong commitments to his girlfriend and wants to show her kindness, patience, and encour-agement. He would love to become a Navy Seal when he graduates.

Jared has a hair trigger temper. He was ultimately rejected by his adoptive mother: she gave up on him. He lives with his adoptive father, a large man who sometimes yells in a booming voice when he is anxious for Jared and his future. Jared has a strong commitment to growth and to being the best person he can be. He is devastated when his Dad worries that he will amount to nothing. Rather than tolerating the hurt, he explodes into despairing rage and self-loathing. His biggest challenge this year has been breaking iPhones by throwing them against the wall or cement. He depends on his iPhone for texting with friends and his girlfriend, especially during COVID isolation, when he had only soccer practices and games for peer interaction. He has gone through six iPhones over the past 5 months, since he always seems to be holding his phone when things go wrong between him and his Dad. He has broken many other bad habits and is dedicated to fixing this problem. He is beginning to realize that this is his problem to fix since there is a limit to iPhone insurance for teenagers. He got a punching bag to take his anger out on, and hopes to instill an internal rule about not throwing his phone when he flashes into rage at his father. He describes his rage as being like a tornado inside him: his fists take over before he can slow himself down. He used to punch holes in walls (which he had to fix himself) but is now working on not throwing and smashing his phone.

Fear Conditioning

Have you ever felt frustrated with someone who just wouldn't "let go" of a trauma they experienced—a powerful abandonment or a disastrous event like rape? Overwhelming experience often persists neurologically in the form of vertical splits (Kohut, 1971). Vertical splits in consciousness, achieved through dread and disavowal, allow patients to both know and not know some painful feeling or memory and probably account for the vicious cycles of numbing and flooding so characteristic of traumatized individuals. Gedo (2000a, 2000b) has worked extensively with dissociative experience and vertical splits in psychoanalysis. He points out that dissociation serves to ward off overwhelming affects while at the same time preserving those same affects on a visceral level via flashbacks. The half-life of fear conditioning in childhood is very, very long. Siegel (1999a) suggests that some traumatization in childhood may become permanent, "as such early experiences of fear may become indelible subcortical emotional memories which may have lasting effects" (p. 133).

Limbic Resonance

We are comfortable thinking about psychotherapy as mind-to-mind play: the patient fantasizes, we have an association and a responsive fantasy, and so forth. With traumatized individuals (who may make up a larger percent of your practice than you have considered heretofore), what counts is emotional, or limbic, resonance. Countless therapists have been mired in impasse with patients manifesting developmental trauma and vertical splits. Without taking a careful history, therapists miss early warning signs of impending distress in their patients with hidden trauma.

In *A General Theory of Love*, Lewis et al. (2000) concluded that therapy for developmental trauma is actually limbic-relatedness shaped to redress early maternal mis-attunement, separation, and attachment experiences gone awry. "The first part of emotional healing is being limbically known—having someone with a keen ear catch your melodic essence" (p. 170).

> Without rich limbic resonance, the child doesn't discover how to sense with his limbic brain, how to tune in to the emotional channel and apprehend himself and others. Without sufficient opportunity for limbic regulation, he cannot internalize emotional balance. Children thus handicapped grow up to become fragile adults who remain uncertain of their own identities, cannot modulate their emotions, and fall prey to internal chaos when stress threatens. Anxiety and depression are the first consequences of limbic omissions. The dominant emotion in early separation's protest phase is nerve-jangling alarm. The brains of insecurely attached children react to provocative events with an exaggerated out-pouring of stress hormones and neurotransmitters. The reactivity persists into adulthood. A minor stressor sweeps such a person toward pathologic anxiety, and a larger or longer one plunges him into depression's black hole.
>
> (Lewis et al., 2000, p. 210)

The authors advise:

> Therapy's last and most ambitious aim is revising the neural code that directs an emotional life.... Overhauling emotional know-ledge is no spectator sport; it demands the messy experience of yanking and tinkering that comes from a limbic bond.... When a limbic connection has established a neural pattern, it takes a limbic connection to revise (and repair) it.
>
> (Lewis et al., 2000, p. 177)

By implication, then, therapy with neglected and traumatized people requires the emotional presence and resonance of the therapist. Unbearable affect deriving from childhood experiences with terror and deprivation is then the currency of exchange between the patient and therapist. Garfield (2003) writes that unbearable affects must first be recognized within the patient's symptoms; next, owned and located with the patient's body; and finally understood in the context of the patient's early childhood experience. "As this three-step process unfolds, close attention to the patient's vitality affects, as the 'music' of his or her day-to-day psychic functioning is helpful" (p. 57). I would add that close tracking of the patient's melody of affects and "unthought known" (Bollas, 1987) is central to the formation of an authentic therapeutic alliance and thus necessary for meaningful therapeutic experience. This is the process of attunement, or limbic resonance.

Limbic resonance is the symphony of mutual exchange and internal adaptation supplying the wordless harmony between a father and his contented baby, between a purring cat and its mistress, between a patient in reverie and his quietly attentive analyst, between two lovers holding hands on a moonlit beach walk.

> From the beginning, the brain is capable of—and in fact is hardwired to—make connections with other brains.... At the neurological level, such a nonverbal, emotional sharing involves the output of the right hemisphere of each member of the interacting pair. As the right hemisphere both sends and receives these signals, the opportunity is created for a resonance of the minds of each of the individuals. At this nonverbal, core self-level, the interaction of self with other becomes mapped in the brain in a manner that literally, neurologically, creates the mind of the other.
>
> (Siegel, 1999b, p. 84)

When the baby fusses, it takes limbic resonance to soothe her; when the cat startles, it takes limbic resonance to get him to purr again; when the patient feels "dropped" and "punctured" by a comment of the analyst, it will take limbic resonance for the analyst to get things right again; when one of the lovers wants to leave the beach to go watch CNN, it will take limbic resonance to restore harmony and avoid an escalation of tensions. Attunement, disruption, and emotional repair are all about limbic resonance.

Thus far we have established that early attachment experience sets the template for emotional self-regulation, attachment style, and the development of underlying brain structures that manage stress hormones and other chemical reactions within the body, arousal level, and memory. Now we will turn to examine the role that the physical/emotional shock response plays.

Trauma and the Shock Response

Underneath everything else is shock. I believe shock is at the bottom of black hole trauma (Grotstein, 1990a, 1990b), most early childhood trauma, certainly separation anxiety trauma, and the attachment traumas we will be reading about. Bromberg (1998) points out that Shakespeare himself wrote about shock in Hamlet, as Hamlet wonders whether death will end what he calls "the thousand natural shocks that flesh is heir to."

> Why is that word [shock] so particularly evocative? Why is it able to unmask the essential quality of human vulnerability that allows us to know what Hamlet feels at that moment—to know in our own souls the enemy that we are all helpless to oppose and possibly unable to escape even through death?
>
> (p. 196)

Bromberg notes that Theodore Reik (1936), an early psychoanalyst who was, Bromberg says, considerably ahead of his time, wrote evocatively about shock:

> *The root problem of neurosis is not fear, but shock.* In my opinion, that problem remains insoluble until fear is brought into connection with the emotion of shock.... Shock is the prime emotion, the first thing that the little living creature feels.... I hold that shock is in general a characteristic of a traumatic situation, fear, one of danger. *Shock is the emotional reaction to something that bursts in upon us, fear the reaction to something that comes with a menace.* Fear is itself a signal preceding shock, it anticipates the emotion of shock in miniature, and so protects us from it and from its profound and harmful effects.
>
> (Reik, 1936, pp. 267–8, cited in Bromberg, 1998, p. 196)

Bromberg also reminds us that Freud made the distinction between a danger situation and a situation that actually becomes "traumatic," stating that it is the subjective meaning of the traumatic situation that is of essence; it is not the *source* of the danger as objectively evaluated that is primary, but whether the affect is subjectively experienced as overwhelming. If the person is psychologically over stimulated to the degree that he cannot think or perceive and instead experiences a generalized flooding of affect—this is what Reik called shock.

> This idea may be our greatest unacknowledged debt to Freud—that what a person perceives in front of his eyes (so-called objective reality) is a construction that is partially shaped by his state of mind, not simply vice versa. "Psychic" reality, the world "behind" one's eyes, is thus in a continuing dialectic with perception, and our success as clinicians with any patient depends on our ability to work at the boundary between...past experience and "here-and-now" experience.
>
> (Bromberg, 1998, pp. 169–70)

Gottman and Notarius (2000) and other researchers are confirming Freud's and Reik's hunches. Using sophisticated brain monitoring equipment, they are finding that the cortex actually goes "off-line" to some degree during flooding, inhibiting the possibility of constructive dialogue for a while. The past, and our present-day, terror-filled construction that the present is just like the past is literally interfering with our present-day brain functioning.

Shock response occurs naturally when we experience life-threatening anxiety. The natural role of shock is demonstrated in the interplay of predator and prey. The animal kingdom has evolved three defense responses to danger: fight, flight, and immobility (freezing) (Levine, 1997). A deer running from a lion has a pounding heart and a fully engaged sympathetic nervous system; just before the lion grasps for its throat, however, it collapses to the ground using the shock of the trauma to freeze in apparent immobility, preparing for the inevitable. In the immobility response, both the animal's sympathetic and parasympathetic nervous systems are highly activated simultaneously. No fear shows on its face. Yet if the lion drags it to its kits without killing it and turns away for a moment, the deer flees toward freedom in an all-out burst of energy.

Levine believes that the recognition of shock is crucial to the working through of trauma. He uses the image of a river to represent the flow of one's life.

> Our bodies are the banks of the stream, containing our life-energy and holding it in bounds while allowing it to freely flow within the banks. It is the protective barrier of the bank that allows us to safely experience our sense of inner movement and change.... Using the analogy of the stream, shock trauma can be visualized as an external force rupturing the protective container (banks) of our experience.... With the rupture, an explosive rushing out of life-energy creates a trauma vortex. This whirlpool exists outside the banks of our life stream of normal experience. It is common for traumatized individuals either to get sucked into the trauma vortex or to avoid the breach entirely by staying distanced from the region where the breach (trauma) occurred. We re-enact and relive our traumas when we get sucked into the trauma vortex, thus opening the possibility for emotional flooding and retraumatization. In avoiding the trauma vortex, we constrict and become phobic. We do not allow ourselves to experience the fullness of what we are inside, or what there is outside. This split-off whirlpool sucks away much of our life-energy, reducing the force of the main current.
>
> (Levine, 1997, p. 19)

Levine's published work on trauma focuses more on acute than on chronic "cumulative trauma" (Khan, 1974), but it applies equally well to the horrific unmetabolizable affects that patients with backgrounds of neglect and disorganized attachment bring to therapy. The problem with cumulative trauma is that the trauma shock stacks up over repetitions and re-livings, and when it is triggered, a person may sequence all the way back to feeling the sensations and the enormity of the critical incidents.

Consider this example. A woman in her mid-40s reported this dream after many associations about being tired of working so hard in therapy, tired of her husband and his lousy attitude, tired of him jumping down her throat yelling at her all the time "out of just nowhere, for no reason*,"* tired of couples therapy, tired of not getting anywhere, tired of feeling stuck. In her dream: "I was taking this really long, four-feet or so long, sausage out of my mouth," she gesticulated, pulling slowly for a long time. After many associations and ruling out the obvious (sexual abuse, divorce), I offered the possibility that this dream represented all the bits and pieces of all the trauma and attachment shock she had accumulated over her life, globbed together in her body and clogging her energy up the way sausage was all globbed up in a wrapper. She burst into tears and stared at me with a glazed, shocked comprehension and nodded, tears streaming down her face for some minutes.

We are all familiar with the classic flashback from sexual abuse, rape, or war trauma. Yet trauma specialists such as Kalsched (1996) have long recognized that trauma

> attacks the very capacity for experience itself, which means attacking the links (Bion, 1959) between affect and image, perception and thought, sensation and knowledge. The result is that experience is rendered meaningless, coherent memory is "disintegrated," and individuation is interrupted…. Whole experience is dismembered.
>
> (Kalsched, 1996, pp. 36–7)

When an emotional flashback of "trauma shock" from early terror is compounded by Hebbian learning (i.e., neurons that fire together wire together) over many repetitions, be forewarned that the intensity of the accumulated shock will be great indeed. Shock interrupts one's ability to stay present, relational, and oriented in present time. Hypervigilance, an exaggerated startle response, an easily roused sense of betrayal by significant others, and an intensity of response beyond that required by the current circumstances, all suggest an undercurrent of trauma shock in the nervous system, one to which the patient may be almost oblivious. Porges coined the term "neuroception" (2001) to describe how neural circuits distinguish whether situations and people are safe, dangerous, or life threatening. He extended his work to examine many clinical applications of polyvagal theory to psychotherapy (Porges & Dana, 2018).

Attachment Shock

When shocks become interwoven with sensory experience, they become fragments and chards of PTSD implicit memory experience. "Unbearable affects can shred the psyche and a whole host of psychosomatic or psychotic symptoms may result" (Garfield, 2003, p. 57). Garfield's specialty is working with psychotic patients, but I believe that unbearable affects, especially the "attachment shock" (Adams, 2006) experience of being dropped, attacked, or chronically startled by an attachment figure are at the very core of traumatic experience itself; it is not only psychotic and psychosomatic patients who suffer from unbearable affects. Most patients with backgrounds of moderate-to-severe childhood trauma have a plethora of dissociative symptoms relating to unbearable affect which go unrecognized, unmetabolized, unseen, and undiscussed. *The shocks of attachment trauma—shocks that occur in the context of relationships that are inherently destabilizing and disorienting—form a grouping of vitality affects that we have just begun investigating.* Clinicians sometimes think of flashbacks as being limited to visual and auditory re-livings of horrific events like sexual abuse or wartime trauma, but the greater preponderance of flashback experiences occur in the context of attachment shocks triggered by relationships with significant others, i.e., "attachment trauma." *Attachment shock flashbacks are physiologically entrained emotional experiences, in reaction to a significant other, that occur in the body long before the mind gets involved and that have to do with not feeling safe. They are emotional memories of inadvertent assault: feeling frightened, dropped, menaced, mocked, confused, disoriented, or terrorized in the early years.*

Attachment shock is central to the understanding of insecure attachment. The following descriptions are taken from a research context (Ainsworth et al., 1978; Main & Solomon, 1990) but have profound implications for understanding preverbal trauma in general and attachment trauma in particular. First, let us take a look at the experience of secure attachment. An infant who has developed *secure attachment* patterns to both parents (for each parent–child relationship has its own attachment pattern) has had repeated experiences of emotionally attuned, predictable, and empathic caregiving responses from her parents that have been encoded implicitly in her infant brain.

The infant has developed a mental model of attachment (Siegel, 1999a) which helps her know what to expect from each parent. Given that there has been a fair degree of predictability in the parenting relationships (what Winnicott termed "good enough" parenting), and that adequate emotional repair was made when the parents did overstress the infant, this infant's implicit memory anticipates that the future will continue to be secure, predictable, and reliable, and that glitches in communication will be worked out and soothed. These youngsters tend to have good social skills and high trust. In the Strange Situation their mothers readily soothe them. They can easily relax into a fantasy that everything will turn out to be manageable. Secure attachment certainly does seem to correlate strongly with social skills later in life (Lewis et al., 2000) and may contribute to what has come to be called emotional intelligence (Mayer & Salovey, 1995; Salovey & Mayer, 1990). We can surmise that securely attached children had relatively little attachment shock experience early in life—to the degree that they were startled, snapped at, or otherwise traumatized by a parent, we can reliably infer that they experienced immediate parental repair and soothing.

Infants with an *insecure-avoidant attachment* tend to have experienced parents who were less emotionally attuned, perhaps more distant or intrusive, non-perceptive, rejecting, and less able to make emotional repair and soothe them when things went wrong. These experiences then become encoded implicitly, and the infants' implicit memory anticipates that the future may continue to be filled with rejection, misunderstanding, and overcontrol. These youngsters tend to be lonely and keep to themselves. In the Strange Situation they turn away from or ignore their mother's return. We can hypothesize that these youngsters experienced a kind of shock in their bodies that Lewis (1981, 1983/2004, 2006) terms cephalic shock: a chronic sense of misattunement that resides in the musculature of the developing infant and later child, creating tension and muscle soreness and a sense of never being able to completely relax. Youngsters experiencing cephalic shock probably had difficulty molding against their parents' bodies or completely relaxing as they were being held, rocked, fed, dressed, bathed, and changed by parents who were not tuned into the nuances of the infants' communications and needs. We will go further into Lewis's notion of cephalic shock in Chapter 4.

Infants with an *insecure-ambivalent attachment* tend to have had parents who were inconsistently empathic, predictable, and perceptive and tended to impose their own states of mind upon their children. As these experiences become encoded, the infants' implicit memory anticipates confusion, unpredictability, comfort, and rejection simultaneously. Consequently, these youngsters are extremely difficult to soothe in the Strange Situation; they cling desperately to their mothers, sob frantically, but don't calm down easily. We can surmise that these youngsters experienced more shocks of mis-attunement, startle, abandonment, and a confusing rhythm of attachment, with enough attunement to encourage the youngster to turn toward the parent figure for soothing and repair, but with no confidence that soothing is forthcoming.

As we have seen, infants with *disorganized/disoriented attachment* tend to have parents who have not only been emotionally unavailable and unpredictable but have also had frightened, frightening and/or disoriented communications with their infants during the infant's first year of life. Main and Hesse (1990) have proposed that a caregiver's own unresolved fears related to past losses or traumas result in frightened or frightening behaviors toward the infant. This frightened or frightening behavior, in turn, creates fear of the caregiver in the infant, which disorganizes the infant's ability to accept soothing from the caregiver as a solution to stress and fear. During the Strange Situation, these infants have turned around in circles; shown acute, bizarre approach/avoidance behavior toward the parent; fallen upon the ground as if to hang onto something solid; or "frozen" in place looking terrified. These experiences are encoded implicitly and developed into a disorganized mental model with multiple, contradictory and alternating dimensions.

Additionally, Lyons-Ruth et al. (1999) have suggested that when a parent consistently fails to repair an emotionally stressed relationship (e.g., fails to respond to the infant's distress communications in a sensitive fashion), the infant *cannot develop* an organized attachment strategy in the first place; without consistent emotional repair, there is no possibility of security or predictability. "The failure to repair is another clear, unambiguous source of alarm for the child" (Solomon & George, 1999, p. 21). With the stimulus cue of being alone with a parent who has been the source of panic, confusion, terror, and alarm, these implicit representations can become reactivated and create a disorganizing and frightening internal world for the infant. We can hypothesize that children with disorganized attachment have been shocked and traumatized repeatedly, leading to a "freezing" trauma response that is somewhat bizarre. These youngsters may well grow up into adults with dissociative defenses to help manage their anxiety level.

> By a child's first birthday, these states of mind, these repeated patterns of implicit leaning are deeply encoded in the brain…. Repeated experiences of terror and fear can be engrained within the circuits of the brain as states of mind. With chronic occurrence, these states can become more readily activated (retrieved) in the future, such that they become characteristic traits of the individual. In this way, our lives can become shaped by reactivations of implicit memory, which lack a sense that something is being recalled. We simply enter these engrained states and experience them as the reality of our present experience.
>
> (Siegel, 1999a, pp. 32–3)

Attachment Shock in the Body

Judith Kestenberg (1965), an analytically trained dance and movement therapist, provides a rich developmentally based window into the bodily state precursors of psychic structure. More recently, Janet Kestenberg Amighi and colleagues (2018) review normal milestones in developmental sequencing and patterning of breath, extension, flexion, expansion, contraction, rhythm, and movement, and then examine the impact of childhood stress on these sequences and patterns. The progression of these milestones provides the nonverbal foundations of relational development. When we have experienced a traumatic childhood, our bodies' movement patterns and rhythms reveal to the practiced eye a damaged sense of self and lack of basic trust through our patterns of muscular tension, skeletal constriction, restrictive breathing, rhythmic movements, and vocalization. Fear is engraved and etched into the cells of our bodies by shock—our posture, our muscle tone, our voices, our movements betray early experiences outside of our awareness. Through authentic movement and dance therapies and other forms of bodywork, including the Feldenkrais Method, cranial sacral therapy, myofacial release, physical therapy, bioenergetics, chiropractic, and rolfing techniques, bodily states can be mobilized and modified adjunctive to depth psychotherapy. I have found that adjunctive non-verbal therapy modalities are powerfully synergistic with the verbal psychotherapy process in facilitating the working-through process of shock trauma in the body/psyche.

Lyons-Ruth and her colleagues suggest the possibility of many different pathways to disorganized attachment and dissociation, among them unresolved trauma and loss without sufficient external support to promote a working-through process. They propose a cat-egory of individuals with disorganized attachment who did not experience frank childhood loss or outright abuse, whose experience of unintegrated fearful affects was rooted in the relationship with a hostile/helpless caregiver. These caregivers tend to get agitated and overwhelmed by their children's distress and fail to soothe them. The authors further surmise that, absent a significant change in caregiving environments or significant new relationships, "the earlier deviant care-giving is likely to potentiate the occurrence of later loss or trauma, as well as to increase the likelihood that the trauma will not be resolved" (Lyons-Ruth et al., 2006, p. 44). In this book we will explore the stories of many individuals who have struggled all their lives with this para-doxical conundrum.

Randomness and Meaninglessness

I believe that Lewis (2006), Grotstein (1990a, 1990b, 1991), Mitrani (1996, 2001), and Mitrani and Mitrani (1997) are on the cutting edge of providing us with visceral metaphors for understanding the lived experience of attachment trauma. By definition, shock is a jolt, a scare, a startle, a fall, a sudden drop, or a terror reaction; shock can daze, paralyze, stun, or stupefy us. We draw a sharp, deep breath inward and almost stop breathing. Grotstein (1990a) believes that "the experi-ence of randomness *is* (emphasis mine) the traumatic state (the black hole) which can otherwise be thought of as the experience of psych-ical meaninglessness…ultimate terror of falling into a cosmic abyss" (p. 274).

Lone Tree
A tree spooked
By its own evening whispers.
Afraid to rustle.
Just now
Bewitched by the distant sunset.

Making a noise full of deep
Misgivings,
Like bloody razor blades
Being shuffled,
And then again the quiet.

The birds too terror-stricken
To make their own comment.
Every leaf to every other leaf
An apparition,
A separate woe.
Bare twig:
A finger of suspicion.

"Lone Tree," p. 60 from *Walking the Black Cat*,
by Charles Simic. Copyright © 1996 by Charles Simic.
Reprinted by permission of Mariner Books,
an imprint of HarperCollins Publishers LLC.

Let us turn our attention to the cumulative trauma of the shock of the random. We are about to explore the not-good-enough caretaking experience.

Attachment Shock: The Broken Container

Siegel's (2020) work on the nascent sense of self suggests that it is through mind-to-mind emotional limbic resonance that we learn who we are, how to feel, and how to regulate how we feel. Bion (1962) suggests that a "steppingstone" in the normal development of a child is having the experience of a "container" to receive and process the jumble of feelings and sensations—mainly painful ones but also painfully excited ones—that the child's brain eventually needs to learn how to regulate. These feelings need to be held and somehow made bearable for the infant, much like a mother bird pre-chews the food for the baby bird and then regurgitates it into the eager youngling's awaiting mouth.

For example, the mother of a young, overtired toddler might know her child needs to sleep, even though he is wound up and over-active. When he melts down in the next few seconds, he will be totally overwhelmed by a cluster of distress that is meaningless to him. If the mother is able to understand that he is exhausted and soothe him instead of correcting him sharply with a "what did I tell you would happen?" and escalating into upset herself, she is metabolizing in herself what the child is not, as yet, able to metabolize. Bion (1962) stressed that it is vital for the mother to use her own mental and emo-tional (and physiological) resources for giving meaning to the mean-ingless because the child has, as yet, no resources of his own outside of his environment. Very gradually the child can begin to take inside himself this repeated experience of having a space in somebody's mind and of being understood. This process is what is meant by the phrase "container/contained."

What happens, then, when the container leaks; when the parent doesn't have a clue how to change or feed him and is afraid to hold him; when a parent goes cold as ice as the youngster cries for a hug, when a parent breaks off contact during a child's meltdown? Krystal's (1988) work on trauma and affect points out that *trauma doesn't just over-load the circuits in some mysterious neurological fashion but is related to meaning making.* What meanings can the infant fashion when an immature father holds it by one arm and shoulder while dragging it around the mall? When a mother bursts into frustrated sobbing at her own ineptness to satisfy this greedy monster clawing at her? When a parental couple silently wishes the child had never been born and leave it to cry alone into the night, perhaps in a closet, and who grudgingly feed and clean it enough to keep it alive, but resent the demands and necessity all the while?

I believe that "attachment shock" is an individual's neural network of the psycho-physiological shock states that have failed to integrate during rapid changes in emotional stability—overwhelming the ner-vous system with confusion, shock, and unmet attachment needs in mind-to-mind contact with primary caretakers in childhood and, eventually, with significant others including spouses. Attachment shock is all about the concrete experience of randomness that accompanies state shifts, that is, changes in emotional stability. An important element of attachment shock is rapid state change accompanied by confusion. A child who sizes up his mother, provocatively slaps her, and gets slapped back is probably not going to suffer much attachment shock. He may be surprised, startled, even cry, but he is crystal clear on what happened. This form of limit-setting happens in the animal kingdom all the time. In the experience of attachment shock, up to four opposing subjective states rapidly oscillate: a strong attachment drive for comfort/safety: "I need you"; a felt sense of danger: "I must escape and get away"; shock at the body level about the abrupt intrusion of (felt) danger into a safe haven of relationship or abrupt withdrawal of safety; and confusion and unsuccessful attempts to make sense out of why safety shifted into danger. In attachment shock, it is impossible to hang onto anywhere or anything firmly; at best, it is as if the ground is pitching beneath one's feet; more likely, the ground has suddenly opened up into a chasm and one is hurtling into the abyss with no forewarning, no understanding of why. Helping adult patients develop an awareness of prodromal warning signs is useful in staving off the full shock experience, for if they can identify it early, it is like pulling the ripcord of a parachute and slowing the momentum of the fall.

Siegel (1999a) believes the brain can be called an "anticipation machine," scanning the environment and trying to predict what is coming next. Thus, in a couples session, the complaint of the "harsh voice" of the spouse, coupled with the scowl/growl of his or her visage may be a description of a traumatic activation experience. For certain individuals with disorganized attachment experience who begin to get shaky at moments of harsh voice/scowl/growl, this prodromal "felt body sense of fear, almost an instinct that something is very wrong here" may be an early warning signal, a harbinger of more intense attachment shock about to come. One patient described it in this way:

At home or in couples therapy, if things start to go wrong between us, it's like a bird is flying around in my head. It's panicked, bumping against the walls the way birds do if they accidentally get inside the house.... I know there's not *really* a bird in my head, but it's the only way I can describe to you the feeling of panic on the edge, it's like a storm is coming. I've learned to tell my husband "there's a bird in my head," and then we know I'm in some kind of shock from what just happened between us.

Attachment shock is an experience of the *body*, as ambivalence is an experience of the *mind*. Attachment shock can feel like being blindsided by someone you trust; it can feel like stepping on solid ice, only to fall in flailing; to jump or fall backwards into someone's waiting arms, only to be dropped (think Ropes Course). I have heard it described as being transported to an amusement park ride like the Cyclone, in which the cylinder spins and the bottom drops, with the unwitting, helpless shockee pinned against the side of the wall for the duration of the dizzying, nauseating ride. In ambivalence, on the other hand, one firmly holds two opposing states of mind in one's grasp, such as loving one's spouse and hating the same spouse; these two states may wriggle and attempt to escape one's hold like a toddler on the way to his bath, but one holds on nonetheless, a bit worse for the wear and tear of all the effort involved, but victorious in the end. Ambivalence is unrelated to the shock experience; learning to hold opposites in mind is a bit like achieving a new yoga position or a new technical skill in sports.

Attachment shocks occur throughout the life span; one of my patients remembers rushing home at age 10 eager to share with her mother what she had learned about the female body in "sex ed." "Guess what's going to happen to me!" she exclaimed, rushing into the kitchen, hugging her mother and the visiting neighbor lady, her words tumbling as fast as they could from her brain out of her mouth onto the kitchen floor. Seconds later, she crawled shamefaced up the back stairs, knowing she had committed an awful offense in her exuberance but not exactly sure what the offense was. Shortly afterwards she made her first suicide attempt in an effort to convey her distress. Her family, unaccustomed to emotional dialogue, ignored her distress and never discussed her suicide attempt with her. Her father was a Vietnam vet and slept with a shotgun under his pillow, occasionally sleepwalking with the loaded gun during a nightmare. This patient learned how to talk her father down but, again, the family never discussed with her what had happened.

Attachment Shock and the Second Skin

Bick (1968) proposed the notion of a "psychic skin" as a projection of or corresponding to the bodily skin: "the need for a containing object would seem in the infantile unintegrated state to produce a frantic search for an object...which can hold the attention and thereby be experienced, momentarily at least, as holding the parts of the personality together" (p. 484). When the parenting is not "good enough," the youngster is totally disabused of infantile omnipotence and discovers that he has no influence, let alone omnipotence. This discovery is shattering enough to rip a metaphoric hole in the psychic skin. Disturbances in the domain of the psychic skin can lead to the development of "second skin" formations through which dependence on the mother is replaced by pseudo-independence. One woman (Jennifer) came to our initial session in mid-summer wearing heavy boots and a leather coat (see Chapter 5). She laughingly explained to me that she used clothing as a pretend barrier to protect herself; she advised me to check out what she was wearing to determine how safe she was feeling and how vulnerable she was willing to be. I brought up the notion of "second skin formations" with her, which fascinated her as it made sense of something she had always known intuitively but not really understood. Within a few weeks she began wearing sandals to her session. In Chapter 1, I mentioned the patient who seized eagerly upon a comment I made about him not having any skin. He rushed to tell me about the lobster in his favorite childhood chapter book who had to shed his shell. The lobster felt horridly vulnerable, you see, but none of his friends understood his anguish or terror. They did not need shells to survive, as he did.

Culbert-Koehn (1997) attempted to link the works of Tustin (1981) and Jung (1970) in her paper on the analysis of "hard" and "soft." Jung believed that when opposites were brought together and contained, a "third" element was produced by the "transcendent function." Tustin wrote about the "third" element emerging from the infant's integration of hard and soft sensations as a way that reality can be processed and the world can begin to make sense. Culbert-Koehn writes about catastrophic anxiety states, presumably stemming from mismanaged birth and psychological catastrophe, which affect her patients' abilities to manage transition points in life and within themselves. However, the implications of Culbert-Koehn's article reach far beyond the birth experience into the attachment experience itself. Hard and soft attachment experiences are hard-wired into memory; each of us filters our interactions with others through the lenses of mental models formed from experiences with early attachment figures from the past. "These models can shift rapidly outside of awareness, sometimes creating abrupt transitions in states of mind and interactions with others" (Siegel, 1999a, p. 34). Nowhere is this condition of rapidly shifting and confusing states truer than in the disorganized attachment relationships of childhood, sometimes manifesting in everyday, relatively banal situations.

A woman in her 50s, for example, who had a difficult childhood with disorganized attachment to her mother and insecure-ambivalent attachment to her father became both excited and distressed after reading Culbert-Koehn's paper. As a therapist, she sensed that the whole notion of integrating hard and soft would be quite salient for her. Because of a shoulder injury, she couldn't just reach into the shower and pull out the shower head to warm the water up before getting in. Alas, this meant she had to allow herself to be hit full blast with a spray of cold water, which she wailed that she could not tolerate. Although she looked and felt ludicrous, she wore her husband's hiking rain jacket into the shower to cover herself and shield her from the "hard" cold jet of water until the "soft" hot water arrived. "Hard" and "soft" have also become the currency of discussion in marital negotiations related to issues of tone of voice, abruptness, quality of touch, and so on.

My patients who struggle to integrate hard and soft frequently bring it up in terms of fear dynamics in their relationships: "We were having a perfectly lovely evening and then she said and I said and suddenly we were having this fractured evening, and it didn't make any sense, and she was in tears and I was shaking inside...." Disorganized attachment experience is the penultimate failure of integration of parallel soft and hard attachment states, woven together by confusion and frenzy. Within a committed relationship, attachment states ebb and flow, shift, and flux within minutes if not seconds of each other, sometimes depending upon the demand characteristics of the situation and how many people are involved. When fear, confusion, disorientation, disorganization, helpless, and hostile emotional states intertwine with "I've asked you two times already who takes the boys to soccer practice, what time is dinner and did you remember to pick up the prescription?" a recipe for communication distress at a minimum seems likely.

Attachment Shock and Second Skin Defenses

Mitrani (1996, 2001) and Mitrani and Mitrani (1997) extended Bick's (1968), Tustin's (1981), and Meltzer's (1975) work on the second skin and adhesive identification in their work with adult patients in psychoanalysis. They observed in adult patients that severe infantile privation could lead them to:

(1) paper over the holes with a patchwork of encrustments, encapsulation, armor, intellectuality, muscularity, and other second skin formations. Environmental failures that the infants were not psychically equipped to deal with become walled off from conscious awareness. These defenses are the price patients from difficult environments pay just to survive;

(2) retreat into a self-made illusory kingdom/prison of omnipotence much like Antoine St. Exupéry's *Little Prince* inhabited to protect the vulnerable baby self from getting bruised, while secretly believing humanity and vulnerability to be a fatal error;

(3) glom onto the surface of others in the hope they will provide sufficient bandaging to the psychic skin to prevent leaking, using people as interchangeable band-aids for as long as they are available to plug the holes. The cultural phenomenon referred to as "serial monogamy" by savvy singles is often revealed, in depth psychotherapy, to be more of an attempt to staunch the flow of uncontrolled psychic bleeding with at least someone, however unsuitable, rather than a genuine search for a compatible partner. Alas, the deepest vitality affects and even the joys of deepest intimacy may be forfeited until the tears in the psychic skin are attended to.

Attachment Shock and the Black Hole Experience

When attachment shocks accumulate, so do the experiences of meaninglessness. The more a youngster experiences himself as unable to forge a meaningful bond with his parents wherein he feels understood and responded to emotionally, the more desperate and bereft he feels. Children naturally assume that it is they who are without meaning, rather than their parent who is deficient in parenting skills, because of the natural egocentric reasoning style of children. Grotstein (1990a, 1990b) believes the experience of meaninglessness, descending as the link breaker of connection, is haunting because it is either eerily persecutory or remorsefully melancholic. This meaninglessness, which may be experienced passively and, paradoxically, impassively or actively, characterizes the "black hole" experience and corresponds to the experience of being cursed, abandoned, damned, and without hope. Emotional abuse, chaotic parenting, and neglect stem from, and lead back into, the whirlpool of the black hole and may spawn in the fertile ground of potential disorganized attachment dyads fed by multigenerational trauma affects. In a meltdown situation, when parents share mind-to-mind negative states with their infants, the parent may start off with the intention to soothe but inadvertently tumble into a trauma cascade, amplifying and co-mingling their own and their infants' distress states in a panic- and desperation-filled escalation into the black hole experience.

Sometimes parents feel so ill equipped to meet their baby's physical and emotional needs that they momentarily just give up and withdraw when intensity crescendos. The sound of a baby crying is biologically designed to be piercing and unforgettable for survival reasons, but many of my patients, who are otherwise highly emotionally resonant people, report that it just sends them over the edge neurologically. Perhaps in some individuals the baby's cries tap into a neural network of their own distress cries from long ago, activating their own unresolved attachment issues.

The threshold of tolerance breach is a critical juncture for a parent in the face of intense dyadic distress. I propose that in dyads involving a parent with a secure attachment style, the anxious/overwrought parent may negotiate the moment to be able to dispel the predator/prey anxiety (Grotstein, 1990a, 1990b) of "kill or be killed," either by calling for help from outside the dyad or taking a deep breath and calming herself or himself down, remaining emotionally aware of the baby as a tiny individual in need of help. Parents with disorganized attachment styles may be at higher risk for overwhelm, as attachment shock circuits begin to activate and different meaning systems get activated. If subsequent kindling of their own unresolved childhood trauma occurs and the parent cannot self-soothe or call for help from outside the dyad in sufficient measure or time to reverse the escalation of tensions, the parent may freeze in immobility shock momentarily as his or her coping resources are overwhelmed. Fight or flight? Depending on their own attachment patterns they may (1) contain, constrict, and withdraw both affectively and cognitively (and possibly even physically), in an enactment of their own disorganized attachment confusion, abruptly severing the mind-to-mind link between parent and infant when the infant needs the parent desperately in order to preserve or regain some composure; or (2) pass some threshold of tolerance and just snap, flooding affectively, enacting part of their own disorganized attachment pattern by crying, lashing out, and passing the flooding response onto the child through both mind-to-mind resonance and sensory contact. As the parent responds in the heat of the crisis, the infant has his own shock responses to process. Immobility shock describes the shock the brain experiences in the moments of "too much-ness" when, from the infant's perspective, the time of impending nervous system overwhelm is long past and annihilation seems at least momentarily imminent. For at least some infants, attachment shock may be the ultimate result if the parent is unskilled at initiating repair to the relationship. The youngster is then left in a shocked state for a prolonged period of time, unable to down-regulate the overwhelming arousal. Animal studies demonstrate that the more times an animal is traumatized into immobility and then released, the more frantic and disorganized the animal's post-release behavior will be (Levine, 1997). We can surmise, then, that disorganized attachment behaviors may be linked to an excess of attachment shock accumulated in the nervous system.

Sometimes characterological issues in the parent offer a pathway to attachment shock. Chronically narcissistic, withholding, or punitive parenting catapults children into an attachment shock, which disrupts any sense of security they may have about their place in the world or in their parents' hearts. In these families, children have to walk on eggshells, be careful what they say, and not dare to be spontaneous for fear of emotional consequences. In this excerpt from *The God of Small Things*, Arundhati Roy captures the chilling quality of attachment shock in a family with a punitive mother, Ammu.

> So why don't you marry him then?" Rahel said petulantly. Time stopped on the red staircase...Rahel froze. She was desperately sorry for what she had said. She didn't know where those words had come from. She didn't know that she'd had them in her. But they were out now, and wouldn't go back in her. They hung about that red staircase like clerks in a government office. Some stood, some sat and shivered their legs. "Rahel." Ammu said, "Do you realize what you have just done?" Frightened eyes and a fountain looked back at Ammu. "It's all right. Don't be scared." Ammu said. "Just answer me. Do you?" "What?" Rahel said in the smallest voice she had. "Realize what you've just done?" Ammu said. Frightened eyes and a fountain looked back at Ammu. "D'you know what happens when you hurt people?" Ammu said. "When you hurt people, they begin to love you less. That's what careless words do. They make people love you a little less." A cold moth with unusually dense dorsal tufts landed lightly on Rahel's heart.
>
> (Roy, 1997, pp. 106–8)

Attachment Shock and Disorganized Attachment: Implications for Psychotherapy

When parents are unable to perceive distress in their child, or are unable or unwilling to respond empathically to that distress, then the child is unable to use his parent to enter more bearable levels of arousal. Thus the child is left to rely upon his own, paltry resources for self-regulation and to experience unbearable emotional states that become encoded in implicit memory. It is these unbearable, shocking affect states of being abandoned, unprotected, confused, and frightened by a parent who cannot relate helpfully to the child's distress that I characterize as attachment shock. Liotti (1999) points out that, although the implicit memories of these early interactions leading to disorganized attachment contain the experience of terror and confusion in the child and the memory of helpless, frightened, and/or frightening affects in the parent, implicit memories of comfort will also be encoded.

"Notwithstanding the barrier of fear and/or aggression in the parent, the disorganized child will eventually be able, in most instances, to achieve proximity (otherwise, he or she could not survive)" (p. 299). Liotti suggests that the meaning structures emerging from implicit memories in which comfort, aggression, and fear dramatically follow each other will necessarily be contradictory and multiple. Disorganized children may construe—simultaneously and with equal likelihood— what they have repeatedly experienced in their attachment interactions as: (1) being frightened and helpless in the face of a menacing parent; (2) being the cause of the parent's bewildering fear, helplessness, or rage; (3) being responsible for comforting the parent; (4) being joined with the parent as helpless co-victims of an inexplicable, invisible external threat. Repeated experiences within disorganized attachment relationships have been shown to be associated with clinical dissociation, in which mental processes fail to become integrated as a whole (Carlson, 1998; Liotti, 1999; Lyons-Ruth et al., 2006; Main & Morgan, 1996; Ogawa et al., 1997).

Attachment shock is the clinical bridge between attachment theory and clinical practice. Disorganized attachment is still in its infancy as a research construct, but its applications to psychotherapy are manifold. Patients bring their unbearable affect states straight into therapy. In group, individual, and especially in couples therapy, I have observed that there is a moment of transition, of critical mass, between "when things were ok between us" and "when things are awful between us." In physics, this principle is called "resonance." Imagine a bridge gently rocked by the wind from side to side. When—and if—the rocking motion reaches a particular frequency, the bridge is vulnerable to shattering. This very event happened in Seattle in the 1970s: high winds escalated vibration in a bridge until it fell apart. Attachment shock in the child, infant, or spouse occurs *at the moment the dyad goes into negative emotional resonance.* All, or at least most, parent–child dyads occasionally reach this point of meltdown. What we see in disorganized attachment is the failure of repair on the part of the parent, which contributes to a build-up of attachment shock in the developing child. The child is left in confused, startled agitation for a period beyond endurance.

My hypothesis is that attachment shock serves as the initiation point for the transitory paranoid states we see in couples, for the negative transference we see in group and individual therapy, and for unbearable countertransference affects of confusion, rage, and panic. Following the principles of neural networks and Hebbian memory, the *meaning* of the startle and dysphoria sensations inherent in attachment shock experience—whether it relates to feeling dropped and abandoned, terrified beyond endurance, shattered, criticized, or horrified—is construed within familiar internal working models. Thus the man who grew up being criticized will plunge into shocked rage at a mere constructive suggestion from his spouse; the woman who felt terrorized as a child will flinch if her spouse moves too quickly into her "space"; the patient who felt abandoned as a child may panic when his girlfriend does not return his calls in a timely fashion. What we have carefully studied as theoretical constructs such as "transference," "countertransference," and "paranoid states," we can now begin to understand also as critical moments in a relationship pivoting on the threshold of attachment shock.

Main and Hesse (1990) have proposed that dyadic interactions involving parental frightened, disoriented, or frightening behaviors toward an infant are inherently disorganizing. They disrupt the formation of an organized strategy because the infant cannot make sense of the internally generated and confusing parental responses that are not in attunement to the infant's needs. Indeed, these responses are, in many cases, counter-indicated, actively destructive, or even random—related to the parents' own pasts rather than the infant's present.

I propose that, similarly, there is sometimes no organized adaptation available for the therapists of patients with disorganized attachment styles because disorganized attachment systems convey frightening, dissociative, and disorienting affects *by their nature* and are at least initially intransigent to soothing. The therapist cannot reliably make sense of the transference or the countertransference in traditional terms and finds the floor shifting beneath his feet just when he begins to get grounded. When terror erupts in the transference, everyone in the room gets goosebumps. My dictionary defines terror as stark fear and as a running from fear. Therapists are sometimes buffeted by the storm winds of confusion as much as their patients are.

Hedges (1994, 2000) describes the terror that children feel when "contact" with the mother's mind has gone awry in the formative years; what ensues is a terror of connection layered over other terrors of loss, of disorganization, of breakdown, of annihilation. Patients who have grown up with disorganized attachment may explode, cling, and withdraw in rapid sequence; risking close contact may result in confusing and sometimes bizarre follow-up responses. Too much empathy can be as disorganizing as too little in this context. Hedges recommends carefully tracking sudden breaks and shifts into and away from intimacy as a grounding strategy for therapists caught in confusion.

In summary, as you will see in the following chapters, taking a careful trauma history at the beginning of treatment is essential. Not just in the sense of "were you beaten or abused?" but what kind of sad or scary things happened during your younger years? Did your mom suffer any losses or traumas while she was carrying you? Was there fighting at home that was distressing? Were you ever in a tornado, accident, or housefire? Did you lose a pet at any time? Who could you turn to when you were sad? Did you feel safe being you? Were there any separations between you and your family, medical or otherwise? Were you ever in a hospital? I ask people to chronicle for me (in writing) ages 1–4, 5–10, 11–14, 15–20, and later in life about life events that might have been stressful. How did you play? What were friendships like? How would I know if you were feeling overwhelmed? If you don't inquire, you might never find out.

Note

1   The chapter title is taken from a Khalil Gibran poem (see Gibran, 1923).

References

Adams, K. (2006). Falling forever: The price of chronic shock. *International Journal of Group Psychotherapy,* 56(2), 127–72.

Ainsworth, M. D. S., Blehar, M. C., Waters, E., & Wall, S. (1978). *Patterns of attachment: A psychological study of the Strange Situation.* Erlbaum.

Amighi, J. K., Loman, S., & Sossin, K. M. (2018). *The meaning of movement: Embodied developmental, clinical, and cultural perspectives of the Kerstenberg Movement Profile* (2nd ed.). Routledge.

Bakermans-Kranenburg, M. J., & van Ijzendoorn, M. H. (2007). Research review: Genetic vulnerability or differential susceptibility in child development: The case of attachment. *The Journal of Child Psychology and Psychiatry,* 48(2), 1160–73.

Balint, M. (1952). *Primary love and psycho-analytic technique.* Hogarth.

Benjamin, W. (1969). *On some motifs in Baudelaire in Illuminations* (H. Zohn, Trans.). Schocken Books.

Bick, E. (1968). The experience of the skin in early object-relations. *International Journal of Psychoanalysis,* 49, 484–6.

Bion, W. R. (1959). Attacks on linking. International Journal of Psycho-Analysis, 40, 308–15.

Bion, W. R. (1962). Learning from experience. In Seven servants. Jason Aronson.

Bollas, C. (1987). *The shadow of the object.* Columbia University Press.

Bowlby, J. (1969/1982). *Attachment and loss: Vol. 1.* Attachment. Basic Books.

Bowlby, J. (1973). *Attachment and loss: Vol. 2.* Separation. Basic Books.

Bowlby, J. (1980). *Attachment and loss: Vol. 3.* Loss. Basic Books.

Bromberg, P. M. (1998). *Standing in the spaces.* The Analytic Press.

Carlson, E. (1998). A prospective longitudinal study of disorganized/disoriented attachment. *Child Development,* 69, 1970–1979; 1107–28.

CDC & Kaiser Permanente. (1998). *The ACE Study.* U.S. Department of Health and Human Services, Centers for Disease Control and Prevention.

Crittenden, P. (1988). *Clinical implications of attachment.* Erlbaum.

Culbert-Koehn, J. (1997). Analysis of hard and soft: Tustin's contribution to a Jungian study of opposites. In T. Mitrani & J. Mitrani (Eds.), *Encounters with autistic states: A memorial tribute to Frances Tustin* (pp. 111–23). Jason Aronson.

de Saint-Exupéry, A. (1943). *The little prince.* Harcourt.

Epstein, O. B. (2022). Primary shame: Needing you and the economy of affect. In O. B. Epstein (Ed.), *Shame matters: Attachment and relational perspectives for psychotherapists* (pp. 46–59). Routledge.

Firestone, L. (2021). Disorganized attachment: How disorganized attachments form & how they can be healed. *PsychAlive.* Available at: www.psychalive. org/disorganized-attachment/.

Freud, S. (1926). Inhibitions, symptoms and anxiety, *Standard Edition,* 19, 235–9, Hogarth Press.

Garfield, D. (2003). The mask of psychotic diagnoses. *Journal of The American Academy of Psychoanalysis and Dynamic Psychiatry,* 31(1), 45–58.

Gedo, P. M. (2000a). Symptoms, signals, affects: Psychotherapeutic techniques with dissociative patients. *Journal of the American Academy of Psychoanalysis,* 28(4), 609–18.

Gedo, P. M. (2000b). To be, and not to be: The concept of multiple function and dissociation. *Psychoanalytic Inquiry,* 20, 194–206.

Gibran, K. (1923). On pain. In K. Gibran, *The prophet.* Knopf.

Gottman, J. M., & Notarius, C. (2000). Decade review: Observing marital interaction. *Journal of Marriage and the Family,* 62, 927–47.

Grotstein, J. (1990a). Nothingness, meaninglessness, chaos, and the "black hole" 1: The importance of nothingness, meaninglessness, and chaos in psychoanalysis. *Contemporary Psychoanalysis,* 26(2), 257–90.

Grotstein, J. (1990b). Nothingness, meaninglessness, chaos, and the "black hole" II: The black hole. *Contemporary Psychoanalysis,* 26(3), 377–407.

Grotstein, J. (1991). Self-regulation and the background presence of primary identification. *Contemporary Psychoanalysis,* 27(1), 1–33.

Harlow, H. (1958). The nature of love. *American Psychologist,* 13, 573–685.

Harris, N. B. (2018). *The deepest well: Healing the long-term effects of childhood adversity.* Mariner Books.

Hedges, L. E. (1994). *Working the organizing experience.* Jason Aronson.

Hedges, L. E. (2000). *Terrifying transferences.* Jason Aronson.

Herman, J. L. (2018). Shattered shame states and their repair. In J. Yellin & K. White, *Shattered states: Disorganized attachment and its repair* (pp. 157–70). Routledge.

Hofer, M. A. (1996). On the nature and consequences of early loss. *Psychosomatic Medicine,* 58, 570–81.

Holmes, J. (1996). *Attachment, intimacy, autonomy.* Jason Aronson.

Jung, C. G. (1970). Mysterium coniunctionis: An inquiry into the separation and synthesis of psychic opposites in alchemy. In *Collected works of C. G. Jung, Vol. 14* (pp. 89–257). Bollingen Foundation.

Kain, K., & Terrell, S. (2018). *Nurturing resilience: Helping clients move forward from developmental trauma—an integrative somatic approach.* North Atlantic Books.

Kalsched, D. (1996). *The inner world of trauma.* Routledge.

Kestenberg, J. S. (1965). The role of movement patterns in development. *The Psychoanalytic Quarterly,* 34(1), 1–36.

Khan, M. (1963). The concept of cumulative trauma. *Aspects of Normal and Psychological Development,* 18, 286–306.

Khan, M. (1974). *The privacy of the self.* International Universities Press.

Kohut, H. (1971). *Analysis of the self.* International Universities Press.

Lebois, L. A. M., & Kaufman, M. L. (2020). Large-scale functional brain network architecture changes with trauma-related dissociation. *The American Journal of Psychiatry,* doi: 10.1176/appi.ajp.2020.19060647.

Levine, P. A. (1997). *Waking the tiger.* North Atlantic Books.

Lewis, R. (1981). A psychosomatic basis of premature ego development. *Comprehensive Psychotherapy,* 3, 91–102.

Lewis, R. (1983/2004). Cephalic shock as a somatic link to the false self personality. https://www.yumpu.com/en/document/read/11428826/cephalic-shock-as-a-somatic-link-to-the-false-self-personality.

Lewis, R. (2006). Frozen transference: Early traumatization and the body-psychotherapeutic relationship. *USA Body Psychotherapy Journal,* 5(2), 18–25.

Lewis, T., Amini, F., & Lannon, R. (2000). *A general theory of love.* Random House.

Liotti, G. (1999). Disorganization of attachment as a model for understanding dissociative psychopathology. In J. Solomon & C. George (Eds.), *Attachment disorganization* (pp. 291–317). Guilford Press.

Lyons-Ruth, K., Bronfman, E., & Atwood, G. (1999). A relational diathesis model of hostile-helpless states of mind: Expressions in mother–infant interaction. In J. Solomon & C. George (Eds.), *Attachment disorganization* (pp. 33–70). Guilford Press.

Lyons-Ruth, K., Connel, D. B., Zoll, D., & Stahl, J. (1987). Infants at social risk: Relations among infant maltreatment, maternal behavior, and infant attachment behavior. *Developmental Psychology,* 23, 223–32.

Lyons-Ruth, K., Dutra, L., Schuder, M., & Bianchi, I. (2006). From infant attachment disorganization to adult dissociation: Relational adaptations or traumatic experiences? *Psychiatric Clinic of North America,* 29(1), 63–86.

Main, M., & Hesse, E. (1990). Is fear the link between infant disorganized attachment status and maternal unresolved loss? In M. Greenberg, D. Cicchetti, & M. Cummings (Eds.), *Attachment in the preschool years: Theory, research, and intervention* (pp. 161–82). University of Chicago Press.

Main, M., & Morgan, H. (1996). Disorganization and disorientation in infant Strange Situation behavior: Phenotypic resemblance to dissociative states. In L. Michelson & W. Ray (Eds.), *Handbook of dissociation: Theoretical, empirical, and clinical perspectives* (pp. 107–38). Plenum Press.

Main, M., & Solomon, J. (1990). Procedures for classifying infants as disorganized/disoriented during the Ainsworth Strange Situation. In M. Greenberg, D. Cicchetti, & M. Cummings (Eds.), Attachment in the preschool years (pp. 121–60). University of Chicago Press.

Mayer, J. D., and Salovey, P. (1995). Emotional intelligence and the construction and regulation of feelings. Applied and Preventive Psychology, 4, 197–208.

Megala, J., Sivakumar, D., Jha, D., Kundu, S., Arora, K., & Gayathri, V. (2021). Epigenetic modifications due to childhood trauma causative of potential mental and physical disorders. *International Journal of Nutrition, Pharmacology, Neurological Diseases,* 11, 41–9.

Meltzer, D. (1968). Terror, persecution and dread: A dissection of paranoid anxieties. *International Journal of Psychoanalysis,* 49, 396–400.

Meltzer, D. (1975). Adhesive identification. Contemporary Psychanalysis, 11(3), 289–310.

Mitrani, J. L. (1996). *A framework for the imaginary*. Jason Aronson.

Mitrani, J. L. (2001). *Ordinary people and extra-ordinary protections*. Routledge.

Mitrani, J. L., & Mitrani, T. (1997). *Encounters with autistic states*. Jason Aronson.

Moss, E., St-Laurent, D., & Parent, S. (1999). Disorganized attachment and developmental risk at school age. In J. Solomon & C. George (Eds.), *Attachment disorganization* (pp. 160–88). Guilford Press.

Ogawa, J., Sroufe, L., Weinfeld, N., Carlson, E., & Egeland, B. (1997). Development and the fragmented self: Longitudinal study of dissociative symptomatology in a nonclinical sample. *Development and Psychopathology*, 9, 855–80.

Pally, R. (2000). *The mind-brain relationship*. Karnac.

Porges, S. W. (2001). The polyvagal theory: Phylogenetic substrates of a social nervous system. *International Journal of Psychophysiology*, 42, 29–52.

Porges, S. W., & Dana, D. (Eds.). (2018). Clinical application of the polyvagal theory: The emergence of polyvagal-informed theories. W. W. Norton & Company.

Putnam, F. (2016). *The way we are: How states of mind influence our identities, personality and potential for change*. International Psychoanalytic Books.

Rains, M., & McClinn, K. (2013). *Resiliency questionnaire*. Southern Kennebec Healthy Start, Augusta Maine. Available at: https://acpeds.org/blog/resilience.

Rakoff, V. (1967). A long-term effect of the concentration camp experience. *Viewpoints*, 1, 17–22.

Reik, T. (1936). *Surprise and the psycho-analyst*. Kegan Paul.

Roy, A. (1997). *The God of small things*. Random House.

Salovey, P., & Mayer, J. D. (1990). Emotional intelligence. *Imagination, Cognition and Personality*, 9, 185–211.

Schore, A. N. (2019). *Right brain psychotherapy*. Norton Interpersonal Series.

Siegel, D. J. (1999a). *The developing mind*. Guilford Press.

Siegel, D. J. (1999b). Toward an interpersonal neurobiology of the developing mind: Attachment relationships, "mindsight," and neural integration. *Infant Mental Health Journal*, 22(1–2), 67–94.

Siegel, D. J. (2020). *The developing mind*. 3rd ed. Guilford Press.

Simic, C. (2003). Lone tree. In C. Simic, *Walking the black cat*. Harcourt Brace & Company.

Solomon, J., & George, C. (1999). The place of disorganization in attachment theory: Linking classic observations with contemporary findings. In J. Solomon & C. George (Eds.), *Attachment disorganization* (pp. 3–32). Guilford Press.

Teicher, M. H. (2002). Scars that won't heal: The neurobiology of child abuse. *Scientific American*, 286(3), 68–75.

Tustin, F. (1981). Psychological birth and psychological catastrophe. In J. Grotstein (Ed.), *Do I dare disturb the universe?* (pp. 181–96). Karnac Books.

van der Kolk, B. A. (1987). *Psychological trauma*. American Psychiatric Press.

van der Kolk, B. A. (2015). *The body keeps the score: Brain, body, and mind in the healing of trauma*. Penguin Publishing Group.

Yehuda, R., & Lehrner, A. (2018). Intergenerational transmission of trauma effects: Putative role of epigenetic mechanisms. *World Psychiatry*, 17(3), 243–57.

Chapter 3

Retreat from the Body
Birth and Beyond

The ability to find coherence and meaning within our life stories is crucially important to our ability to connect with others. Unresolved trauma and loss create an enduring vulnerability in our brains to flooding by unprocessed images and sensations of terror and betrayal (Siegel & Hartzell, 2003). Such flooding interferes with our ability to find coherence and construct meaning in our life story. Chapter 2 explored the impact of different kinds of attachment challenges and how they create states of mind rife with chronic shock. Even before attachment injuries become dominant, however, if failure occurs in a child's supportive environment, some children turn away from their body and its needs and dissociate the mind as separate from the body. Children who struggle with overwhelming experiences sometimes withdraw into their mind, what Corrigan and Gordon (1995) called the mind object. Alternatively, they may fail to develop any shock absorbers or methods of self-regulation, bouncing from overwhelming anxiety to dissociation and back again. "The infant whose caregiver has been unable to provide basic regulation around fearful arousal fails to develop a coherent attachment strategy for reducing physiologic arousal in the face of moderate stress, leading to under- or over-activity in the stress-response system" (Lyons-Ruth et al., 2006, p. 70).

In their review of literature on the etiology of dissociation and disorganization, these authors propose that "hidden traumas of infancy" (p. 70) related to neglect and/or fear arousal, although perhaps more subtle than outright abuse, engender physiologic consequences similar to the threat responses that are salient for older children and adults. They also point to another version of "hidden trauma" in the form of "quieter" caregiver failures such as withdrawal from emotional contact,

DOI: 10.4324/9781003262367-5

role-reversal, unresponsiveness to the child's overtures, and maternal depression, all of which appear to be the caregiving responses most implicated in pathways toward dissociation.

To date there is much clinical debate around topics of complex trauma, developmental trauma, and developmental trauma disorder. *For the purposes of this volume, developmental trauma relates to cumulative trauma from subtle neglect, mis-attunement, and ongoing stress during childhood that derives from environmental failure and unavoidable stress rather than maltreatment, but nonetheless derails the development of self-regulation, self-esteem, and sense of safety with others.* These youngsters grow into adults who experience disruptions in affect regulation, disturbed attachment patterns, rapid shifts in emotional states, heightened anxiety and traumatic expectations, chronic shame, and a sense of ineffectiveness in the world. They often are quite accomplished professionally and are at a loss to explain why they feel so incompetent emotionally. "Hidden traumas of infancy seem to contribute to the early hyper- or hyporegulation of stress responses mediated through the limbic hypothalamic-pituitary-adrenocortical (HPA) axis" (Lyons-Ruth et al., 2006, p. 70). Vivid clinical examples of these phenomena in individuals with histories of early subtle trauma compounded over years of cumulative trauma will, I believe, bring these concepts alive to the interested reader.

Beginnings

Medical traumatization during childhood, exposure to serious physical or mental illness in a family member, and of course sexual and physical abuse (not the focus of this volume) profoundly disrupt children's sense of physicality and empowerment. Depending on how sensitive and attuned parents are to the child's experience, as well as the degree of previous traumatization, the impact of exposure to medical trauma can range from benign to catastrophic. Toxic stress is unsoothed stress: much stress can be managed by well-timed soothing and a nurturing, holding environment. A lack of reliable soothing sets children up for lifelong developmental trauma. The challenges of identity formation, images of the body-self, and relationships to peers can all be profoundly affected by body or family experiences that make one

feel apart from and different from others. Especially in early adolescence, any experience of different-ness from one's peers almost always
impacts the development of sexual confidence.

If you think about it, no greater state shift exists than the birth
experience. Catastrophic anxiety states presumably stemming from
a complicated birth can affect peoples' ability to manage transition
points in life and within themselves (Culbert-Koehn, 1997). Hard
(distressing) and soft (comforting) experiences seem to be hard-wired
into memory.

Birth Trauma: Heather

Many experienced psychotherapists note that special attention should
be given to the processing of nonverbal remnants of trauma that occur
at birth (Culbert-Koehn, 1997; Hopper, 2003; Winnicott, 1958). These
therapists have found that birth traumata frequently color patients'
experience without any awareness (Janov, 1983). The majority of
therapists, however, rarely prioritize inquiry on these matters.

I saw Heather three times a week for psychotherapy over 11 years.
Heather had been born with an undiagnosed broken collarbone to a
very unpredictable mother and a remote father. She was reportedly
inconsolable during her first three weeks of life until her injury was
diagnosed.

Both she and I were perturbed by a pattern we lived out together.
She became easily distressed with me unless I could hold her perfectly
with my mind and voice. If my voice was slightly chipper in the waiting
room as I said, "Hello, come on back," on a day when she was feeling
that she would be better off dead, she could lapse into one of her eerie
silences. She would respond to anything short of perfect understanding
of her current emotional state by falling into a remote, brooding, and
scary silence that would last for weeks or sometimes months, possibly
"dorsal collapse" (Porges, 2018). Other times she could simply snarl at
me to shape up and quit being so damn disconnected, or ruefully laugh
at herself for being so impossible.

What was so fascinating about our journey together was the way in
which we eventually negotiated around both her and my attachment
shock. During such periods she would frequently not show up for her
appointments, which I found intolerably disconcerting. I frequently

work with adolescents and young adults, however, and when they fail to keep their appointments, I do not become nonplussed the way I did when Heather no-showed. The internal chaos I experienced when she did not show up can be understood by a sense within my body that I was failing her in some way. For about 7 years, she and I had no idea what would precipitate these periods; she insisted she did not feel puni-tive during these periods, but rather "detached" and "not alive."

Heather had two preferred fantasies during these periods. One involved being an astronaut on the outside of a space shuttle and having the gravity belt that held her onto the outside shell of the spaceship come abruptly unattached. She would then just float further and fur-ther away, melting into the silence and the sounds of her breathing. In this fantasy, she experienced no anxiety and never ran out of air: it was as if she were abruptly back in the womb. Her second fantasy also involved a transition moment: she would beg me to shoot her in the head so her head would explode. The central aspect of the fantasy was the violent sensations of the shot going off (perhaps the sounds of her bones breaking?). We never exactly worked out the meanings of this fantasy, except that it symbolized her own rage, her intolerable level of stress and disorganized attachment, and her birth trauma.

Over the years we were able to talk frankly about my experience of her abrupt "disappearances" within and from the sessions, my attempts to discern what had just happened, and my attempts to make repair (which she typically characterized as my turning somersaults to try and engage her). I would feel a sinking feeling, sometimes bordering on panic, when she would abruptly drop into one of those silences. I would search the past few minutes trying to reconstruct what may have occurred, probing for possible errors or any content from our last session that might help explain what was happening. I imagined she would kill herself, that she was lost beyond reach, that she was gone forever. I so desperately wanted to find a way to stay in control of this dive into the dark by understanding with my mind, rather than by "going along for the ride." I eventually realized my feelings had as much to do with my own early abrupt abandonment experiences and early losses as it had to what was happening in the room with Heather.

For her part, Heather was able to talk about how she came to rely on me as a second skin for her. She experienced the shock of my occa-sional mis-attunement as a devastating loss. She gradually began to talk about these periods as the emergence of the "dead baby" within her. Gradually we made sense of these events in terms of her traumatic birth and early infancy. Eventually we were able to talk frankly of the dead baby who could not die but also could not be soothed, a baby who had had to endure unbearable experience by herself.

Heather is now a mother in her own right. She is deeply attuned to her daughter's emotional experiences. Heather faces intolerable anguish, however, whenever her daughter is suffering physically or psychologically. It is as if Heather is trying to vanquish her own childhood suffering by providing for her cherished daughter a perfect childhood.

The Basic Fault: Adoption and Prematurity

The obliviousness of our profession to the impact of adoption and prematurity is most striking. Birth is stressful enough without the added complications of prematurity and adoption. Michael Balint, a prominent psychoanalyst in the 1950s and beyond, noticed that traumatic experiences during the early years, especially mis-attunement and other attachment injuries, created a fault line in the individual's body-psyche that was important to address. His "basic fault" (1968) is a concept patients relate to readily—a sense that something is inexplicably wrong with them.

For babies destined for adoption, the experience of being separated from their birth mothers is agony, even when the adoption is well intentioned. Infants are acclimated to their mothers' voices *in utero*, and the disappearance of the familiar makes the birth experience all the more stressful. Almost every adoptee feels abandoned deep down and has some fantasies concerning "why?" "how?" and "what if?" As a child psychologist, I have discovered that the separation from one's birth mother leaves indelible fingerprints of rejection and despair in most adoptees. Most adopted children have fantasies about how life would have evolved with their birth mothers, but typically these fantasies fade by adulthood. Even—and especially—those who deny any impact of adoption (I was one of those) discover an internal dark night of the soul when they finally wrestle with the demons of those early moments of severed bonding. Neonatal intensive care unit (NICU) nurses have told me that they are well acquainted with the despair in newborns who are awaiting adoption.

Finally, in 2020, popular culture has at least begun to pay attention to the complexities of adoption for both birth mother and baby. A popular television show *This Is Us* (Fogelman, 2016–2022) ran a 3-year story arc on the emotional struggles of an adoptee named Randall. His adoptive mother had just given birth to triplets, one of whom died during the birth. That same night, a fireman brought Randall to the hospital as an abandoned child. The story was that Randall's birth mother had died and that his adoptive parents-to-be, devastated at the loss of one of their triplets, jumped at the chance to take Randall home with them. He grew up cherished and beloved in his family but yearned to understand why he had been abandoned.

Over several years viewers learned the story of Randall's birth mother and father. Randall was Black while his siblings were Caucasian. The show dealt with both adoption and race issues with sensitivity, but the several-year-long story arc exploring his distress around his birth parents was compelling. Over the years, viewers (and Randall) got to know the backstories of both his birth mother (who had not, in fact, died) and his birth father, and their struggles with guilt and shame about not having been able to raise him. Once the circle was completed and Randall, too, understood what had happened, a lifetime of angst lifted.

In 2021, Gabrielle Glaser published *American Baby*, a story about the adoption "industry" in the postwar decades. From the cover: "The shocking truth about postwar adoption in America, told through the bittersweet story of one teenager, the son she was forced to relinquish, and their search to find each other." The far-reaching impacts of adoptions are heart-wrenching and powerful. Yet many clinicians underestimate adoption as an important adverse childhood experience.

Silent Ravages of Adoption: Mother and Son Reunited after 30 Years

In 2016, I was given a unique opportunity to work with two individuals who taught me about the inner workings of adoption from both sides. Judy was 17 when she got pregnant by accident, and the birth father preferred that she get an abortion. Judy decided to carry her son Steve to term and give him up for adoption. Her family was normotic (Bollas, 1987), preferring to fit into society and not look too deeply into feelings. Thus, Judy arranged the adoption on her own and found Steve the most loving adoptive family she could find. Steve adored his adoptive family but was nonetheless restless and unhappy. He complained to his therapist that there was something ineffably wrong with him. He had secretly and always thought of himself as garbage, despite being raised with adoring parents. His parents frantically tried to soothe him as an infant and toddler, but he had trouble calming down. In an odd twist of fate, he and his birth mother were reunited; on a whim Judy contacted the agency that had placed Steve and reached out to him. They met briefly and then encountered each other by chance in the Los Angeles Airport. They decided this coincidence had happened for a good reason, and Steve's therapist referred them both to me to work on their relationship.

For many months Judy flew hundreds of miles to have biweekly "re-union" sessions with her beloved son. Steve had recently lost his adoptive mother and was still grieving but was ecstatic to finally have a chance to work on his relationship with Judy. Judy, for her part, was a contented wife and mother who was determined to forge a bond with her long-lost son, trying desperately to assuage her guilt at having given him up for adoption and to soothe his distress.

At first, their sessions were a dream come true. Each was "in their own corner," mostly. Judy wanted in the most earnest way possible to reassure Steve that she had never wanted to reject him. Steve sobbed and raged about the agonies he had felt for most of his life and about his sense that he was somehow flawed despite having felt loved by his adoptive parents. He begged for reassurance that she loved him still; she begged for forgiveness and relief from the terrible guilt she suffered for sending him away. What shocked and upset both of them the most was the discovery that Steve's adoptive parents had not gotten him immediately after his birth. Instead, he was mandated to foster care for five days.

It is difficult to describe these sessions in words. I have worked with many profound people over many years, yet these sessions were transcendent, full of joy at reunion and despair about their awful separation. Although both had full lives with jobs, spouses, and children of their own, they treated the therapy space as sacred and worked just on their feelings toward each other. Without exploring it first in therapy, they impulsively decided that their families would take a cruise together and spend Christmas together. Both adventures proceeded uneventfully; the families liked each other and enjoyed their time together.

However, underneath it all was dread. Predominant was their terror that accidentally one of them would say something wrong and inevitably they would be wrenched apart. What was healed would be broken, this time forever. Inevitably they handled this dread by "doing" (turning a dreaded passive experience into reality by seizing control) and had a massive blow-up on a phone call with each other. Steve was raging at Judy and she gave up, hanging up on him and retreating into familiar misery. Each had an individual session with me recounting their terror and hatred of the other, insisting that the situation was impossible and that they were inconsolable. Judy retreated into guilt and Steve into rage. Each worked with their own therapist until 3 years later when they reapproached me.

This time their mission was repair and reconnection. Both were in training programs to become therapists. Steve wanted Judy to know that he understood her agony as a 17-year-old, that he absolutely forgave her for running away from him, and that he took ownership of the formidable and inconsolable infant rage he had thrown at her. Judy owned up to being afraid of her feelings, afraid of his anger, and forgave him for blowing up at her. During our second session I brought up the elephant in the room: what about the blow-up they had engineered? We talked about Winnicott's (1974) "fear of breakdown," the concept that one fears a past event that has not quite been experienced. They were so worried about losing each other again that they made it happen, survived it, and were no longer quite so terrified. They were nervous talking about it and surprised by how easy it was in reality to discuss and understand. We used the image of river rafting as a metaphor: the waves might toss and turn us about, but we were in no danger of drowning. Any misstep would just be a hiccup, not a catastrophe. With a sigh of relief, they relaxed. Steve was no longer a bereft, raging infant, and Judy was no longer an overwhelmed teenager giving up her baby. This go 'round there were two adults in the room comforting each other and rejoicing in each other's lives. There was terrible pain, yes, but there was also delight as they discovered that they could be authentic with each other without destroying each other.

The NICU

If a child is born too early, he or she is often placed in a neonatal intensive care unit (NICU), where they must endure about 70 stressful and painful procedures a day. Only in the twenty-first century is research being done on developing protocols for pain control in these infants, and interventions—such as cocooning—being introduced to cut down on the level of overstimulation. Until recently babies in NICUs were seldom touched with gentleness and were bombarded with assaults for weeks on end: needle pricks in their heels and scalps at all hours of the day and night, bright lights 24/7, invasive intubation just to keep them breathing, and a cacophony of machine beeping. The compounding of NICU hospitalization with adoption experiences makes for a very stressful introduction to life. As a survivor of both NICU care and adoption, I have chronic oversensitivity to light and sudden sound; despite all my work, I still have a biological startle reaction to these stimuli.

Neonatal intensive care nurses are familiar with the deep depression overlaying premature babies' struggles to live or die within their units, especially when their spiritual and biological ties to their birth mothers have been abruptly severed in anticipation of adoption. Babies are exquisitely tuned to their mothers' voices, heartbeats, and other familiar sounds like music; the loss of familiarity leaves these babies unusually vulnerable and ungrounded. J. K. Eekhoff (2019) feels strongly that NICU experience is underreported and missed by psychoanalysts as a critical incident that disrupts the formation of the self. She spends much of her volume on trauma and primitive mental states, exploring the analysis of adults who started life in a NICU: as infants, her patients "were traumatized at birth by being born medically compromised and separated immediately from their mothers. They faced death as they were born" (Eekhoff, 2019, xvii). It has become clear to researchers that NICU experiences are "not only a source of (necessary) physical trauma for premature infants, but also of unavoidable, prolonged periods of mother-infant separation. Yet this situation has not become a major area for research on early attachment processes" (Polan & Hofer, 2018).

The NICU in Traumatic Play

A young boy I worked with was preoccupied with fantasies of sticking needles in the head of my golden retriever, who worked alongside me in my playroom when children requested her presence. He insisted that he *must* have needles to stick into her head and was irritated that my playroom had no suitable substitute. He said my dog "needed" the needles desperately but couldn't say why. He was frequently in trouble in school for tantrums and rage, but the peculiar form his rage took in my playroom had all the hallmarks of traumatic play.[1] I checked with his mother, who confirmed that, as a preemie he was hospitalized for quite a while, and because of some surgery had to have needles stuck in his scalp for many days. She brought in his birth book that had many pictures of him with needles in his head. Once we shared this with him in a play therapy session, he lost all interest in torturing my dog.

Developmental Trauma from Medical Traumatization

Much has been written about sexual and physical abuse, but medical experiences in childhood are frequently overlooked antecedents to attachment disruption, blocking children's ability to experience family—indeed life—as a safe harbor. Even loving families overwhelmed by medical issues are often helpless to titrate the level of distress their youngsters are forced to endure. Overwhelming experience, whether in the self or in a significant family member, stresses the nervous system of a developing child and results in encapsulations of traumatic experience that exist side by side with the high-functioning self. As a consequence, children often try to escape from the body-self by fleeing into their minds, sacrificing vitality in the process but managing to "look" resilient. Shock becomes encoded within the physical structure as a compartmentalization of trauma. Lyons-Ruth et al. (2006) present a clinical example of a patient with high anxiety and subtle dissociation who was hospitalized without warning at age 4½ for a serious infection. His parents dropped him off at the hospital promising to be right back but left him there and returned only once a week. This clinical example of "…a frightening childhood experience in the context of a nonabusive family, provides a vivid illustration of how the pivotal absence of a regulating parent–child dialog may be related to dissociative phenomena" (pp. 80–1). Although initially this traumatic experience seemed to account for all his abandonment anxiety and dissociation, "[i]t was not until much later in the treatment that he and his therapist more fully appreciated how deeply he felt his mother's sense of helplessness and anxiety throughout his childhood and how role-reversed his relationship with his mother had been and continued to be" (p. 81).

The following pages will provide examples of how both chronic and acute medical experiences during childhood can become layered into the body-self and form a foundation for exploration and treatment in psychotherapy. It is unfortunate that therapists rarely inquire into such experiences when they embark on a new psychotherapy adventure.

Toddlers and Restraint: Jordan

A woman who attended a workshop I was teaching on this topic had a daughter who, a few months before, was refusing to get married to the man she loved because she was terrified of the blood test and of having a baby. She was a preemie child who had endured countless "hard sticks" in the neonatal unit; additionally, she had had a terrifying emergency room experience as a toddler that involved multiple attempts to draw blood while she was being restrained. Once her mother put the pieces of this mystery together for her and told her the story of what had happened to her, her terror was able to fade into the past and she was able to look forward to marriage and parenthood. The "state of mind" of terror from repeated blood draws was put in its proper place in her past experience and no longer flooded her in the present.

Levine and Kline (2006) teach that restraint procedures can be among the most frightening experiences for children of all ages who are vulnerable and in pain. They lay out a treatment protocol for the tracking and regulation of acute shock in the nervous system. Let us examine the potentially deleterious impact of the "papoose board," a device used in emergency rooms to immobilize a frightened, struggling child. The child is often separated from his parents and placed on a rigid board, at which point three sets of restraints are tightened around him to hold him still. If the injury involves the head, the child's head is often draped completely so that he cannot see out, with only the part of the head or face that needs injections or stitching exposed.

One of my friends circumvented the potential trauma of this restraint for his son by refusing to leave the room as directed and by defiantly slipping his own head under the drape, so that he could whisper soothing words in his child's ear. Another friend recently managed to keep steady eye contact with his toddler Sean during the papoose board ordeal, also refusing to leave him alone with a strange and frightening doctor to have his scalp sewn up. Nonetheless, Sean detests being restrained and would become frantic whenever his parents held him to help him regain control. After his father heard about traumatic reactions to the papoose board, he suddenly realized that Sean probably would do better not being restrained at all. The parents bought a hospital set and are doing play therapy with him on what happened to him to help him come to terms with the experience.

As I shared my concern about restraints with colleagues, one listener became agitated, remembering how her daughter was restrained in pediatric intensive care on such a board after open-heart surgery at 7 months of age. Although of course the daughter had no knowledge or memory of this experience, her mother became intrigued at the realization that perhaps this is why her daughter had become such a dedicated intensive care nurse. This theme of the power of early experience is replicated repeatedly across the many thousands of individuals who have endured frightening medical experiences in early childhood.

Jordan, a sensitive and articulate 15-year-old with athletic and intellectual gifts, was referred to me for defiant behavior and acting out. He was stealing his parents' credit cards and using them to fund video game purchases and to look at pornography. He was quite creative in these efforts, scaling the side of his house so he could drop into his parents' bedroom when they were downstairs. His parents were loving and committed parents and professionals. Jordan's father had had an overbearing father and had no tolerance for disrespect. Jordan was full of rage—at his older brother who he claimed had always hated and resented him; at his father for being rageful and controlling; and at both his parents for not recognizing the importance of videogaming during the COVID-19 lock-down, for not understanding that his sleep cycles didn't allow him to go to sleep by 10 p.m., and for being inconsistent about rules and consequences.

Jordan's first 3 years of life had been difficult: he had had stomach problems due to undiagnosed milk allergies and had undergone a year of multiple spinal taps due to high fevers. His screams were so awful during the many spinal taps that his mother got sick and almost fainted in distress. I did projective testing with him to help him understand himself better and to give me an idea of what I was facing. His projectives showed deep empathy and considerable rage. He was thrilled when I pronounced him the angriest youngster I had ever tested. Finally, he felt understood.

We talked at length about the helplessness he had endured and how it had shaped his nervous system toward having some control, any control, of his life. He profoundly resented his parents' attempts to impose arbitrary controls on his waking and sleep behavior that felt unreasonable to him. The more they tried to get him to stop videogaming during the COVID-19 crisis, the more he felt desperate to play at all hours of the night. He felt hopeless about getting his parents to understand him or respect him.

His older brother had not rebelled at all and had joined an ashram to pursue a meditative lifestyle for a time. This youngster (the brother) excelled at rock climbing (as did the parents) and loved being around his parents. Jordan despaired of getting his parents to understand that he was different from his brother but not bad to the core. He was one of the most insightful teenagers I have ever worked with. He was drawn to psychedelics because his friends were doing them but understood immediately that he was at risk for bad trips because of his early life. As his parents relaxed their attempts to control him, he became bored with videogaming, weary and exhausted at his lack of sleep, interested in broadening his horizons, and is working on a novel. He is eyeing a young lady whom he sees as compatible, in the hope of dating her. While still rebellious, he realizes that controlling his pride and learning to repair injuries will be a lifelong learning endeavor for him if he wants to have successful relationships. He sees me weekly and is in family therapy, having found an ally in his family therapist. As of this writing, he is in a much better space with his family and is well on his way to growing up to be a responsible young man. I don't think we could have made the progress we made without understanding the role that medical intrusiveness to the point of "torture" had played in his development.

The Cumulative Trauma of Multiple Childhood Surgeries

Children and adolescents who have to undergo multiple surgeries are forced to confront and endure circumstances of physical impairment that many people don't face until their 60s or later. The sense of alienation from peers and a longing to be like others only compounds over time. Attachment issues become highly relevant when the youngster is frightened and in pain.

In the early 1950s, the prevailing opinion was that infants did not feel pain. Open-heart surgeries and other invasive surgeries were routinely conducted on infants without anesthesia. When young children were hospitalized for surgeries, their parents were allowed only very limited visits. Many hospitals provided no opportunity at all to visit children 3 years or younger for their first month in hospital. Both medical professionals and psychiatric experts pooh-poohed attachment researchers who were reporting inconsolable agony and despair and progressive deterioration in these young children who were not allowed the comforting presence of their parents.

A harrowing documentary called *A Two-Year-Old Goes to Hospital* (Robertson, 1952) was filmed depicting a toddler's responses to distress at being separated from her parents. Her umbilical hernia surgery was uneventful, and she did get some anesthesia (although it was given rectally, which upset her greatly). This film was instrumental in changing hospital practice to allow rooming in and more frequent visitation by parents. Three stages of separation distress paralleling Bowlby's (1969, 1973, 1980) were eventually delineated by James and Joyce Robertson (1989). In the first, protest, children evidence distress, crying, and visible upset; next is despair, as the child begins to withdraw from contact with caregivers, apparently giving up hope that the parents will return. Children become easier to manage during this period and appear to be settling in, no doubt fueling the prevailing attitude that the children cope just fine if upsetting visits with the parents are curtailed. Finally, children enter the third step of separation distress, a denial/detachment phase during which they interact placidly and superficially with their environment, but hardly seem to know the parents when they return. In today's terminology we would view these children as having learned to dissociate. Relationships with others appear to turn shallow and untrusting.

Mark

Even by the late 1950s, visitation hours with hospitalized children were sharply curtailed. One of my patients, Mark, was hospitalized multiple times for surgeries on his club foot, beginning at early infancy. His mother was not allowed to visit him but merely to observe him through a window. He remembered the confusion and sharp agony (while recovering from one of his later surgeries) of feeling bereft, outraged, and confused about why she was not coming to visit. He gradually learned to dull the pain of his suffering and fury, and developed the character armor of an affable, witty man who was an eternal optimist, sometimes to his own detriment.

Mark tried to vanquish his early helplessness by determinedly pursuing a positive outlook. Because of his vulnerability to dissociation and his optimistic world view, his business was embezzled by an office manager who had earned his trust. He was taken advantage of by several of his employees. His wife was insightful but often dysregulated due to a difficult childhood herself, and his adopted son who had bipolar disorder would become violent, but Mark maintained the illusion that everything was fine at home and with the world. His mother died after a long illness, but Mark took her loss in his stride while the rest of his family fell apart. When a friend of his died abruptly in a tragic accident involving the Chicago "L," Mark appeared to handle the tragedy with amazing resilience. He threw himself into his work with renewed vigor and determination. He withdrew from engagement with his family, however, and seemed to shut off his feelings. Only when he began to develop heart symptoms did he begin to come to terms with his panic, fury, and inner despair.

Two more experiences of exposure to multiple surgeries will be explored in detail below. The first example is Jill. Jill's mother was not allowed to room in with her in the hospital but became hyperfocused on Jill's dysfunction and disability once Jill returned home. She remained relatively unable to comfort Jill or support emotional expressivity through what must have been Jill's hellish experiences of struggling with disability and multiple surgeries throughout childhood.

The second example is Sylvia. Sylvia grew up with a mother who wanted a Martha Stewart lifestyle and spent most of her time trying to fix up the house to compete with her peers. Although she loved Sylvia and her brothers and sisters, she was so emotionally withdrawn and depressed that she could not be emotionally attuned to what they needed. When Sylvia underwent a series of knee operations in her late adolescence, she became increasingly pessimistic about ever being able to ask for comfort. This became the central theme of her psycho-therapy with me.

Jill

Jill worked with me throughout her 30s and 40s and into her 50s. I saw her in twice-a-week individual therapy and in group. She also had weekly art therapy with another therapist, a body therapist, and a spiritual director who worked in coordination with the rest of her treatment team. She was an utterly delightful but slightly shy, lonely, and self-conscious woman who struggled to overcome a childhood of feeling different than other children. She grew up with a father who was somewhat odd and remote, and a compulsive but doting mother. At birth, Jill had suffered some brain damage that permanently affected one of her legs. She needed about 20 surgeries throughout her childhood to gradually lengthen her leg and untwist her foot. Jill relied heavily on stoicism and dissociation to get herself through the hospitalizations. She observed early in her hospitalizations that the children who put up a fuss got the worst care from the nursing staff on the orthopedic ward, so she was a "good patient" who cooperated fully. She remembers dissociating on the children's ward, so she wouldn't have to listen to the other children's screams. Like many slightly dissociative individuals, she had an extremely high pain threshold. Her parents had a distant marriage and were not particularly warm people, but Jill loved them both and felt loved in return. Her mother dedicated herself to Jill's physical rehabilitation so she wouldn't be too different from other children. Nonetheless, the life metaphor Jill used was "growing up with my face pressed to the glass," watching other children run and play and interact.

In her individual and group therapy, Jill's "good patient" mask finally crumpled. Themes of protest and despair permeated her work. She did her best to make other group members dislike her but failed utterly. (Jill's group experience is explored more thoroughly in Chapter 7.) Themes of being damaged shadowed her psychotherapy. She was afraid to masturbate, fearing that she would damage her genitals—her mother had said something to this effect to her when she was in a bathtub at age 3. Even as an adult, she was convinced that her genitalia were somehow defective and different until I showed her a book addressing this very fear. She was afraid to read fantasy fiction because she was terrified she would go crazy, like her uncle at the state hospital who had schizophrenia. Her parents had taken her to visit him every weekend throughout her childhood, even though he was usually delusional and hallucinating. She hated the visits and faced them with dread. She grew up with the understanding that there was something wrong with her brain (she described it as having a hole in her brain) and dreaded anything else going wrong with it. We spent much time addressing her conviction that she might go crazy if she allowed herself to feel, read fantasy, or be creative. In art therapy she completed a series of drawings about her damaged body-self, depicting herself in a cringing posture that aptly captured her style of relating to others.

As we explored her cautious, self-conscious style of communicating, I wondered aloud if I didn't annoy her sometimes. She grinned uncharacteristically and said contemptuously "Jill is afraid to be alive but I'm not! I'm Yuk, and you annoy the shit out of me sometimes." This was the only time the Yuk part of her ever spoke with me. Yuk was the encapsulated, side-by-side part of Jill that carried vitality and rage. In art therapy she began to produce a series of drawings by, for, and about Yuk. Jill was terrified to make messes, but the Yuk side of her loved finger paints and all sorts of messy things. On one occasion when I knew I would be replacing my office carpet the next day, I offered Jill magic markers and finger paints to do with as she pleased. She politely thanked me, saying she could never do something as bold as that, then changed her mind and gleefully colored and painted all over my carpet.

Although Jill was, by and large, very restrained, the Yuk side of her held a great deal of anger. One day when her feelings of rage became overwhelming, I offered her an old phone book to tear up. With delight she ripped the book into shreds and left the mess for me to clean up. At that time, I was working with a great many abused young children who each had a large pickle jar in my playroom filled with all sorts of messes. Finger paint was mixed up with scraps of paper and sometimes foul-smelling substances, all of which helped manage and contain bad feelings and memories. Children could deposit horrible feelings and memories in the pickle jars and leave them safely locked up with me.

Jill didn't want to do a pickle jar but did draw a series of ginger jars to hold all her bad memories about the surgeries and subsequent alienation. Yuk quickly became less encapsulated and more an everyday part of Jill; as she did so, Jill became livelier. For the first 10 years of our work together, she only experienced satisfaction with a session if she had been able to cry and be comforted by me. Eventually, she learned that there were other ways to feel emotionally connected: we could laugh or reminisce together. It became increasingly clear that she had felt desperately isolated and under-nurtured, even within her loving family.

One frustration Jill had was the visibility of her affliction; she walked with a limp, wore orthopedic shoes, and increasingly had to wear a clumsy, mechanical leg brace to get around. She was never able to "pass" as an able-bodied individual. When illness or disability occurs in later life, the illness can be one island of self-experience among many. When illness and disability have existed since birth, they wreak havoc with sexual and social identity.

Jill focused much of her fury and resentment on her face, believing herself to be ugly and unattractive. She had one great love during her 20s, but after this relationship didn't work out, she pretty much gave up on men and on herself as a sexual person. Her sexual fantasies were permeated by her surgery experiences. Her central fantasy involved being in an operating room-like space, with a disembodied voice calling out various sexual demands to her. This fantasy must have mirrored her experience of dehumanization by her doctors, who had always paraded her as a "fascinating case" in grand rounds.

In the early years of her therapy, she was disembodied, over-intellectualized, and hell-bent on making the case that she was too ugly to date and too damaged to ever be a parent. Her supposed ugliness became a huge group issue, as well as playing out between us in the transference.[2] She would call me up after the group ended complaining angrily about how unfair it was that I was so beautiful and she was so ugly. She was less interested in comfort and reassurance than she was in torturing me with her resentment. We eventually made sense of her suffering: she always felt different than other girls and so left out of activities like sports and dancing. Growing up, she seemed always to be recuperating from some awful surgery and unable to participate even minimally in such events. Like me, she grew up during the "straight hair" zeitgeist of the 1960s, while she (as well as I) struggled with unruly, curly hair that wouldn't be sleek and glossy no matter what we tried. She was fascinated to learn that I had struggled with despair about my hair as much as she had.

After a few disappointing dating experiences, Jill had decided to give up permanently on men. At this point she was also questioning her ability to ever be a parent. The group wondered why she didn't consider adoption. Three years later while in her 40s, she left group to become the proud mother of a baby from China, who is now a college graduate.

Jill was going to end her therapy when she found a lump in her breast and underwent a mastectomy, chemotherapy, and radiation. Throughout her lifetime, Jill had rarely felt treated like a person by her doctors, until she got cancer. For the first time, she felt taken seriously by her oncologist and radiation oncologist, who treated her body as only one dimension of her multifaceted personhood. She felt liked, admired, and respected—almost cherished—by these caring professionals who treated her like a person instead of a case. I met her mother at the hospital on the morning of Jill's surgery. She became distracted and uncomfortable when I expressed concern and understanding about how hard this must be for her. I offered her some time to talk with me, but she declined, feeling obvious discomfort at my offer.

Jill experienced a breakthrough in expressing her feelings while recuperating from the surgery. One day when the nursing staff was particularly lacking in timely arrival with pain medication and food, Jill staged a strike. She sat in the middle of the hallway and was as obstreperous as possible, considering she was in pain and rather shy. When she was admitted to the hospital, I gave her a stuffed dog to hold onto during the hard times. She named him Andrew and still keeps him to this day. I visited her every day and even made one home visit, which touched her visibly. A good friend of hers kept a bedside vigil with Jill during her chemotherapy, keeping her spirits up when possible, babysitting her daughter, and comforting her when she was vomiting or nauseated. The presence of her friend made all the difference for Jill. Her trials were still a nightmare, but she was not alone. She also took great pleasure in "passing" as a well person with this illness. No one could tell she had cancer unless she told them. She had an experienced hairdresser who fixed her up with a great wig during the worst phases of her chemotherapy.

Jill stayed in therapy until she passed her 5-year post-cancer checkup. Mostly she used her therapy during these years to explore parenting issues (especially how to manage her daughter's expressivity and sexuality), to voice envy of her daughter's sturdy athletic body, and to bemoan her unsuitability for dating. Her daughter is spontaneous and lively and has never had trouble expressing her feelings to her mother. Since Jill had no idea how to respond in a healthy way to her daughter's emotional expressivity, we did some family sessions in the playroom where I modeled an imaginative, playful response to her daughter's ire. At first Jill would squirm because her daughter had figured out that if she expressed feeling inadequate in any way, her mother overreacted. Feigning suicidal despair became a way for Jill's daughter to get an emotional reaction from her mother. Jill was horrified by the way I handled her daughter's pretend suicide threats. I would gleefully join with her in her fantasies, asking about guns, knives, jumping off cliffs—comparing and contrasting the suffering involved in each choice. Her daughter knew I was calling her bluff but enjoyed my playfulness. Eventually, Jill got over her fear, and we worked on the two of them finding healthier pathways to emotional connection.

Even if Jill grudgingly acknowledged that she wasn't really unattractive, she maintained that she was still a single mother after all and didn't have much free time, unlike the other mothers who all had husbands to love them and help with the kids. Although her self-attack never fell away entirely, she learned to catch herself with a grin. She also noticed when she was spacing out or being unconnected. The demands of rearing a daughter have forced her to be more emotionally present. Despite the brace on her leg, she took her daughter on a six-week tour of China and also tackled an extended van camping trip with several other families. She is not sure she will ever date but is beloved by all who know and cherish her, me included.

Sylvia

Sylvia curls up on my new couch, huddled right into the corner so as to be close to me. She doesn't realize it yet, but the new couch is allowing her to melt into our relationship for the first time. My old couch had reinforced seating that had turned out to be quite uncomfortable: Even when I persuaded 10-year-old patients to jump up and down on it, it refused to yield into softness. Sylvia struggles with exhaustion, depression, and chronic pain from a congenital knee condition that makes her legs hyper-mobile.

She was in her freshman year at college when her knees got so bad that she had to undergo surgery for the first of many times. Her life's passion was dancing, and her knees were interfering. She became a master at ignoring pain. As she put it, what was the point of noticing it? She stopped expecting any kind of comfort at all from her mother. During her 20s, Sylvia had intermittent periods when she could be a dance instructor and put herself through college. As she got older, the periods of doing well began to shrink; constant pain and physical dysfunction were her constant companions. By the time I met her, no matter how much surgery and physical therapy she pursued, she could never get strong enough to be able to go for pleasure walks or swims, much less go out dancing.

Sylvia knew that her mother loved her, but also that her mother was too depressed to really get to know her. For example, once as a teenager Sylvia actually managed to ride a bicycle 20 miles and rushed home to share her accomplishments. Her mother interrupted her, changing the subject. In outraged indignation Sylvia had challenged, "Don't you want to hear about what I did?" and her mother snapped "Not really." Arts and crafts interested her mother somewhat (she would praise Sylvia's sewing), but Sylvia's physicality wasn't something she could relate to.

Sylvia's multiple knee surgeries began when she was away at college, but she remembers even then her mother's getting off the phone when she tried to talk about her pain level or frustration at being unlike other girls. A lithe and lean beauty, Sylvia never had any trouble attracting men or finding boyfriends. As so many lonely girls do, when she focused on finding a boyfriend, she used the strategy that worked so well with her mother—not having any needs at all. Obviously this strategy was doomed from the outset, so when she finally would begin to depend on a boyfriend, he would freak out and leave her. She felt alienated from other girls who didn't have to struggle with surgeries and physical pain.

She also believed that they had better relationships than she did. By some stroke of inspiration, she finally broke this pattern and married a man who was nurturing. When I met Sylvia, she was in her late 30s. She had survived cervical cancer and radical surgery, as well as several more surgeries to reconstruct the damaged tissue.

Several years before I met her, Sylvia and her husband had adopted two toddlers from Columbia who had been so badly neglected (possibly abused) that even responding to love was difficult. From the outset Sylvia knew that her children were somehow different than other children. Her son was highly manipulative and her daughter, superficial. Sylvia had been in therapy during the adoption process and had kept trying to tell her therapist that something was wrong. Her therapist dismissed Sylvia's concerns as new mother anxiety and assured her that the kids were fine. They were friendly and sociable and utterly adorable when the therapist met them. She would refocus the conversation on Sylvia's work goals and friendships. Like Sylvia's mother, her therapist had missed Sylvia's signals and focused on other issues.

Like any other mother confronted with the dilemma of knowing that something was amiss with her children, Sylvia became obsessed with a search for answers. When her husband found a new job in a different state, Sylvia discovered that her concerns about her adopted children were not just made-up worries. A specialist in adoption and attachment difficulties confirmed her worst fears: her children couldn't bond.

It was the therapist treating Sylvia's children who referred her to me, knowing that the parenting process for these children was going to be so difficult that Sylvia needed her own support. Sylvia was devastated when she found out the children's diagnosis was reactive attachment disorder. Their treatment process was exhausting. Both parents had to work hard at blocking their children's manipulations and superficiality so that they could begin to feel the rage and anxiety about their early neglect. The children's rage was so intense, it sometimes took both parents holding a child in full body restraint to keep actual injury from occurring. The older child, a boy, took out much of his rage on his little sister. He threatened to kill her and their parents while they were asleep. He had to sleep with a lock on the outside of his bedroom door. While he grew more and more outspoken and bold with his violence, his little sister began to shrink into shy superficiality. She was terrified all the time because her brother was always on the edge of violence.

During the first month of therapy, Sylvia showed up unexpectedly at my office. I happened to be free, and as I walked into my supposedly empty waiting room greeting her with a confused smile, she threw herself, weeping, onto my shoulder. Her son was getting increasingly violent, and she was worried he would injure or kill his little sister. She was in physical pain from restraining him and at her wit's end about how to cope. As we got to know each other, it became a running joke between us that of course Sylvia couldn't allow herself to need me. At the first sign of any distress, she would instantly dissociate and forget what she had been talking about. Over time she began to signal me that she had an ache in her chest or offer some other clue that she was having a big feeling. The first of these "big feelings" occurred when I made a connection between her yearnings for love from her children (who couldn't tolerate the slightest affection or physical touch) and her deprivation with her mother. Initially she dismissed her distress about her mother's underwhelming response to her psychological and physical pain, but gradually she began to realize how profoundly her mother's inability to resonate emotionally had affected her. Over time, Sylvia began to be able to cry a bit during her sessions, always dismissing herself as a whiner. She began to face her anger with God for tricking her into having hope for a normal life.

Lonely as she had been in college, she felt alienated from all the other parents who complimented her children for being so charming. Charming superficiality paired with covert violent aggression in her son and severe avoidance in her daughter only vaguely resembled the relatedness of other children. Sylvia felt envious of all the mothers who had normally responsive children. She raged at God for betraying her. After their son spent several months in a children's psychiatric hospital, the family discovered he had many neurological problems which made it even harder for him to manage his anger or to bond. He hated his family and, most especially, his sister. After a serious car wreck with his mother in which the car was totaled, Sylvia's son asked her what would have happened to him if Sylvia had been killed. "You would have been picked up at school by a neighbor," she replied. Would the neighbor let him eat sweets and watch as much TV as he wanted, he wondered? Sylvia replied, "probably." In all seriousness, he said then that he wished she had died in the car wreck because he never got to eat enough sweets or watch enough television with her around. He had liked the psychiatric hospital better. Eventually he was sent to live as an only child with a favorite aunt, and actually did fairly well there when he was able to get all the attention. Now that her raging, terrifying brother was not around her all the time, Sylvia's daughter Carla was free to discover her own feelings.

Carla had spent much of her first 2 years of foster care bundled in a backpack with her face covered. Although she spent many hours in physical contiguity with her foster mother, she had little eye contact with the world, much less her mother. She was superficially compliant but really drifted through life, frantic about being out of touch with people. She hated it when Sylvia or Daddy touched her or tried to talk about feelings, yet demanded their constant companionship. She didn't know how to play by herself and would become agitated if not engaged with a play date or her parents. Gradually she became able to express her need for emotional contact and begged Sylvia to sleep on a mattress beside her. She began deliberately breaking rules and ignoring requests as a tentative way to broach her anger. She would scratch at her parents on the rare occasions that they would have to hold her, shouting that she hated them, while her body slowly melted into relaxation. As she began to realize her fears of abandonment, she became increasingly engaged emotionally with her parents. Hugs, tears, whining, reassurance, and temper outbursts all became commonplace as Carla began to emerge from the shell of isolation that had encased her all her life. She had become a real girl.

But back to the couch: Sylvia began to let herself cry sometimes but continued to be exhausted and depressed. She no longer called herself a crybaby or a whiner; indeed, she had to learn from me that whining can be an early indicator of attachment, as it represents a protest against distress. I insisted on her being compassionate with herself, and she sneered at me for being a bleeding heart. While she was thrilled that Carla was awakening as a person and as a daughter, Sylvia struggled to find time for herself. She either slept too little or too much. Finally, she demanded to know why God was letting her body hurt so much. Words popped out of my mouth that startled us both: "God,"

I said, "wanted her to experience the touch and warmth of Rebecca," her physical therapist, who truly cared about Sylvia's physical pain. This could be a pathway for healing the little girl inside, whose mother didn't want to hear about her. For once, Sylvia didn't joke or become sarcastic. She said her heart hurt, and tears flowed freely.

Accidents in Childhood: Potential Incubators of Developmental Trauma

Scaer (2005, 2014), a noted neurologist and pain specialist, has come to believe that attachment trauma, emotional regulation, the autonomic nervous system, acute and chronic shock, and physical traumata are intertwining phenomena that manifest as traumatic diseases (fibromyalgia, chronic fatigue); a tendency to dissociate from the body-self; and a vulnerability to chronic pain syndromes. Trauma in early life increases vulnerability to subsequent trauma, such that even minor vehicle accidents can trigger years of chronic pain in individuals with histories of abuse or multiple traumas. Without explicit intervention on the level of chronic shock, even children from loving families can experience psychological derailment from traumatic medical experience.

Three clinical examples illustrate the impact of childhood accidents on three individuals. Cassie experienced her first disillusionment in her idolized father when they were in a car wreck together. She struggled for years with the fallout of the event until she sorted it all out in physical and psychological therapy. Gillian grew up in a loving family, but a terrible accident catapulted her into a burn unit where she learned to dissociate from her bodily experience and disavow all need. Susan was sensitized to pain during her long stay in a neonatal unit. Always feeling anxious and unlovable, her sense of self was really shattered after she was in a terrible bicycle accident as a 9-year-old.

Cassie

Six-year-old Cassie was sitting in her favorite seat in the old Buick, right next to her Daddy whom she adored. Her mother was far less warm by nature, and Cassie turned primarily to her Daddy for affection. She was singing a song that her Daddy had taught her when he started acting sort of scary. He began swearing loudly at the driver in front of them to get the hell out of his way. As their car raced ahead toward the on-ramp, a Cadillac was perched at a dead stop before them. Cassie realized that the car wasn't going to get out of their way. Somehow, her Daddy (who was known to take a few drinks now and again) hadn't seemed to figure that out yet and was now swearing at God as well as at the other driver. (Cassie knew from her Catholic school teachers that swearing at God was a serious sin.) Seat belts hadn't been invented yet, so in the seconds that stretched into minutes between herself and slamming into the Cadillac, Cassie scoped out the best way to throw herself under the dashboard. All she could remember about the aftermath of the accident is that the man whose car got hit was really, really mad and had almost come to fisticuffs with her Daddy.

Later in life Cassie came to therapy wanting help with her marriage. She would fly into a panic whenever her spouse was approaching another car rapidly and ask for a bit more distance because she was starting to shake. If he didn't slow down, she would involuntarily cry out to her Daddy. Her husband would snap at her when this scenario occurred, thinking she was accusing him of being a bad driver. His anger would only make her more agitated. We explored the possibility that she was having flashbacks instead of being critical or controlling of her husband. He became much more receptive to her input after this explanation was proffered to him. As Cassie began to look deeper inside herself, she realized that in her young mind she had made a connection between her Daddy's swearing and the crash: she thought God was punishing them.

She hadn't let herself learn how to drive until her mid-20s because she was so frightened of going fast. This accident had shaped her physiology, spirituality, and her sense of self in one fell swoop. The accident also was the first time Cassie remembered feeling disillusioned by her father. She had always nearly worshipped him as her rescuer from the sterility of being alone with her mother. Late in her therapy she had to wrestle with the realization that he wasn't quite the white knight in shining armor that she had created in her mind. The accident was an incident we kept returning to throughout her therapy as a touchstone and marker of a psychological watershed. Cassie had always believed she hadn't really been hurt much in the accident, but discovered in physical therapy for a sore knee, back, and pelvis that her pain went away after she had worked all of this out with her treatment team and me. The work on her body allowed her to make sense of things that verbal therapy alone could not have accomplished. The torque in her spine unwound to correct for the twist it had taken when Cassie had thrown herself in the car—her neck and shoulders had twisted to the right as her left knee had careened into the dashboard floor.

Gillian

Gillian grew up in a warm, loving Irish family. There were always relatives about, sometimes too many living at once in the small brownstone, but Gillian always felt loved. When she was 11, she was in the basement when the gas heater exploded, burning her severely. At the burn unit, her grandmother cautioned her to be very, very brave and not cry so as not to upset her mother. Gillian didn't cry. Indeed, she learned at this tender age to disown her own needs almost entirely. When I met her she was struggling with fibromyalgia. She had a terrible time getting any quality of sleep due to the pain that would awaken her and keep her from getting deep sleep.

A pediatrician, she was the most gifted woman I have ever met at working with preschoolers. She adored children and understood their needs intuitively. She also understood the dilemmas of their parents and put them at ease immediately. How ironic it was that Gillian was not nearly as empathically attuned to her own vulnerabilities as she was to the needs of others. Despite her sleep deprivation, chronic pain, and her tendency to skip meals, she protested that she was doing fine, that she wasn't ignoring her body entirely. We worked out a deal involving her putting a black pebble in a bowl on the far side of her bed every time she awakened from pain. She was stunned to realize how frequently she was waking up every night. As we continued talking, she discovered that she seldom asked herself what she really needed. She had dissociated almost entirely from her body-self. She instituted a ritual of sitting quietly in a chair several times a day, asking her inner self what she needed. Was she tired? Hungry? Achy? Did she need to stretch or take a walk? She was intrigued to discover how effectively she had learned to tune her own needs out after the burn unit. She became a master at self-care as a result.

Susan: Earthquakes in the Body

Susan reported a recurring dream that had haunted her since childhood. Bad guys were trying to break into the house she was in, and she had to try and hide. She remembered how stirred she was by the story of Anne Frank, and she imagined the dream was about her. In the dream she pulls down a ladder to the attic and climbs up, pulling the ladder up after her and locking the trap door. Frantically she scans the attic floor, looking for any hiding place. She spies a door that might lead into a closet and opens it. A bunch of clothes are hanging in the closet, but she pushes through the clothes and finds yet another door, this one too small for the bad guys to enter. She locks the closet door behind her and crawls through the little doorway into a tiny room with a slanted roof and a skylight. After she locks this door too, she sighs with relief: she is safe. When I ask her about the slanted roof, she remembered looking at houses with her parents when she was about 9 years old. Her favorite of the houses (although not the one her parents chose) had an entire attic playroom with a slanted roof and skylights in the ceiling.

After talking about the dream, Susan suddenly remembered to describe a real-life version of the dream that she had experienced several years before. She lived in a small house by herself in a neighborhood that was being terrorized by a man who had raped more than 20 women. Susan asked for a consultation with the police department about how to make her house safer. The police recommended that she key lock her wood windows, to make them impossible to open. Since it was springtime, she key locked them open about two inches to let the fresh air in. The week after she completed this task, the rapist began to stalk her. In the dead of night, he removed every one of her window screens, only to discover that every window was locked. Her mail was delivered to a mailbox on the outside of her house, and apparently the rapist had discovered her name by intercepting her mail. The night he removed her window screens, he left her a snarling, furious voice message about his frustration with her windows, and promised her that he would get to her somehow. She promptly turned over the message tape to the police, who stepped up their surveillance of her house. She still couldn't sleep, however, until she had the idea to install locks on all her inner room doors. In effect, she was recreating her dream. Her bedroom was locked in an area that was also locked from other areas of the house; she slept in a room within a room within a room. She was able to sleep better once the locks were installed, and within a few months the rapist was caught and sent to jail. Her answering machine tape constituted crucial evidence.

Susan's early life had been difficult: Destined for adoption, she was born to a businesswoman who was horrified at the baby she carried. She was born prematurely and spent several weeks in a NICU. She was frequently babysat by her maternal grandmother, who had fled at 18 from another country and didn't really understand how to relate to a sensitive baby like Susan. At 2 years old, Susan bit her grandmother after being slapped for dawdling. The grandmother shook her violently, and the family chronicled this event as the day Susan "turned into the devil." Although intellectually gifted verbally, learning to read before starting school, Susan tended to be a klutz and was seriously uncoordinated. Both in the neighborhood and at school she was anxious enough that she was an easy target for bullies. She did develop close girlfriends, but secretly envied the girls who had natural self-assurance. Her mother didn't like her very much and preferred Susan's more sophisticated cousin, who was the daughter she wished she'd had. She often wished aloud that she had adopted a different daughter who was more like herself.

Susan was very close to her father; they played card games together for hours and took walks. She excelled at academics but was seriously uncoordinated at athletics. Her father had had polio as a youngster and was unable to help her with sports, but he loved boating and took Susan out boating with him every weekend. Eventually he grew impatient with her inability to learn how to tie nautical knots, no matter how many times he showed her how. She felt mortified but couldn't hold the spatial loops in her mind. She hadn't learned how to tie her shoes until the third grade and was always lost spatially, probably remnants of shaken baby syndrome from her maternal grandmother's violence. Fortunately, her father's parents adored her, and she spent many weekends with them.

What follows is a chronicle of Susan's bodily disintegration after apparent wholeness, illustrating the compounding of developmental trauma in a high-functioning patient. When menopause hit, Susan's new husband rejected her. During that time, her car was totaled by a deer. An avid hiker and runner, her body suddenly fell apart. Her journey back to wholeness illustrates the power of chronic shock to fracture the developing self by encasing it in shame and self-attack. The step-by-step description in the following pages chronicles Susan's journey through a bicycle accident and its aftermath in the emergency room, lifelong repercussions of these events, and their ultimate manifestation in chronic pain.

1. *Her body fell apart.* Susan was in her late 40s, a veteran of many years of therapy with several competent therapists. Her last two therapists had moved away, however, and she needed support while she was trying to figure out what was happening to her body. She used to be a hiker and runner, but suddenly had difficulty even managing walks. In the throes of abrupt sexual rejection by her spouse, she plunged into a massive, shock-induced depression. Then a deer jumped onto her car during rush hour traffic, knocking out all her mirrors and windows and leaving her stunned and shaken. Although she was not seriously injured in the car wreck, she rapidly developed mysterious chronic pain in her pelvis, tailbone, and back that was to persist for many years. She was working with a sophisticated treatment team[3] to keep herself at least somewhat functional while she tried to make sense of what was happening to her. As it turned out, all three precipitating factors (menopause, car wreck, feeling sexually damaged) were compounding developmental trauma from a terrible bicycle accident Susan had had when she was 9.

   Scaer (2005, 2014) notes that emotional and physical disintegration after minor car wrecks (like the deer incident) probably connotes earlier, unprocessed developmental trauma.

2. *The bike accident.* Susan had only had her new bike for a few months when a neighborhood bully chased her down the street, threatening (as usual) to kill her. Susan hadn't yet learned to call his bluff, and fled on her bike, pedaling pell-mell toward the safety of home. She lived on a hilly street, and her steep driveway was lined with jagged rocks. As she raced for her garage, her speed accelerated and she careened out of control, veering into the rocks. She was flung off

her bike and, after bouncing off her tailbone, flipped over and slid face down about 8 feet along the jagged rocks. In shock, she crawled off the rocks and wandered in the house, blood dripping down her thighs. Her father scooped her up in his arms, grabbed her mother and drove Susan to the emergency room, soaking eight bath towels in blood. While her parents were shunted off to the waiting room, Susan was assessed. Her vagina and rectum were seriously torn, and she was bleeding profusely. With not a moment to spare, the staff proceeded to sew her up with no sedation and only some Lidocaine shot into her vagina. Terrorized, ashamed, and confused by what was happening to her private parts, Susan could not cooperate with the doctors; she fought with all the adrenaline she could muster. It took a team of six to physically restrain her while a seventh doctor sewed her up. She passed out at least once and once fell off the table struggling. She remembers the doctors and nurses yelling at her to stop struggling or she would die, which only made her all the more frantic.

3.   *Fragmented memories.* After the emergency room ordeal, her memories were somewhat fragmented. Susan always remembered some of the details of this terrifying experience but had dissociated other details. She vividly remembered that the accident occurred just before Christmas. Her uncle Bob was staying with them over his college break, and he brought home some special chemicals that he sprinkled over the fire to make pretty colors. The kindness he showed her during this visit was the only indication she ever received that any of her family took her trauma seriously. She "knew" what had happened to her, but didn't really remember hitting the rocks, sliding across them, or how she came to be in the emergency room. She did remember hearing her parents ask the doctors how damaged she would be sexually and whether she would ever respond normally during sex, tolerate intercourse, and be able to bear children. She didn't remember the answers to these questions—perhaps she simply didn't understand the words they used.

4.   *Shame.* For 2 weeks after the accident, her mother (hardly a paragon of warmth and maternal instinct) would crawl under Susan's sheets at night with a flashlight and apply antibiotic cream

to her vagina and anus to keep the areas free of infection. Susan remembers begging to handle this procedure herself, because she felt so violated, traumatized, and ashamed by the way her mother did it, but her mother insisted on doing it. Six months after the accident, Susan was once again horrified to discover blood on her legs and panties. Away at horse camp, she hadn't noticed anything amiss until a group of other 9-year-olds began making fun of her for having a period. Her mother had been warning her that menstruation was going to happen soon because she was becoming precociously mature, but Susan simply couldn't cope with the blood or the facts of life that her mother kept reminding her about. She began hiding used Kotex anywhere she could in her bedroom in a feeble attempt to ignore what was happening to her. Her mother would confront her angrily about this disgusting habit, demanding an explanation. All Susan could do was cry. She simply couldn't handle the responsibility of menstruation, the relationship of her vagina to sexuality, and the flashbacks from her accident, so she tried to make it all disappear. In addition to the evidence of her shock-induced denial of the necessities of menstruation, Susan had blotted out the awful pain the accident had caused her, the sense of being defective and damaged sexually, and her sense of horror at the traumatic, rape-like initiation into her sexuality. After putting the pieces of the accident together in treatment during her 50s, freely allowing herself to finally "hit the rocks," Susan went through an awful period of six weeks during which her body literally resounded with physical pain. Following that, she began to be able to free herself from her lifelong sense of shame.

5. *Phobia and rescue.* During the months that followed her return from the horse camp, Susan spent the time sneaking sweets and hiding in the basement, daydreaming all day about an elaborate fantasy of a young woman lost in the mountains who was rescued and tenderly nursed back into health in the wilderness by a Canadian Mountie.[4] After she fainted in church during Easter services the following spring, Susan developed a sleep phobia that lasted for 2 years. The sensation of falling asleep would prompt her to jerk awake in alarm. After having a dream about the Devil putting his hand on her pelvis, she compounded her sleep phobia by becoming

phobic about the Devil (she had grown up as a Catholic). Only after she sprinkled holy water all around her bed was she able to try to go to sleep. She became convinced that the Devil was looking at her all the time (she discovered that when she rubbed the inside corner of her eyes, she would experience something she imagined as the Devil watching her). She also became frightened of looking in a mirror, afraid she would see him there. Her phobia of looking in mirrors lasted well into her college years.

6. *Dental horrors*. Her early sense of horror, overwhelming pain, and violation was compounded by a series of unbearable dental experiences. At age 4, Susan had to have a filling. The dentist told her to hold very still while he drilled, but she couldn't. When the drill hit a nerve, she jumped and bit him. He slapped her, calling her a brat. Needless to say, she became afraid of dentists. At age 5, she developed a tooth abscess that required extraction under surgery. Her beloved grandmother gave her a necklace to wear to the surgery, promising her it had powerful protective properties. The anesthesiologist promised her that she could keep it on, but it was missing when she woke up, never to be found again. She was devastated. Then she had her tonsils out, and once again felt betrayed. The doctor had promised her she could have as much ice cream as she wanted after the surgery, but she was too sore to even try one bite. Her parents were traveling as they often did for business, so she was left in the care of a relative. She felt profoundly betrayed by the adults she had trusted.

    Susan's mother didn't know how to give her security but did give her something she loved to eat for school lunches—brown sugar sandwiches. By age 11, Susan had had three sessions of fillings. This dentist did give her a shot of Novocain each time, but she would scream and throw up after each of 12 fillings. The dentist assured her and her parents that she was quite numb and couldn't possibly be feeling anything, that she was just being fearful and dramatic. However, when she finally approached a dentist again in her 20s, the dentist discovered that it took three Novocain shots to even begin to numb her mouth. She had literally experienced pure nerve pain as her childhood dentist had drilled on her.

7. *Developmental trauma disorder*. Not only did Susan have separation trauma from her birth mother at adoption and weeks as

an intubated neonate in a NICU, but she also experienced add-itional separation trauma from her adoptive parents who traveled a lot for business, leaving her with various relatives. Her paternal grandparents were not available to babysit—her grandfather was a world-class violinist who traveled abroad much of the time; her grandmother taught piano and etiquette at a prestigious girls' school in a nearby city. So, Susan stayed for weeks at a time with a revolving door of aunts who lived nearby. Susan disliked these relatives and dreaded family get-togethers with them, although she had no memories of maltreatment other than having once had her mouth washed out with soap. She grew up as an awkward, anxious child who was bullied and insecure.

So the bike accident had merely been the icing on the cake. Because of untreated pelvic, coccyx, thoracic, and foot trauma from her accident, Susan began to move more awkwardly through space, even forgetting how to walk sometimes. To improve her pos-ture, her parents enrolled her in a ballet class, where she suffered untoward humiliation by being so much taller and more inflexible than her peers. Her awkwardness and periodic limping merely fed bullying by other girls.

8. *Finding meanings for pain.* The significance and details of all Susan's medical experiences emerged in physical therapy, body therapy, somatic experience therapy, and continued psychoana-lytic therapy, as she cycled through various states of chronic pain and somatic dysfunction. Her memories of the bicycle accident and dental traumas appeared to launch a series of tooth infections that followed. Susan then had to endure, one-by-one, the trials of 15 root canals and three dental surgeries. Her endodontist and oral surgeon speculated that she must have cracked all her teeth during the impact on the rocks. Fortunately, both were experts at pain management and gave her appropriate sedation and anesthesia for each procedure.

Susan had tried to talk about the layering of traumatization in her life in her previous therapies—the NICU, the bicycle accident, emergency room experience, sleep phobias, and menstruation embarrassment—but somehow none of these topics, nor her pre-mature birth, her adoption, dental traumas, the violation by her mother, and her damaged sense of sexuality were explored very deeply. Only when she began combining psychotherapy with somatic body work with kinesiologist specialists and rolfers did the meaning of these symptoms begin to make more sense.

Her recurring dream about a room-within-a room-within-a-room also began to come clear. The dream was communication of desperate terror and dissociative states: she couldn't bear to face the emotional and physical fallout of the stressors she had endured, and thus had created layers of dissociative defenses to shield herself from the impact. These defenses all fell apart with the advent of the deer-instigated car wreck, menopause, and sexual rejection by her husband. He told her she smelled bad, and despite numerous checks and reassurances by her ob-gyn that her genitalia were completely healthy and normal, she felt devastated by the ruthlessness of her husband's disgust and aversion to her. (Solomon and Tatkin (2011) explore sensory disgust as the *sine qua non* of avoidant spouses.) He was fed up with her chronic pain and trauma work: "I just thought you were somebody normal. I want the old you back, the one who could hike and ski with me for hours."

Couples therapy was a disaster, as the man she adored ranted about her defects—physical and sexual. "Why can't you just respond to what I like to do, why do I have to learn to do what you like sexually? Sex becomes an engineering project with you!" Despite the genuine love between them, her husband could not wrap his head around developmental trauma or the need to sort it all out. Retired young, he just wanted a companion who could play as she used to. Sadly, they split up. Menopause made her feel crazy, bereft as a woman. Once again, she felt damaged and defective sexually, different from other women, and immersed in shock. With these multiple triggers pressing against her defenses, Susan's brain couldn't keep up the layers of defenses. As one of her healers put it, "Once there's a straw that breaks the camel's back, we have to unpack the whole damn camel."

Susan described her body dysfunction as resembling "earthquakes in the body," since it seemed that every day her body had a different symptom profile that would leave her pelvis twisted in different directions depending on what she was feeling. "Earthquakes in the body" was also an allegory for all the emotional upheaval occurring internally. Susan's experience, although bizarre in many ways, was not really mysterious or idiopathic to her alone. Goodwin and Attias (1999) note that dissociative states and post-traumatic anxiety may manifest first in episodic, inexplicable bodily crises that accompany the psychological reworking of childhood trauma. One of their patients, who was working through chronic pain mixed with chronic shock, described her body experience much as Susan did: "Like a tornado, twisted, distorted, expandable and shrinkable like an accordion, weak and malleable like putty. Fragmented, in pieces, millions of pieces, tiny granules, as if it had been vaporized" (Goodwin & Attias, 1999, p. 231).

9. *Dissociation and pain.* When early childhood distress isn't adequately contained or soothed by a significant other, the emotional and physical pain in the body can become too intense to be tolerated or integrated, resulting in two different kinds of dissociative responses[5] that may occur within a single person at various stages of their healing. If the child was also mirrored as bad, demanding, and defective (as Susan was), integration cannot occur. Later in life, as dissociation is cleared away during intensive psychotherapy, it is not uncommon for patients like Susan to become traumatically overwhelmed: she had to face the realities of her impoverished, terrifying, and chaotic childhood. Years of traditional talk therapy with some of the best clinicians in town had built up ego strength and offered much insight but had sadly underestimated the ravages of traumatic anxiety that culminated eventually in Susan's bodily breakdown in midlife.

> This traumatic pain becomes a "not-me" experience of franticness, upset and lostness...the child is left in a chronic state of disembodiment or embodied in a damaged, not-whole, fragmented unhealed body. The terror, isolation and unimaginable loneliness of this condition produce the Type I [overwhelmed by pain] and Type II dissociative responses [avoidance of the body and denial of pain]
> (Goodwin & Attias, 1999, p. 227).

As an adult, Susan never struggled with pain until menopause hit. Before then she had had endless endurance physically; she had always been a Type II dissociative. After menopause and spousal rejection, Susan became a Type I dissociative: she couldn't get out of pain no matter how hard she tried. Having been a NICU baby lowered Susan's pain threshold, which made the descent of constant pain all the more overwhelming. Susan gradually emerged from the nightmare of chronic pain, sexual shame, and unresolved trauma. Unwinding the interwoven pieces of attachment experience and childhood physical suffering can facilitate a patient's facing their experience in the present rather than remaining fractured into dissociative pieces.

Developmental Trauma from Illness in the Family of Origin

Exposure to serious illness in a sibling or parent can be a terrifying experience. As Dobrich (2021) skillfully illustrates in her examination of survivor siblings, the inability to ask penetrating questions, to challenge relentless optimism within the family, and to openly mourn the lived family experiences that could never come to pass, create a form of dissociation she calls "unexperienced-experience."

> As is well established in the trauma literature, dissociation and survival are tightly linked—and because the presence of a chronic, often life-threatening and always life-limiting, condition in a family member creates a traumatic loss to everyone involved, we'd expect dissociation to play a large role in a family's capacity to adapt…unexperienced-experience is different from the experience that is inhabited because the fragmentation disrupts mentalization forging and solidifying a reliance on a dissociative structure…. Survivors break the unbearable into barely manageable bits and are left with a plethora of unexperienced-experience as they grow into adults.
>
> (pp. 19–20)

The therapy experiences of Raine, Cyril, Isabelle, Carlie, and George will demonstrate the intertwining of their attachment distress and development when as children they had to cope with serious illness in their families of origin. The horror of coping with unbearable experiences such as a terminal diagnosis, serious illness, or poor prognosis can tax and deplete the resources of any family, no matter how loving. Raine was a toddler when her little brother was diagnosed with a terminal illness at birth; she and her parents coped by fleeing into the haven of intellectuality. Isabelle's father struggled with Type I diabetes and was prone to flying into rages when his blood sugar was low; she was the only family member who could convince him to eat at such times. Her terror of feelings was palpable. Cyril was the introverted big sister of an extroverted little boy Chris, who struggled with hemophilia. Carlie grew up in the shadows of a father diagnosed with stage IV cancer and a brother with schizoaffective disorder. George grew up with a violent brother who was schizophrenic.

Flight into the Mind; Insulation against Catastrophe: Raine

Raine was a 42-year-old patient from a loving family. She had been diagnosed with obsessive compulsive disorder (OCD) and generalized anxiety disorder, but her art therapist, the group, and I suspected that she was also somewhat dissociative. I saw her only in group (for more details about her group experience see Chapter 6). She had been preoccupied since early childhood with fears that she would get leprosy. She herself made the analogy to psychic skin; it was as if her skin never grew in solidly. When she was 1 year old, her little brother was born with serious complications, among them cerebral palsy and severe retardation. Doctors did not believe he would live to be 2, but her parents kept him at home until he died at age 30. Several years ago, her father collapsed with a stroke, and afterwards was confined to a wheelchair, unable to speak. He died the following winter, just before Christmas.

Raine grew up feeling much adored, but the sunshine of her idyllic childhood was shadowed by her parents' agony over her brother's illness. For the first 2 years of his life, Raine's parents spent almost every waking minute with him, fearing each one was his last. Raine determined to not be a burden on her aggrieved, doting parents, suppressing her needs and, whenever possible, her feelings, attempting to live in her mind. Her brother was prone to rages and acting out. Raine's parents doted on both their children, so Raine suppressed nearly all her aggression and irritation with her brother.

Raine felt different from other children in her rural area because, like her parents, she was an intellectual. She rarely brought anyone home because her brother was such a handful. As an adult, she began therapy after enduring open-heart surgery, realizing that she had to begin to let herself have needs. She was skeptical about whether therapy had anything to offer her that her mother, spouse, and friends didn't provide. Her mother, whom she talked with a couple of times a day, was also highly skeptical about doctoring in general and psychotherapy in particular.

Raine was terrified of her feelings, fearing that she would go crazy. According to her family, she had begun to recoil from touch when her little brother was born. We have speculated that she couldn't help but absorb her parents' terror since she spent much of her toddlerhood in a hospital while they kept a death vigil. Her parents kept "a stiff upper lip" and a positive mental attitude, which offered no opportunity for sharing or mastering their grief, despair, and horror.

As a child, Raine translated the helplessness of her inchoate terror into an active coping strategy that could offer reassurance: she developed obsessions about various catastrophes that her mother could address. Her mother had served as her *de facto* therapist, reassuring her steadily that she was intact, not crazy, not bad, not going to get AIDS or leprosy, and was not going to hell. Raine later came to understand that her terror represented preverbal experiences that were impossible to metabolize. Throughout her life she was worried that she would get AIDS and leprosy. She also was convinced that she was destined to go to hell. Raine thought it was relevant that both leprosy and AIDS connote feelings of being untouchable. She began to realize that she never really thought she could grow up or that she could cope.

She related to others in a highly intellectualized manner but joked about an internal little girl locked in an internal closet because "she" is screaming all the time. (She later forgot having said that.) She had difficulty tolerating her group's frequent stories of disappointment in their parents and insisted that her parents were perfect and her childhood idyllic. However, she began to recognize that she absorbed her parents' terror about her brother's fragility through every pore. She painted frenetic but compulsively organized pictures of her "feelings," each with a solid black swash of paint demarcating two different sections or zones of feeling. Try as she might, the black swash always crept in, although she insisted it meant nothing. The group invited her to relinquish her highly abstract, intellectualized style so that they could sense her "heart and soul." She believed that feeling her feelings would be a pathway to madness. She had retreated into her mind as an escape hatch where she had some control (Corrigan & Gordon, 1995).

Flight into Books

Raine describes her parents as brilliant, loving intellectuals who coped with tragedy with brave stoicism. Like many other overwhelmed children, she turned to books and reading for solace. In the following excerpt (Spufford, 2002), a man reflects on the way in which compulsive reading during his childhood years created a wall of words and images that served to insulate him from the horrors of his little sister's lingering terminal illness and his mother's bone degeneration. Reading provided him with a psychic skin that felt impermeable to the blows of reality. As he fought to establish some territory in which he could feel *apart from* the vulnerability that imbued his very existence, he had to steel himself against even the idea of fragility. The worlds which engaged him were those of heroes and magic that vanquished evil. When I first read this passage to Raine, she burst into tears of comprehension:

> And ever since, I've hated vulnerable people. ...so, when I read stories obsessively as a child I was striking a kind of deal that allowed me to turn away. Sometime in childhood I made a bargain that limited, so I thought, the power over me that real experience had, the real experience that comes to us in act and incident and through the proximate, continuous existence of those we love.... I learned to pump up the artificial realities of fiction from page to mind at a pressure that equalized with the pressure of the world, so that (in theory) the moment I actually lived in could never fill me completely, whatever was happening. For the first years of the bargain, my idea was that good writing should vanish from attention altogether while you read it, so that the piped experience pressing back the world should seem as liquid and embracing—as unverbal—as what it competed with.... Still, when I reach for a

book, I am reaching for an equilibrium. I am reading to banish pity and brittle bones. I am reading to evade guilt, and avoid consequences, and to limit time's hold on me: all thoughts far from prose....

(Spufford, 2002, pp. 14–17)

Talismans of Power

In addition to being a compulsive reader, Raine shopped—another active strategy designed to offer reassurance that catastrophe doesn't lie around the next corner. Raine and her spouse made a good living, but Raine overspent with compulsive shopping, which she indulged in whenever she felt anxious. She bought many books, of course, but it is her relationship with jewelry that was most fascinating. Whenever she was stressed, she bought and held onto jewelry. She bought a new, larger purse so that she could carry all 15 pounds of jewelry with her wherever she went. She clasped at least one piece during most groups. She at least partly believed they were powerful "talismans" that would keep her safe in a form of magical thinking. She tried desperately to predict the future and braced herself for it, pointing to her father's life-impairing stroke and ultimate demise as proof positive that bad things will happen if she didn't prepare for them. Christmas was highly stressful for her, as her little brother's death, and her father's stroke and his death 2 years later, occurred within a few days of Christmas. She wrote the following:

"What are you searching for, what are you missing, what are you trying to replace?"

My husband's and my psychiatrist asked that this morning, of my compulsive shopping (mostly for jewelry), a years-long obsessive-addictive behavior that has run us into $20,000 (plus or minus) of credit card debt.

I have run up $20,000 of credit card debt. I. Did. That.

The psychiatrist's point was that my husband, through compulsive computer gaming, and I, through shopping, are sublimating real feelings into these activities, which then in turn fuels feelings—anger, shame, irritation, for example—that circle right back and bite us on our proverbial asses. Maybe those are my words, but that was his point.

They [the pieces of jewelry] have to be special, they have to stand out, they should have a history, and they're best when associated with a memory, or cluster of memories.

My mom gave me this bracelet; it has little silver Scotties on it because she had two Scotties when she was a girl.... My husband bought me this heavy silver antique-looking bracelet, a gift for our first anniversary. I bought this puzzle ring two years ago during my first trip to the mall—one of my first forays into the public world—after my open-heart surgery to replace a defective valve.

They're talismans, you see.

Talisman: A stone, ring, or other object engraved with figures or characters, to which are attributed the occult powers of the planetary influences and celestial configurations under which it was made; usually worn as an amulet to avert evil from or bring fortune to the wearer; also medicinally used to impart healing virtue; hence, any object held to be endowed with magic virtue; a charm—http://dictionary.oed.com.

I know this because I've hunted and hoarded talismans as long as I can remember. The object of obsession, ideally to be carried on the person at all times. I, ahem, carry a cache of my jewelry with me most days, juju against regularness, boredom, loneliness, sorrow [terror, catastrophe]. I was fascinated with [Tolkien's] ring of power, Thomas Covenant's white gold, Popeye's cans of spinach, Felix's magic bag. When I was 7 or 8, I bought my mom a gold-tone and red-plastic ring and attested to her as to how it was a magic ring. I wasn't playing make believe; I was serious. She kept it in a drawer in the living room, where I would occasionally take it out and handle it and wonder at its powers.

February 4, 2005 (personal communication)

Raine gave an inexpensive ring to all the women in her group as a talisman and brought books that she hoped would be helpful to members who were suffering. In addition to sharing books with group members, Raine occasionally brought in tea and DVDs of particular television series that she had experienced as soothing and reassuring to loan to someone who is having a hard time.[6] Over time Raine became much more emotionally expressive in the group. Once she was able to get mad at me because I had given her group siblings attention and ignored her entirely, when she was on the brink of a disaster at work. We tried doing individual therapy together, but Raine didn't find our work particularly useful. Unless I have supernatural healing powers, I don't have enough to offer her except for a useful idea now and again. She couldn't quite figure out why I care about my patients or why they care so much about each other and me. She fretted that she was missing out on some important dimension of human relationship that she couldn't quite get her mind around. She couldn't imagine missing me when I was out of town. Although she acted compassionately by bringing soothing gifts to other group members, she didn't experience compassion or tenderness. The books, tea, and DVDs were simply practical interventions that might mitigate another's distress; she hated seeing distress. She was terrified that her mother would die soon—she had reached her 70s and wouldn't see a doctor despite Raine's urging. Raised during the Great Depression, Raine's mother learned to be stoic, matter of fact, and pragmatic. We meet Raine again in Chapter 6.

A Good Little Girl Who Didn't Make Waves: Cyril

From the outset, Cyril denied her competitiveness and aggression and let her little brother have all the toys and attention. Suppressing all competition is another way to achieve active mastery over the passive experience of being outshone. Teenagers who are unsure about getting a date for the prom, for example, will frequently scorn the whole notion of dancing, announcing themselves as contemptuous and uninterested. Once Cyril's brother Chris developed hemophilia, Cyril began to make herself increasingly invisible. Chris was the daredevil of the family despite his medical challenges. He and his pals were inevitably pulling dangerous stunts around Cyril, who was sitting in the background, anxious and appalled. She would ultimately get in trouble for the mischief from her parents when they found out about the escapades. The children spent much of their childhood with their grandparents. The grandmother struggled with some kind of schizoaffective disorder and the grandfather was emotionally remote and a drinker. They never intervened, no matter how dangerous the stunts became. Suppressing the instincts of a tattletale, Cyril never told her parents what was going on, and willingly took the heat for Chris's misdeeds. When Chris went into active decline in his late teens, family life revolved entirely around his increasingly poor health.

After he died, Cyril and her parents were bereft. Cyril described her 20s as a period of deadness; she could barely remember herself during those sad, lonely years. She was working on a doctorate. Cyril was now the only child of doting parents and felt suffocated by their needs for attention from her. Her mother had grown up in another country in a large, closely knit family. All the relatives lived in the same neighborhood. Boundaries, even the concepts of boundaries and personal space, were totally foreign to Cyril's mother. Endless confrontations and discussions didn't help. Although Cyril's father was sympathetic to her struggles with boundaries, her mother continued to function in the same, joined-together-at-the-hip fashion. She couldn't imagine why Cyril wouldn't want to spend every weekend and holiday with her parents. If Cyril left a family get-together earlier than the family had anticipated, Cyril's mother sulked.

Finally, Cyril moved to another city to provide herself with some autonomous existence. She didn't tell her parents much, if anything, about her private life, knowing her mother would want to be part of it—another active coping strategy to deal with the helplessness of merger and invasion. Once, Cyril planned with her parents' permission to have a Fourth-of-July party at the family's nearby lake house. Her mother arranged to have the kitchen redecorated during the very same weekend, barging in on Cyril and about ten friends while they were engaged in the usual leisure activities of thirty-somethings—flirting, smoking, drinking, and general partying. To Cyril's vast amusement, her mother grabbed herself a handful of a tray of "special" brownies that one of her friends had baked.

In group, Cyril slowly learned about boundaries and competition. She noticed that, at bars and parties, she ceded all the attention to her more flirtatious girlfriends, even if a man she was interested in was present. Then she would sulk and become passive aggressive. In art therapy, she constructed a wall from old stones, keepsakes and jewelry—a concrete representation of her desire to have a more individuated, defined self. Unfortunately, she contracted Lyme's disease and became incapacitated, withdrawing from group, school, and much of life. To her credit, she works steadfastly with her art therapist to this day.

No Words—Daddy's Little Helper: Isabelle

Isabelle came to me in her early 20s. I am known for my ability to work with individuals who have trouble putting their feelings into words, and one of my groups was particularly suitable for individuals who struggle with emotional expression. Isabelle was exceptionally self-critical and preoccupied with being a good person. As she grew away from the protected environment of being in school, she hit a wall of personal inadequacy. She felt her peers far outstripped her in their life accomplishments. She had no idea what to do with her life and felt empty: "I don't feel like a full being." Complicating her struggles was a neurological problem with encoding memory. Neurological findings were negative, but neuropsychological evaluation revealed significant deficits in memory and both nonverbal and verbal reception. She envied people who could remember and articulate their inner experiences with ease. Alone with me, she struggled to tell me what it was like to be her, but essentially did fine. In group, she froze with terror and felt she had nothing of value to offer. Yet, the first time she saw a new picture I had commissioned for above the group sofa, she exclaimed, "There's holiness behind the paint!" Indeed. More than 60 friends had written notes of blessings for me and my patients. The artist had glued them to the frame before applying paint, and the blessings were invisible underneath the oil paints coating the frame. Isabelle was a mystic!

Isabelle's father was diagnosed with Type I diabetes when Isabelle was little. She remembered his flying into violent and unpredictable rages because of blood sugar problems. Isabelle remembered hiding under the dining room table to escape his notice during such times. As she matured, however, she developed the knack of cajoling her resistant, belligerent father into eating. Soon, only Isabelle could get him to eat when he was out of control. Since entering college, Isabelle lived away from home, leaving her father's problems to her brother and mother to manage. He stopped responding to her cajoling during her visits home and suffered neurological damage from his frequent diabetic seizures.

Isabelle's mother was a warm and loving woman who came from a difficult childhood herself. She didn't know how to help Isabelle articulate her inner experiences while growing up and wasn't particularly introspective herself. Isabelle was terrified of having unacceptable feelings and berated herself for being self-centered and unfulfilled. I have speculated with her that she suppresses resentment and other negative feelings because she didn't want to turn into her father. She censored herself brutally in the group, dismissing all her thoughts as unworthy and trying desperately to hide from the shame she felt when she compared herself with other group members. Isabelle's older brother was also a bit lost in life; his therapist fired him because he wasn't able to "use therapy productively." I suspect he faced some of the same issues Isabelle did. While Isabelle's brother dated rarely, if at all, Isabelle was in a secure relationship with a kind and loving man for many years, whom she found boring but safe and predictable. She summoned up the courage to leave him because she couldn't envision a life with him, whereas he was ready to start a family. Isabelle braved the challenges of online dating, anxiously second-guessing herself and wondering whether she had made a terrible mistake. After years of self-doubt, she went off to graduate school in social work and married a young man she met there. When her father died recently, we met, just to catch up. She was amazed at the growth we had catalyzed together: her past was a mere shadow of her present self. For more about Isabelle's group work, see Chapter 7.

Body as Retreat: Defiance and Play

Individuals who experience uninterrupted adequate parenting in their early years have the advantage of neurological resilience. Although severe life stressors can overwhelm their coping abilities, these youngsters learn to ground themselves and calm their anxiety through physicality and athletic play. Whether they are competing in a horse show or just losing themselves in the delight of a great ski run or tennis match, their intense focus on the task at hand frees them from worry.

I came across an interesting piece of research on the phenomenon called "the yips" many years ago but was never able to relocate this source. In this study, college students whose brains were wired to PET scanners were given an opportunity to compete at miniature golf. The top 20 or so would compete again, only this time the researchers upped the ante: the students would supposedly be viewed live on national television, and a huge prize pot was offered. Analysis of the top performers' brain scans was intriguing. Those who were able to compete well under these stressful conditions had similar brain scans to what they had in the first competition. In those who panicked during the second competition, whole areas of their brains had gone black under the stress, and their scores suffered as a consequence. Somehow the top performers were able to preserve their sense of play and utter absorption even under stress. Carlie and George both had the ability to immerse themselves entirely in bodily experience to escape anxiety.

Daredevil with an Attitude: Carlie

I only worked with Carlie for 2 months, over the college summer break. Her mother, a previous patient of mine, noticed how unhappy Carlie seemed to be after her first big relationship began to have problems, and suggested Carlie meet with me over the summer. When Carlie was 2, her father was diagnosed with stage IV carcinoma. Much of her early childhood was spent by his side in hospital rooms while he aggressively fought to live. He went into a lasting remission, but then her parents divorced, and her mother remarried some years later. Then Carlie's big brother began to fall apart. In the midst of terrifying rages, delusions, and runaway attempts, he fled into polydrug use to medicate his anxiety and flunked out of school. After many false starts and some therapy, he was diagnosed with schizoaffective disorder and received effective medication. He was able to go off to college only a couple years after his peers did.

With all the emotional storms ravaging Carlie's life, it was no surprise that she was highly anxious. During the short time I knew her, she was terrified of noises in the house when she was alone, nightmares, rejection by her peers and boyfriend, and thunderstorms—all things she couldn't control. She said she felt like a little girl when she was anxious but like an almost-grown-up the rest of the time. Her warm relationship with her mother was her saving grace. Her own father was an extremely busy financier who traveled around the world and was difficult to talk with about personal things. Yet he was proud of Carlie's equestrian skills and academic achievement. They had never really talked about his battle with cancer or her brother's mental illness.

Carlie found active strategies to cope with her disequilibrium and to defy the terror besieging her. She was a world-class equestrian, excelling in the worlds of cross country and hunter-jumper. A preternatural calm descended over her when she saddled her horses and entered the competition ring. She loved the thrill of jumping and was blasé about her many falls. She had an exquisite sense of her horse's subtleties and was a sought-after horse trainer. Carlie's stepfather was the sort of man who didn't really understand children very well. She resented her stepfather's somewhat domineering presence in her household and made no bones about telling him so. When he barked out orders to wait on him or to clean up his messes, she openly defied him. He frequently accused her of being disrespectful, but her mother backed her up. They told him if he treated Carlie like a person instead of a caricature, the two of them would probably get along better. She hated living at home over the summer because his presence made life feel oppressive. She yearned for the days when it was just herself and her mother. We speculated together that the sense of oppression he brought into the family might echo some of the dread she had experienced around her ill brother and father.

Carlie and I spent much of our time together trying to make sense of the terror deep inside her, her sadness about her brother's suffering and inner chaos, and her relationship with her boyfriend. Ultimately, she decided to break off the relationship with her boyfriend. When I last spoke with her, she was taking advanced lifesaving and negotiating her second job as a waitress. At the hint of being taken for granted (and hit on for a sexual favor) by her first restaurant employer, she abruptly quit and aimed higher, for a really nice restaurant and the hope of more ethical management.

Wolf in Sheep's Clothing: George

George was the son of a psychiatrist, an irony we frequently chuckled about. His older brother had been schizophrenic ever since George was in elementary school. He had secretly terrorized George in their shared bedroom with both malice and violent rages. George remembers years of terrible anxiety during his childhood: time would constrict, and objects or people would shrink or expand. Sometimes nothing felt real to him, and he worried that he was going crazy too. George turned to his body for solace. Athletically gifted despite a slight frame, he was coordinated and excelled at every sport he attempted. Times of bonding with his family were rare but precious for George, usually occurring during ski trips. The rest of the time he felt lost and resentful that his parents couldn't understand what he needed from them. In the eyes of his parents, George's brother was simply emotionally challenged; they failed to notice that George needed some protection from him. In and out of institutions for most of George's life, the brother continued to live at home between bizarre and violent episodes of full-out psychosis. George remembers breaking his arm at college and sending the x-ray and casting bill home, hoping someone would ask *him* about how he was doing, but his parents assumed that he was fine.

When I first met George, he was sad over a breakup. Although on the outside he presented as confident and successful, on the inside he felt empty and inadequate. He was terrified that he was secretly a fraud. I saw him in both individual and group therapy for about 10 years. In our first few years, George would beg me to help him articulate his inner experience. He could master almost any physical or academic skill with ease, but introspection and self-expression were agonizing for him. The metaphor he used was feeling like a fish, trapped on the sand and gasping for breath. He needed me to gently lift him up and place him in the water again, that is, find the words for him.

His family rarely discussed feelings, although they allowed George's brother to rage and tantrum about envy and competition vis-à-vis his little brother. If the family made a plan revolving around George, his brother was sure to sabotage it. George was secretly furious with both his parents. For several years he withheld love from them, refusing to send birthday cards or to return phone calls. During one of their rare visits to Texas, George brought his parents to meet with me as a family. They were stunned to realize how starved for affection George was. When he tried to describe his sense of playing second fiddle to his brother's madness, they stammered weakly in the brother's defense. When I encouraged his parents to hug George at the end of our meeting, they hung back, clearly anxious about how to undertake this difficult task. George's mother was a caricature of Martha Stewart, adroit socially but startlingly lacking in warmth. When George was home visiting, she would follow him around the house, fussing when he would leave a glass out and erasing any sign of his existence in the name of cleanliness. She was a perfectionist, and George could never figure out how to please her.

George's dating life was a disaster. Determined not to get his heart broken again, he used an active coping strategy to protect himself from vulnerability and helplessness—he became a conqueror. He studied women's needs and became a proficient lover, breaking up with them the moment they began to rely on him. We understood this pattern as both generalized hostility toward women and as a method of avoiding true vulnerability and commitment.

In his fourth year of three-times-a-week therapy with me, George's hostility and yearning finally turned toward me[7] when I told him I was going to stop putting the fish back into the water and instead allow him to struggle with finding his own words. He harangued me regularly about the 30 seconds I took between sessions to stop by the bathroom, protesting that I was stealing time from him. During this period, I had broken my ankle and was in a cast. He "accidentally" kicked my cast on a number of occasions.

Omnipotent strivings emerged (a passive into active coping strategy). He imagined jumping out of an airplane without a parachute. He took risks skiing and with his sports car. He bragged that he was going to conquer even me someday, winning my heart and forcing me to marry him although dating a patient would be against my ethics. He would micro-analyze my facial expressions and triumphantly belittle me whenever he sensed I was feeling vulnerable. To preserve my own capacity to think and in an effort to develop an active coping strategy for dealing with his relentless aggression, I suggested we try therapy with him on the couch, an arrangement that allowed him to look out the window at trees (he loved nature). This arrangement also helped me to escape what had become an endless bait-and-retreat pattern between us (him baiting and me retreating).

By this point George was dating someone seriously. Being on the couch allowed him to look inward for the first time and notice his inner experiences. We learned that he tended to induce feelings of inadequacy in his girlfriend, me, and other group members rather than to face these feelings in himself (a defense against vulnerability called projective identification—inducing unwanted feelings in others in order to control the feelings). He entered a period of profound despair, lamenting that he felt like an empty gas tank without a nearby gas station. With the group's help, he began to see that his difficulties with vulnerability, his inability to tolerate inadequacy, and the long-simmering resentment inside him were limiting his growth. Against the group's urging, he went out and bought a huge diamond ring for his girlfriend, cockily insisting she wouldn't be able to resist his proposal. The group told him he didn't really love her enough yet to propose to her. He was flabbergasted when she turned him down flat and felt a bit crazy inside. When his omnipotence failed, he was forced to face the vulnerability of his childhood. Over the next few years, he returned again and again to the nightmare of his childhood with his brother. He grew by leaps and bounds as he began to let himself love deeply and let go of years of resentments and secret inadequacy. This time, when he excelled at work, he was able to take credit for his actual accomplishments rather than secretly feeling like a fraud. The next time he proposed to his girlfriend, she accepted with delight. He left therapy shortly after the wedding. We both teared up as we said goodbye.

Remnants of Chronic Illness: The Art and Music of Joni Mitchell

Catastrophic illness during childhood makes an indelible imprint on the developing self. Singer/songwriter Joni Mitchell faced death three times in her first decade of life. At age 3, she suffered a ruptured appendix, which had to be a terrifying and painful experience. At 8, she endured two deadly bouts of measles, along with chicken pox and scarlet fever. At 9, she was hospitalized with polio. By that time, she was already smoking cigarettes. Little is known about her family life, except that she disliked formal school and preferred taking art classes. At 21, she was abandoned by her boyfriend while 3 months pregnant and starting her musical career. She gave her daughter up for adoption, lamenting that she could not care for her. She wrote at least one song about her. Always both musically and artistically inclined, Mitchell poured herself into storytelling through painting, photography, and singing. She started her performance career by singing in her children's hospital to the other patients. Her last album, *Shine*, was released in 2007.

Songwriting and other storytelling efforts attempt to find meaning within arbitrary, senseless, and sometimes cruel medical interventions designed to preserve life, seeking to repair the damage that illness has perpetrated on the unfolding of a life.[8] Three kinds of illness narratives represent attempts to master the vulnerability of traumatized experience (Frank, 2013): recovery narratives, chaos narratives, and quest narratives. Recovery narratives tell a story through the wounded body, sharing the dread and perfidy of illness while offering hope in the telling and listening. Chaos narratives resemble unresolved attachment styles; hope is denied by the steady infusion of hopelessness and traumatic affects, sensations, and images. Quest narratives share a person's hopes and fears in an attempt to find meaning and resolution.

Mitchell's songwriting side-stepped bodily experience for the most part, focusing on dreams, heartbreak, and the passage of time. In interviews she acknowledged that she sang her sorrow. About *Blue*, her 1971 album, she described herself as defenseless, unable to present a false self to the world that conveyed strength and poise.

Her poetic stream of consciousness lyrics are laden with the loneliness of winter, the power of fear, love's loss, dreams and the struggle to find hope within disillusionment, and the shame and distress of a mother who had given her child up for adoption. Mostly her songs can be understood as quest narratives to preserve hope and meaning amid catastrophe and heartbreak.

Although Mitchell's lyrics represent illness narratives only metaphorically via songs like "Trouble Child" and "The Sire of Sorrow," her visual artwork was steeped in somatic imagery, resembling more of a chaos narrative. Many of her paintings created as album cover art echo the ravages of her struggles with post-polio syndrome. Post-polio syndrome attacked the nerves and musculature of her left hand and arm, leaving them so weakened that the traditional chording of folk-style music was impossible for her. Jazz chording was easier for her left hand to accomplish, hence her unique style of blending jazz with folk melodies. Since eventually the weight of a traditional guitar was too formidable for her left arm to manage, she used a personalized guitar, weighing only two and a half pounds, to create much of her music. The trauma to her left side is well-integrated into her cover art for her albums and CD cases. *Ladies of the Canyon* depicts a woman with no left arm; *Clouds* depicts her holding a red flower up to left side of her face with explosions peeking out from behind her; *Hejira* also has one oddly disembodied hand. Even the pastoral scene of *For the Roses* depicts her left arm as slightly obscured.

Most recently she has turned to photography to portray graphic insults to the body. Mitchell would probably object to this characterization, insisting that neither her art nor her songwriting is autobiographical. Yet her one song about psychotherapy represents furious resentment at being labeled as suffering. She titled her 2006/2007 exhibit of triptychs "Green Flag Song." Its themes were the ravages of war, revolution, and torture.[9] Although her recent art and music has been dedicated to the ravages of Mother Earth by mankind, in allegory it can also be understood as her own disallowed protest about the cruelty, randomness, and dehumanized suffering of a body ravaged by both acute and chronic illness, beginning in early childhood. Her triptych show is somewhat graphic and brutal, with photographs of dismembered bodies and images of death created from ghostly green-and-white negative images photographed from her dying TV set.

Psychotherapy deals directly with the quest narrative by encouraging the telling of stories and the creation of personal meaning. With many of my patients, I work in team treatment with art therapists, who help in non-verbal modalities such as sculpture, painting, collage, and drawing. Over time I have learned to be alert to indicators of bodily experience in the artwork of trauma survivors by listening with my eyes as well as my ears to what they are telling me. I hope Joni Mitchell will forgive me my armchair analysis of her powerful body of work in the light of developmental trauma. I have always been an admirer of hers.

Notes

1 Terr (1990) studied the play of traumatized children. One of her findings was that children who engaged in perseverative play are often expressing a troubling experience without realizing they are doing so.

2 Transference is the process in psychotherapy whereby somebody unconsciously redirects feelings and fears onto the therapist/patient relationship as a way of communicating about and mastering them.

3 In their exhaustive chapter on the management of somatoform symptoms in traumatized patients, Loewenstein and Goodwin (1999) recommend that somatic and psychotherapeutic practitioners of such patients function in a coordinated treatment team. It took the combined efforts of a multidisciplinary treatment team, along with a highly motivated patient, to fully unwind the layers of physical and psychological adaptation to shock trauma that had accrued over 40 years. Kinesiology, physical therapy, body therapy, and psychotherapy all have in common a recognition that experience accumulates in layers, that it is organized and rigidified in structural/muscular adaptations, and that the dismantling of structures built over a lifetime takes step-by-step, patient analysis. Psychotherapists, physical therapists, and clinical kinesiology practitioners have long known that the brain is an organ of adaptations. Dan Siegel, pediatrician and psychiatrist, believes that all forms of intervention may be successful psychotherapy to the extent to which they enhance change in relevant neural circuits. Cozolino (2002), writing about neuroscience and psychotherapy, notes: "We appear to experience optimal development and integration in a context of a balance of nurturance and optimal stress" (pp. 62–3). He notes that both top–down (from cortical to subcortical and back again) and left–right (across the two halves of the brain) network communication and neural information loops promote optimal information flow and integration. Top–down integration includes the ability of the cortex to process and organize emotions generated by the brain stem and the limbic system; left–right integration allows us to put feelings into words and to construct integrative narratives that allow us to consider feelings from the past in conscious awareness in the current present. Neuroscientists believe that repeated simultaneous activation of neural networks requiring integration with one another most likely aids in their integration. Increased integration across neural networks parallels a patient's increased ability to experience and tolerate thoughts and emotions previously inhibited, dissociated, or defended against. The ability to tolerate and regulate affect creates the necessary conditions to live fully in the present, instead of being imprisoned in the past.

4   This fantasy was modeled after one of her favorite stories: *Mrs. Mike* (a true story of a woman, the wilderness, and rescue by a Mountie) which was published as a popular children's book in 1947 by Benedict and Nancy Freedman, and turned into a movie in 1949. Children's books often capture the essence of struggles to survive, which hold special appeal for youngsters who have faced hard times.

5   Once her dissociative defenses began to unravel, Susan became unable to regulate the intensity and duration of affects and their somaticization into pain syndromes. During her 6-year treatment, her physical condition altered daily, ranging from athletically competent (solid core muscle functioning, able to run, hike, do the stairclimber and weight train) to relatively impaired (mild to moderate chronic pain, unable to pick up anything over 2 lbs, level walks only), depending on what she was processing somatically and emotionally. Goodwin and Attias (1999) describe two patterns of intertwined somatic and cognitive/affective disturbance that typically occur in the same patient over a period of treatment:

> In both types, the individuals' narrative of physical and emotional pain is characterized by gaps, distortions and minimization. In Type I initial clinical presentations, "patients may construct a self-image around the pain and frantically search for a medical diagnosis to ward off further knowledge of the actual traumatic origins of the pain.... In Type I situations, the pain sensation remains, but its meaning is lost. ... In the Type II situation, the individual copes by stepping out of the body, leaving behind both the traumatic circumstance and the bodily container of physical and emotional pain. Complications here result from the denial of the real body and include sensory loss, depersonalization, overwork, neglect of self-care tasks and accident-proneness...
>
> (p. 224)

Like Susan, many Type II patients initially present as high-functioning, dissociative caregivers and overachievers who love to exercise but are out of touch in essential ways with their bodies. Once they get in touch with their bodies, through treatment or by experiences of unmanageable pain such as those triggered by car wrecks, they somaticize increasingly and become overwhelmed by traumatic affects as their dissociative structures are slowly dismantled (shifting into Type I patterns).

6   "Buffy the Vampire Slayer," "Angel," "Firefly," "House" have in common a struggle against the intrusion of unpredictable evil that threatens to swamp the coping resources of the protagonists. The heroes of the series all prevail, however (except in "Firefly," which ended prematurely). Other trauma survivors have described a similar relationship with the Harry Potter universe of books and movies.

7   The turning of yearning and hostility toward the therapist is, as mentioned above, called transference. When split-off feelings come into the therapeutic

relationship, they can be more readily metabolized and ultimately processed. Although I was encouraging George to use me "ruthlessly," as a child uses his mother, I also needed to find some way of managing these feelings, as they poured onto and into me, so that I could be helpful.

8 Frank (1991), a cancer survivor himself, explores the power of storytelling to help individuals come to terms with serious physical illness.

9 See Peter Frank (2006) in the essay that accompanied the catalogue to the "Green Flag Song" exhibit that opened on November 11, 2006 at the Lev Moross Gallery in Los Angeles.

References

Balint, M. (1968). *The basic fault*. Northwestern University Press.

Bollas, C. (1987). The *s*hadow of the *o*bject. Columbia University Press.

Bowlby, J. (1969/1982). *Attachment and loss: Vol. 1*. Attachment. Basic Books.

Bowlby, J. (1973). *Attachment and loss: Vol. 2*. Separation. Basic Books.

Bowlby, J. (1980). *Attachment and Loss: Vol. 3. Loss*. Basic Books.

Corrigan, E. G., & Gordon, P. E. (Eds.). (1995). *The mind object*. Jason Aronson.

Cozolino, L. J. (2002). *The neuroscience of psychotherapy: Building and rebuilding the human brain*. W. W. Norton & Co.

Culbert-Koehn, J. (1997). Analysis of hard and soft: Tustin's contribution to a Jungian study of opposites. In T. Mitrani & J. Mitrani (Eds.), *Encounters with autistic states: A memorial tribute to Frances Tustin* (pp. 111–23). Jason Aronson.

Dobrich, J. (2021). *Working with survivor siblings in psychoanalysis: Ability and disability in clinical process*. Routledge.

Eekhoff, J. K. (2019). *Trauma and primitive mental states: An object relations perspective*. Routledge.

Fogelman, D. (Creator/producer) (2016–2022). *This is us* [TV Series]. NBC.

Frank, A. W. (1991). At the will of the body: Reflections on illness. Houghton Mifflin Company.

Frank, A. W. (2013). The wounded storyteller. University of Chicago Press.

Frank, P. (2006). *Green flag song* [Exhibit catalog], Lev Moross Gallery.

Glaser, G. (2021). *American baby: A mother, a child, and the shadow history of adoption*. Viking Press.

Goodwin, J. M., & Attias, R. (1999). Traumatic disruption of bodily experience and memory. In J. M. Goodwin & R. Attias (Eds.), *Splintered reflections* (pp. 223–38). Basic Books.

Hopper, E. (2003). *Traumatic experience in the unconscious life of groups*. Jessica Kingsley Publishers.

Janov, A. (1983). *Imprints: The lifelong effects of the birth experience*. Coward McCann.

Levine, P. A., & Kline, M. (2006). *Trauma through a child's eyes*. North Atlantic Books.

Loewenstein, R. J., & Goodwin, J. (1999). Assessment and management of somatoform symptoms in traumatized patients: Conceptual overview and pragmatic guide. In J. Goodwin & R. Attias (Eds.), *Splintered reflections* (pp. 67–88). Basic Books.

Lyons-Ruth, K., Dutra, L., Schuder, M., & Bianchi, I. (2006). From infant attachment disorganization to adult dissociation: Relational adaptations or traumatic experiences? *Psychiatric Clinic of North America, 29*(1), 63–86.

Polan, H. J., & Hofer, M. A. (2018). Psychobiological origins of infant attachment and its role in development. In J. Cassidy & P. R. Shaver (Eds.), *Handbook of attachment: Theory, research, and clinical applications* (pp. 117–32). Guilford Press.

Porges, S. W. (2018). *Clinical applications of the Polyvagal Theory*. W. W. & Norton Co.

Robertson, J. (Producer). (1952). *A two-year-old goes to the hospital* [Film]. Robertson Films.

Robertson, J., & Robertson, J. (1989). *Separation and the very young*. Free Association Books.

Scaer, R. (2005). *The trauma spectrum: Hidden wounds and human resiliency*. W. W. Norton Company.

Scaer, R. (2014). *The body bears the burden: Trauma, dissociation and disease*. Routledge.

Siegel, D. J., & Hartzell, M. (2003). *Parenting from the inside out: How a deeper self-understanding can help you raise children who thrive*. Jeremy P. Tarcher/ Penguin.

Solomon, M., & Tatkin, S. (2011). *Love and war in intimate relationships*. W. W. Norton & Co.

Spufford, F. (2002). *The child that books built*. Metropolitan Books.

Terr, L. (1990). *Too scared to cry*. Harper & Row.

Winnicott, D. W. (1958). The capacity to be alone. *The maturational processes and the facilitation environment* (pp. 29–36). International Universities Press.

Winnicott, D. W. (1974). Fear of breakdown. *International Review of Psycho-Analysis, 1*, 103–7.

Chapter 4

No Safe Harbor
Children of Perdition

"Perdition" refers to hell, complete destruction and ruin. Our world these days has run amok with pain on a global level as well as in the hearts and souls of our children and adolescents; in a sense, it has "gone to hell." Our youngsters seek confirmation and mastery of the harshness of their world in reality shows like *Survivor* or *The Voice*. The shows mirror the little deaths, horrors, and tragedies of life in 60-minute bite-sized pieces, far easier to swallow than a Columbine, a World Trade Center, a Waco, or an Oklahoma City. Shock is no longer shocking; or really it *is*, but if we caricature it, mock it, and make it grotesque, then we can turn passive into active experience and pretend we are on top of it all. The word "terror" has been so overused it has lost its meaning. In our consulting rooms, there is no remote control, no laugh track, and no commercial break. Just 45–50 minutes of undiluted Stephen King without the palliative of "this is just pretend." Treating patients with chronic shock states and other fallout from difficult childhoods is a little bit like walking into the wrenching horror of post-Saddam Iraq or the dreary re-building of war-torn countries. Although the reign of terror has fallen, the aftermath is almost as overwhelming as the tyranny itself. When an entire country has operated according to the rules of disorganized attachment, with randomness, arbitrary cruelty, terrorization, and unpredictability of norms, every citizen is a prisoner of war, a survivor of political torture, or a refugee from horror.

Unless we are trauma specialists, we may not think of ourselves as having "trauma" patients in our practice, but we do. Most clinicians consider "trauma" patients to be disaster victims emerging from sites like Columbine, Oklahoma, or the World Trade Center, or as soldiers

DOI: 10.4324/9781003262367-6

after battle. Then there are the ubiquitous crime victims, who perhaps were physically or sexually abused as children, trafficked, or assaulted as an adult. What about more subtle, "small t trauma"? Like disaster recovery dogs who are sensitive to the faintest sounds of a survivor buried under tons of rubble, we therapists can deepen our repertoire of listening perspectives to sense the faint hallmarks of shock experience in our patients' material.

For example, as we saw in Chapter 3, even one unmetabolized disastrous medical experience in a youngster's life can set up shock reverberations that persist throughout the life span. Imagine, then, the impact of the thousands of individual shock experiences that accrue in a disorganized attachment relationship with a non-empathic parent. Our patients with disorganized attachment experience are the *sine qua non* of trauma patients. Their flashbacks are not of bombs and blasts, but of broken connections, harsh rebukes, silent tears, rages against the self for not being better, and deafening screams of unrelenting distress and confusion. Our patients with unbearable affects have come to depend upon us as reliable dance partners in this grim waltz with the macabre. They have had to tolerate the unbearable paradox (Pizer, 1998) of stillness and escape, just as their companions in war-besieged countries have had to do. Their nervous systems have been relentlessly barraged and besieged by the aftershocks of unattuned parenting.

The Living Dead: Gail

The patient who speaks endlessly, desperately, of wishing he were dead is perhaps casting out for an anchor somewhere to stop the ceaseless falling, with his therapist's recognition that he has been dying psychically for years. "Dead thoughts" inhabit a different terrain than suicidal ideation. I often ask new patients if they wish they were dead, and they look at me warily, worried I will demand a suicide contract or hospitalize them if they are truthful. Benedetti, in a published interview with Koehler (2003), speaks of a kind of countertransference he calls counter identification in which the therapist empathically identifies with the patient's preverbal pain, forming a bridge between nightmare and possibility that leads to the creation of a new self, a mutually constructed identity: "The counter identification comes...from the present-day feelings the therapist has towards a psychically dying human being" (p. 80). Psychic dying is the penultimate agony, a torture of relentless reproach for being alive, without foreseeable relief or surcease. Ferenczi (1931/1980) described psychic death very movingly:

> When a child finds himself abandoned, he loses, as it were, all desire for life.... Sometimes this process goes so far that the patient begins to have the sensations of sinking and dying.... What we here see taking place is the reproduction of the mental and psychical agony which follows upon incomprehensible and intolerable woe.
>
> (p. 138)

Benedetti's "psychically dying human beings" spend a lot of time in my office. Gail, a 39-year-old mother of twins, came to me after 19 years of therapy with four therapists. She had come from a chaotic family with disorganized attachment on both sides, a teenage mother, a psychotic grandfather, and an alcoholic stepfather. Not only had her stepfather run over a family pet when he was drunk, he repeatedly tried to strangle Gail's mother in front of her. When violence would erupt at home, Gail would flee to neighbors' homes, trying to be as unobtrusive as possible so they would let her stay until the violence at her house ebbed. School was a nightmare for her. Although she made straight As, the other children tormented her endlessly, sensing her anxiety and vulnerability. Figuring out a strategy to avoid being waylaid and beaten up on her way home from school was a daily challenge. Her earliest memories were taking care of her mother "because she seemed to need it so much." She once found her mother curled up in the shower, sucking her thumb, overwhelmed with bills; the electricity had been shut off for a few days. A medical professional, Gail was divorced, a stable and loving mother determined to provide for her children what she had not had. Her "ex" wanted nothing to do with the children and had given up all custody rights. Like her father, whom she never met, Gail's "ex" was an absent presence for her children. Like her mother, Gail had married at 17, far too young. When overwhelmed, she "lost" moments to hours of time, which frightened her greatly.

I learned long ago to differentiate between "dead thoughts," "suicidal ideation," and suicidal plans. "Dead thoughts" contain unbearable affect states that are not yet "known" or "named." Although the dreaded remains unknown—what Stern (2003) calls "unformulated experience"—the psychically dying person senses that whatever it is he cannot quite name, it is dreadful. "Dead thoughts" are a way of beginning to "know" what cannot yet be felt, described, or remembered; dead thoughts are also a way out. When I first met her, Gail felt enormous shame about confiding her "dead thoughts" to me, not wanting to be a burden, and was amazed when I differentiated "dead thoughts" from suicidal ideation and suicidality; I told her I wanted to hear all about her dead thoughts. Her dead thoughts were a great comfort to her—they offered a way out of intolerable agony. When she was 8, she had nearly drowned in the ocean. She vividly remembered the relief of sinking into blackness, hoping her hard little life would now stop. She remembered no sense of panic or will to survive but did remember being disappointed when she was revived. Thus, thoughts of death were for her what heroin is to a heroin addict: a wonderful peacefulness, one which she actually had tasted before.

Gail was an attractive, lively mother. Her ACE score was 8, a hallmark of severe toxic stress. She grew up with inadequate parents who were always fighting, and Gail felt she needed to fix them somehow. She had a charming smile, which she resorted to in a self-deprecating way whenever she felt vulnerable. She blamed herself for "being a burden" to me, although I didn't feel particularly burdened by her at all. She was afraid to cry, because "If I cry, I will just end up having to take care of someone." She tried too hard to be a "good" patient and to take care of me. When I intercepted these maneuvers, she giggled in embarrassment and looked down at her lap. She often sat curled up in a big easy chair, her feet tucked up underneath her. On other occasions she lay or sat, Indian style, on the couch, looking out the window. Her eyes cast about for anywhere to look but at my face, especially when she felt herself beginning to "disappear." I have a large reef aquarium in my office, and sometimes she looked at the fish to ground herself and try to get present at the end of a session. She had many gradations of experience on the spectrum of dissociation. "Being not present" always seemed to begin with her hands, for reasons we didn't understand. She learned to tap her hands and remind herself that they belong to her (Levine, 1997) when she began to lose sensation.

Eventually she linked her hand tapping to a robbery/assault experience and her subsequent disavowed rage. As she entered her house with a broken window several years before, she had become terribly angry at the invasion and devastation to her house. She began screaming at the (presumably) long-gone robbers as she viewed the detritus of her family's Christmas. The Christmas tree was thrown aside, presents ripped, broken, and stolen. In a fury at the wreckage she saw before her, she had slammed her hands against the wall. Moments after her outrage, she was physically and sexually assaulted by two armed men who had been quietly hiding out in a back room. Laughing at her helpless screams of terror and fury, they tied her hands behind her and took turns kicking and sodomizing her. She was knocked out and came to in the hospital with a severe concussion. Her children had returned from their friend's house and the friend's mother had called EMS. When I visited her in the hospital she was shaking and shrunken, croaking in a whisper. She worried about the impact on her children of finding her unconscious body. Together we arranged for them to see a therapist to debrief and recover from this nightmare.

Every time Gail experienced anger of any kind, her body felt pain in the places that had been violated. She was terrified that she had permitted herself to act in violence like her stepfather had, although no one got injured except her. It seemed as if Christmas, the only holiday she had enjoyed as a child, was ruined forever. I bought her a Christmas ornament that was quite unusual and urged her to hang it in a prominent place. When flashbacks threatened, she could look at the ornament and link it to "me" and "now," a transitional object to help her stay grounded in the present.

At my encouragement, she used my voicemail as a container of sorts, to hold her unbearable experiences. We agreed I would call her back if it was convenient and would not if it was not. Most often she let me know she preferred no callback, but was just "checking in," our euphemism for using my voicemail to try and become more present. This arrangement seemed to work for both of us. Incidentally, I do not offer this arrangement to more than one patient at a time (van Sweden, 1977), lest I become resentful at the intrusions into my personal time.

When her twin children were at a sleepover, she would sometimes call me frantic, lost, and agitated. If I happened to answer the phone or call her back immediately, she might well have "come to" in her car in a location she did not know. Horribly ashamed, she was often seriously dehydrated and on a back road somewhere in a rural area.

I would tell her to drive to a gas station and ask for directions back to the main freeway. She felt exhausted and discouraged about going through this again: "This is no way to live. I need to figure out how to stop doing this, or just stop everything. I can't stand this. I can't stand never knowing when I'm going to dissociate, I feel so out of control."

When I saw her next, she talked of urgently needing to find a way to get control over dissociating. One part of her wanted to live, another to die. Part of her wanted to be hit by another car; another part of her would get her lost on a country road to keep the body alive—the car wreck plan would fail. We talked about dissociating as a little death. I told her she had already died a thousand times, over and over again throughout her lifetime: every time her grandfather became psychotic, every time her mother lashed out at her in hysteria, and every time her stepfather tried to kill her mother. No wonder she wanted it all to just stop. I pointed out that losing time was one way of making the unbearable feelings stop, but that she just ended up exchanging one awful feeling for another. She was terrified I would make her sign a suicide contract, knowing she might break her word. My trump card was my gentle reminder that her children would never recover from their mother's suicide.

She was caught in an intolerable dilemma: she blamed herself and her anger for the assault: "If I hadn't gotten angry maybe they wouldn't have hurt me." She turned her anger in on herself: "the only way out is to die." I cautioned her to be very patient with herself, that working slower is really faster, that we couldn't hurry things along. I then talked about how shock lived in her very pores, and about how awful shock feels, and she burst into tears. The "shocky" state of mind had never been crystallized in words for her as a state of mind that could be shared, or thought about, or even known before. It was so familiar to her that she couldn't believe she'd been in therapy for much of her life and it had never been named before.

Of course, our work had just begun. At times she has been legitimately suicidal; she twice made deliberate, serious attempts to end her life by car wreck. However, she was committed to her children and her therapy, and determined to not end her life for at least the foreseeable future. She lost time less than she used to. All her self-states spoke with the same voice and identified as Gail. Being able to talk about parts of her wanting to be dead was the essence of our work together, even as she dedicated herself to being the best possible parent to her growing twins.

States of Mind: Faces of Shock

States of mind are created within the psychobiological states of the brain and other parts of the body. Thus, attachment shock experiences are rooted in the brain and viscera. Damasio (1994, 2003) has suggested that changes in bodily states are perceived and represented in the brain as what he calls "somatic markers." Siegel believes that somatic markers may be one of the keys to felt emotional experience:

> Our brains create a representation of bodily changes that is independent of the present-day response. A thought can be associated with an emotional response containing a somatic marker that has been generated internally. This is a representation of a shift in bodily state created by our brains from imagination and past experience: an "as-if" loop, in which an internal stimulus (such as a thought, image, or memory) can activate an "as-if" somatic marker…. Memories of emotional experiences evoke "as-if" somatic markers, which can feel as real as direct bodily responses and can deeply enliven the associated imagery of the recollection…. An "as-if" somatic marker reveals how the process of imagination or memory can elicit a sensory response, which then initiates a cascade of fear-related associations that may be quite debilitating. This may be one way in which unresolved posttraumatic conditions continue to perpetuate frightening reactions from long ago; such individuals feel as if they are being traumatized over and over again.
>
> (Siegel, 1999, pp. 143–4)

Siegel (1999) postulates that we know how we feel based in large part upon the nature of these somatic markers, and that some people are more aware of their somatic markers, and thus their feelings, than others. "Impaired input of the right-sided sources of somatic markers would functionally lead such individuals to be consciously unaware of their bodies' response. They would therefore not be able to know easily how they feel…" (p. 146).

Shock is a somatic marker that is rarely recognized or named unless the sufferer is wandering around in a daze after a car wreck or other medical tragedy and is noticed by trained medical or psychiatric technicians. Otherwise, shock goes largely unnoticed, especially in children. Child psychiatrist Lenore Terr (1990), who came to specialize in acute trauma, was amazed after the Chowchilla kidnappings of a school bus full of children to hear the children described, not just by the media but by child psychiatrists, as doing "fine." Those children were not fine, will never be fine again. Probably many were not even "fine" before the incident.

Thinking and reading about shock is a bit like entering the *Twilight Zone*. Those readers who grew up in the 1960s will recall the fine job Rod Serling did of preparing us for what we were about to experience: a sense of the topsy-turvy, of things not making sense, of horror and nightmare, and things that go bump in the night. I hope I can live up to Serling's legacy as your narrator, inviting you to temporarily immerse yourself and your imagination into a new, uncomfortable zone of experience—the shock zone. In this chapter we will review five dimensions of attachment shock experience that create hellish states of mind—a misnomer, really, states of *brain* would be better—that come with a lifetime guarantee of suffering.

"Cephalic shock" (Lewis, 1981, 1983/2004, 2006) is the experience of knowing that the world is not a safe place to rest your head, and that you and only you are responsible for keeping yourself "okay." The consequence of this "state of mind" is chronic tension, particularly in the neck and shoulders, and a sense that peace of mind is ever elusive. Lewis coined this term in his work as a body therapist.

"Abandonment shock" is the state of mind that unexpected radio silence would bring to NASA astronauts circling our planet: confusion and an ominous dismay that all is not well. When we were learning about contributions to disorganized attachment relationships in Chapter 2, we looked at separation and loss as contributory experiences, in addition to a parenting style of momentary or prolonged "abdication," which leaves the child in a state of feeling abandoned and unprotected. This state of feeling abandoned and unprotected is the essence of abandonment shock.

"Shattershock" is, at its worst, the state of mind of a torture victim who just breaks down and surrenders to his captors, with little left but a shattered psyche. In families with patterns of disorganized attachment, a similar shattering experience can occur in the developing self of a vulnerable child. We will see how an agitated child with a parent who feels helpless, rejecting and/or out of control can result in an escalating negative "resonance" which overwhelms the child's capacity to adapt.

"Soulshock" is the trajectory of tragedy that ensues when a child has to make sense of bizarre behavior, malevolence, and madness in a parent. The Red Queen of Lewis Carroll's (1865) *Alice in Wonderland* was a model of dangerousness, paradox, and disorganized attachment; she was intrusive, bizarre, and served up arbitrary rules *à la carte*. Our patients who had to tolerate bizarre paradox and arbitrary randomness in childhood now must rely upon us to help them navigate the monstrous mindlessness of their cosmos.

"Potential shock" is the anticipation of inescapable shock, that feeling we describe as dread. As our brains scan for familiar landmarks of potential danger, our nervous system, our musculature, and our viscera register the toll. Dread dwells in the body, casting shadows of doubt and foreboding onto our minds and psyches.

Cephalic Shock: Frozenness and Static Tension

When babies have parents who go in and out of rhythmic attunement or just never quite get it right, the infants are forced to adapt to the shock of being *handled* rather than being able to relax into the safety of being securely *held*. These infants are thrown back on their own immature nervous systems to maintain balance and homeostasis instead of being able to rely upon their parents in a relaxed fashion. A bioenergetics therapist named Robert Lewis invented the construct of "cephalic shock" to describe the impact and the lifelong consequences of being "handled" instead of being "held" as a developing child. Lewis (1981, 1983/2004, 2006) suggests that one of the results of constant disequilibrium is that infants sense their physical precariousness and the forces of gravity. They prematurely struggle to pull their head and neck up and away, instead of relaxing into bliss the way their more secure counterparts do. Cephalic shock preserved in the musculature and body/mind is the result.

Lewis observed in his bodywork with patients that certain patients carried far more tension in their neck and shoulder musculature than others. When the tense patients gradually learned to relax their heads into his hands, as he sat behind them, they often would break into sobs of relief and talk about how they had never felt supported before; they had always to hold themselves up and could never just relax into a sense of peace. Another way to understand the dilemma of these infants is to imagine the difference between falling asleep in the familiar comfort and stability of your own bed and falling asleep on a sling three thousand feet up the side of a mountain, tethered to the rock face by a few pieces of metal. Experienced rock climbers learn to sleep on such slings while ascending a challenging mountain face. So, too, we learn as infants to accommodate to the kind of parenting we have, no matter how ill-suited it may be to our developmental needs. As he writes about cephalic shock, Lewis (1983/2004) comments on a series of mother–infant interactions videotaped by Brody and Axelrod (1968), observing that the infants of less empathic mothers were "…chaotically assaulted by dysrhythmic, gross mishandling" (p. 7).

> These infants will have to find a way *to hold on, hold together and hold against* the parents who cannot provide it with auxiliary ego i.e. to fight gravity prematurely and unnaturally. The dissonant handling creates a chronic state of disequilibrium or shock. …
> This becomes the no-peace-of-mind syndrome, because there is no piece of the head and mind within that is ever free of the burden of holding its world together.
>
> (Lewis, 1983/2004, pp. 2–3)

Lewis postulates cephalic shock to describe severe falling anxiety, a chronic state of disequilibrium. As described above, this physiological shock state is due to an immature nervous system exposed to unempathic handling, as the infant recognizes that attuned contact and environmental support are unavailable or inconsistent. He notes that the child literally relies upon cephalic bracing to support itself gravitationally before it has the ready musculature to easily do so. Lewis (1981) reminds us that Winnicott believed that failures of holding brought infants to the brink of unthinkable anxieties, one of which was a sensation of infinite falling. A newborn infant will first flinch backwards then rapidly throw out his arms in a desperate grasping motion whenever he senses himself about to fall; this motion is termed the Moro reflex. The evolutionary purpose of this reflex is to enable the primate to fully grasp onto its mother's body, by first opening the chest and arm musculature in a flinch which facilitates the grasp motions that immediately follow. Thus, the baby can be observed to scream in alarm, flinch, and grab toward the mother in a nanosecond. Lewis (1983) notes:

An infant will startle, i.e., exhibit a Moro reflex, whenever a subtle change in its equilibrium occurs. The reflex will be triggered by sudden movement, noise or temperature change or even by its own energetic crying. The handling to which a borderline parent inadvertently subjects an infant creates a chronic state of disequilibrium or shock, if you will, that is far beyond the shock that the infant can discharge via the Moro reflex. This is the unique shock of unempathic handling, a daily occurrence repeated perhaps hundreds of times a day in the course of feedings, diaper changes, etc.

(p. 8)

Lewis further notes that neuro-psychophysiological research data is beginning to document what happens to infants who experience traumatic overarousal. Neuroscientists report that patterns are laid down in the infant's immature nervous system, which become part of its hard wiring. Such structures, both neural and at the same time psychological, become imprinted into the circuits of the infant's cortex and limbic system as a state of frozen fear. When an infant is at the limit of what he can tolerate biologically (e.g., what Lewis would characterize as cephalic shock), the state of threat registers and moves through brain stem, midbrain, thalamic, and eventually cortical areas, engraving long-lasting damage (Perry, 1997). Lewis (2006) points out that daily cephalic shock during holding, changing, and feeding in earliest infancy renders the developing infant vulnerable to other shock trauma later in the developmental cycle:

The same caretaker who cannot respond to his infant in a well-attuned, emotionally responsive way in the earliest months of life, will tend to have long-term difficulties with the child as he matures. The child will not be well-attuned to on a core bodily level, or genuinely engaged with on an intersubjective level.

(p. 21)

Lewis notes at least phenotypic similarity between the stunned infants on videotapes from the 1960s whom he labeled as suffering from "cephalic shock" and the frozen youngsters presenting with disorganized/disoriented attachment behavior (Main & Solomon, 1986). In the presence of frightening or unattuned parental behavior, the children exhibit prolonged freezing and slowed movements. Schuengel et al. (1999) described an unusual infant observation example during their attachment research that seems to fit both these models:

Oddly enough, although apparently frightened by her infant, Mrs. R treated her in a cold and harsh manner, perhaps as a way to control her fearfulness. Deborah reacted with disorganized behavior. On one occasion, she heard her mother approach and displayed an asymmetrical facial expression by pulling one corner of her mouth down. ...When Mrs. R stood before her, ready to pick her up, Deborah looked up with a fearful facial expression. Her eyes bulged, her mouth was open, and her shoulders were tense. ...4 months later, Deborah did not show disorganized behavior and she was actually classified as secure. There was unusual behavior at the second reunion, however. Deborah cried and signaled weakly to be picked up. After being picked up, she stopped crying, and Mrs. R kneeled and held the infant in an awkward position. Because her mother put Deborah in this position, it cannot be coded as disorganized behavior. But it is odd for a secure infant to stay immobile when in an uncomfortable position on her mother's lap. Normally, secure babies sink in comfortably....

(p. 84)

The following clinical example depicts cephalic shock manifesting in states of confusion and disequilibrium. Although the concept of cephalic shock originated in the domain of body therapists, as developmental trauma becomes layered over the years, psychological manifestations occur as well.

Confusion and Disequilibrium: Cadence

Cadence was the second child of a single 23-year-old mother. Her brother George was 8 years older. The mother was a poly-drug user who tried her best to care well for her children but had little support. The mother's parents had died in a car crash while Cadence's mother was carrying Cadence *in utero*. They left her enough money in their inheritance to get by, but most of it was tied up in generation-skipping trusts for their grandchildren's education, future therapy, and medical expenses.

Pictures of Cadence as a baby were painful to look at. She was held in awkward ways by her mother and brother and looked uncomfortable and distressed. We spoke often and frequently about how insecure this must have made her feel. Child-care was often provided by Cadence's older brother George along with an assortment of babysitters. Although by and large he meant well, George sometimes amused himself at Cadence's expense by dangling her upside down. He had loved hanging upside down on the jungle gym when he was little. As he got older, he enjoyed doing flips on the trampoline and skating the rails on his skateboard. Since he was so athletically gifted, he was not fully aware that he was torturing Cadence when he swung her upside down. He was a bit more emotionally sturdy than his sister because his grandparents had taken care of him almost full time for the first 4 years of his life; Cadence had not been so lucky.

Both Cadence and George excelled at the Catholic school nearby. School served as a welcome refuge from the confusion Cadence experienced when her mother was "high" and not making much sense. In first grade, for example, Cadence proudly announced that she had learned that the world was round! Her mother, high on cocaine, argued with her, pointing to the landscape around them as evidence that the world was flat as far as she could tell.

Not being able to discern truth from fiction, Cadence swam in confusion much of the time. One afternoon she came home worried and uneasy. She was learning about "sin." The nuns wore white "bibs," and her favorite teacher had a brown stain the size of a quarter on her bib.

Thinking rather literally, Cadence confided to her brother that Sister Mary Louise was going to hell because she had a mortal sin on her soul and started to cry. George found her worry hysterically funny and teased her for weeks.

As children are wont to do, Cadence's peers zeroed in on her vulnerability to confusion. One of their favorite pranks in elementary school was to tell a joke that really wasn't funny and then laugh uproariously at the punchline to see who fell for it. Of course, Cadence laughed awkwardly because everyone else did, only to find herself once again the target of ridicule.

In fourth grade, her class took a field trip to the county fair. Cadence gamely lined up with the other girls to get on a ride called "The Hammer." Four girls at a time got into a basket on each end of a long lever. The lever swung up and down causing the baskets to whirl in all directions. To her peers' infinite disgust, Cadence began screaming and begging the operator to stop the ride and let her out as she projectile vomited all over the basket's other inhabitants. She earned the moniker "vomit girl" which followed her through high school.

Cadence's brother was a gifted storyteller who helped her fall asleep at night with entertaining stories about magic carpets. He had a soothing voice, and she could fall asleep instantly listening to his tales. Despite his quirks, she knew deep down that he loved her and would protect her in a way her mother couldn't. One night when she was about 10, he was tripping on acid with some friends and found himself in charge of Cadence while his mother was out and about with a boyfriend. George left his buddies gaming on the Xbox while he put his little sister to sleep. His stories grew bizarre and frightening as he spun tales of enchanted bees who would swarm her and carry her off on the magic carpet, encase her in wax, or drop her into enchanted flowers that would devour her. She became agitated and begged him to tell "normal" stories, but he just laughed and called his friends in to join the fun. They never hurt her physically or sexually but tormented her nonetheless by joining in on the bizarre storytelling. She retreated into shock and swore never to do drugs herself, a promise she kept.

I knew Cadence through a girl's developmental trauma therapy group that ran throughout the girls' high school years. All their parents were distracted and emotionally absent. After the first year of this group, all the parents stopped paying, but (oddly) allowed their daughters to continue in the group at their own expense. The group members were firmly bonded to each other and to me. When their parents refused to fund their therapy, they begged me to keep the group together until they graduated high school. They all paid me what they could afford, and never missed a session. Seldom have I had a more committed group of teenagers so invested in their therapy. Their goals were to:

1. survive until they could leave home without getting seriously entangled in romantic relationships.
2. avoid getting caught up in the colored bracelet codes at school. One color meant "I will only make out including heavy petting"; another meant "I refuse to do anal sex but anything else goes"; a third meant "I only do blow jobs," and so forth.
3. not get pregnant.
4. avoid getting lost in the drug culture extant in their schools (heroin was the drug of choice with their friends).
5. do the best they could at school with an eye toward earning scholarships to college.

All eight girls created successful and meaningful lives. All of them graduated high school with honors and managed to attend colleges far from home. Cadence continued to struggle with developmental trauma but ultimately sent me invitations to her graduation from medical school and to her wedding. She proudly brought her daughter to meet me, holding her securely and carefully. Her daughter's middle name was Kathleen.

I could relate personally to Cadence's struggles with confusion. From the moment I read about cephalic shock, I knew it had much relevance to me—why, for example, I would freeze in moments of distress. Late in life, I took up a form of competitive bridge called duplicate bridge. I paid an expert to play with me and teach me the ropes. I would fall apart inexplicably when I didn't understand the bidding of my opponents or when the expert got irritated with me for making a stupid mistake. Shocked by my own distress, I would hide out in the bathroom for a few seconds until I could regain composure, get out of freeze, and stop crying. My instructor was terrific at bridge and could explain what was going on at the bridge table. He was also quite fond of me and respected my profession. However, he was highly competitive and sometimes was confused or embarrassed by my overreactions at the bridge table. He had truly forgotten what it was like to be a beginner: how could a brilliant academic like me make such a dumb mistake or fall apart over a bridge game? Truly he had forgotten (over 60 years) what it was like to be a beginner.

Abandonment Shock: Being Unseen, Overlooked, or Forgotten

Have you ever been stood up? Remember the feeling as time crept by and the dawning horror that your friend, date, whoever, *wasn't coming*? There's a moment of wondering "Do I belong here? Have I misplaced myself?" As an adult this experience is but a momentary flicker, a wink by the Fates reminding us that we exist at their whim. But to a developing child, *the experience of no longer existing in someone else's mind is devastating.* Many children describe waiting at school for a parent to pick them up until, defeated and embarrassed, they drag back into the school for help, feeling forsaken. This is why solitary confinement and shunning are such devastating punishments. Infant studies (Tronick, 1989, 2007) show that a mother's immobile face (under research instructions to remain impassive to her infant for a few moments) is among the most frightening of stimuli.

Consider this experiment. A mother is in a room with a video monitor that transmits a "live" feed of her baby. The baby is in another room with a video monitor transmitting a "live" feed of its mother. The mother and baby respond to each other's screen images; they are playing in real time with one another. While the live feed is running, the babies are surprisingly content, considering that their mother is not physically in the room. Contrast this to what happens when the feed that appears on the baby's monitor is not in real time, but on tape delay: the mother's words and behavior are from one minute before. It is the same "good mother," *only not a "good mother" in relationship with the baby's mind.* The baby collapses in despair.

The research activity was carried out with many mothers and their babies. When the past images—those from one minute prior—were shown, the babies all collapsed. When the live images of the mothers resumed, the babies became animated and resumed playing with their mothers (Moore, 1992, dissertation videotape). This brilliant research—art imitating life—has enormous implications for what happens when a mother simply goes through the motions of parenting and isn't really "there" because of postpartum depression, drug use, mourning, a sibling being in the hospital, or any number of other causes. When I describe the videotape to my patients, or let them watch it, they are typically touched and moved by the sensitivity to the mind-to-mind resonance apparent in the bodies and faces of these infants. It is difficult to describe the profound impact of abrupt abandonment shock in mere words. The ramifications of this research are manifold: depressed, distracted mothering is sensed instantly by babies, who then go into collapse. If the mother is chronically depressed or anxious, disorganized attachment in her child often follows (Solomon & George, 1999).

Abandonment shock is the frozen keening of the bereaved, mimed in silence by confused, disoriented actors moments after their stage has collapsed, their director among the missing. The Romanian poet Marin Sorescu (1936–1996), captures the leaden frozenness of shock:

> The Tear
> I weep and weep a tear
> Which will not fall
> No matter how much I weep.
>
> Its pang in me
> Is like the birth of an icicle.
> Colder and colder, the earth
> Curves on my eyelid,
>
> The northern icecap keeps rising.
> O, my arctic eyelid.
>>   Matter, C. (2016) *Poetry Analysis of Marin Sorescu.*
>>   Used with permission from Prezi, Inc.

What makes the tears freeze invisibly on the arctic eyelid? There are many different pathways to nowhere and non-existence. An absent or inattentive mother, extended separation from the mother, acute loss of the mother, or being threatened with rejection for needing or clinging to the mother can set up abandonment shock in the child. If connection arrives and disappears randomly and unpredictably, or abrupt severing of relied-upon connection takes place due to death, illness, physical withdrawal, or emotional constriction, babies are traumatized and experience abandonment shock. "Constriction appears to be a 'desperate' mental strategy that prohibits segregated attachment models (simultaneous vertical splits) from becoming activated and, thus, blocks painful attachment material from flooding consciousness" (George et al., 1999, p. 339). For infants, a constricted parent means the absence of a soothing, reassuring, solidifying presence.

Bowlby (1980) conceived of the attachment system as integrated with physiological homeostasis. Once a maternal bond has been solidified, the mother is the first line of defense against stressors of all denominations. Actual or threatened loss of the mother then becomes a source of acute distress. Once searching, calling, and crying fail to recover the absent mother, the child is faced with the threat of both emotional and behavioral collapse. When parents do not respond favorably to attachment behaviors on the part of the child, the youngster has to find some way to achieve proximity, even if soothing is not forthcoming.

Research on disorganized attachment demonstrates that the frightening or frightened attachment figure is an inherently paradoxical stimulus to the child. Because any cause for alarm will activate the need for protection and thus the attachment system, the child is compelled both to approach and withdraw from the same person. Main and Hesse (1990) have proposed that the infant's unresolvable conflict is reflected in the tortured approach/avoidance/freezing behavior that is at the core of disorganized attachment behavior. The abandonment shock lies in the realization that no soothing can be had despite the desperate yearning. The "soothing mommy" that might periodically be available has temporarily been displaced by a "scary, rejecting mommy" and no matter how hard the mother later tries to soothe the toddler, the toddler's brain cannot shift rapidly enough from the "scary mommy" model to allow soothing to take place. The "soothing mommy" is gone, for now.

A more everyday source of abandonment shock in the child is traditional separation anxiety. Abandonment shock runs the full gamut between the toddlers furious "you lost me!" at the grocery store (duration 90 seconds) to the more serious variety echoed for me in a *Twilight Zone* television story from the 1960s (recounted a little later). Unfortunately, the current cultural zeitgeist legitimizes a form of behavior termed "ghosting" that stimulates abandonment shock in everyone to a limited degree, but at a traumatic level for those who are vulnerable or who have become deeply attached. "Ghosting" is a tactic used within the dating world these days to avoid accountability or messy emotional interactions. Especially prevalent in online dating situations, ghosting behavior is a form of passive aggression that involves one partner's disappearing from contact with no explanation at all. No phone call, email, or even a text. A recent television series, *Madam Secretary*, tackled this issue in a several-episode arc in 2018, telling the story of a mother (political figure and former CIA analyst), a father (ethics consultant to a military college and former CIA analyst), and their son Jason, a likable young adult who feels suffocated by his romantic partner but doesn't want the stress of going through a formal break up. He just "ghosts her," ignoring her frantic calls and texts, until his parents let him know that this behavior is not okay. He argues that this is how things are done these days. My patients in this age group report, like Jason, that most of their friends feel little remorse about "ghosting," despite how awful it feels to be on the receiving end of abrupt disappearances. For persons who are ghosted, there is no closure, no way to make sense of what happened; they are left to wonder what went wrong. We will look at a clinical example of ghosting when we meet Westin and Gillian later in this chapter.

The 1962 *Twilight Zone* episode that I mentioned above was called "Little Girl Lost." It depicted a young girl who disappeared into another dimension in the wall behind her bed. She found herself in an eerie kaleidoscopic emptiness of Picasso-like topography, peopled by no one but herself. Disoriented, she could occasionally hear disjointed calls from her frantic parents, and they could hear but not see her. They sent a pet dog in after her, in the hope that he could lead her back. If my memory serves, she crawled from angle to jutting angle with her dog, trying to locate a way back to her parents' voices. As the hole behind her bed slowly began to close up (presumably forever), her father somehow got hold of her ankle and yanked her back. No doubt my memory has distorted this episode somewhat to conform to my own personal nightmarish experience of abandonment shock: I was a toddler during my mother's long hospitalization after her surgery. My surrogate caregivers had little warmth, compassion, or calm to spare. My father reportedly walked the floor with me sobbing each night when he returned from the intensive care unit, which went on for months. I was 14 months old, entering a critical period for separation distress. At age 12, I was perfectly aware of the relationship between the *Twilight Zone* episode and my own early-age circumstances and all its implications; yet I checked behind my bed to make sure the wall was really solid for years after watching the show, never without feeling a bit silly.

(Note: After writing this I looked up the episode to see how true to life my memory was of this television story. Interestingly, the only details I altered mentally were the visual topography. Instead of being "hard," sharp-edged angles, the other dimension was like a "soft" set of inter-nested bubbles, concave, convex, vaguely blurry, and luminous. I suspect I shifted the story set to conform to my own agitated memories of "hard" surfaces predominating in my early life instead of "soft," soothing ones.)

Abandonment shock is the horror of going under the water for the third time, life's ebb bubbling madly, while no one is watching. A friend of mine, who felt she was in an impasse with her therapist, had the following dream just after she began therapy with an analyst who, she felt, understood her better. "I was in the swimming pool in the back yard of my former therapist's office building. He and his therapist friends were chatting about their investments as I began to choke and drown. I screamed for help, but they kept chatting away, not noticing my distress. Blacking out, I was lying on the bottom of the pool, terrified. One of his retriever dogs leaped into the pool and dragged me to the shallow end, whereupon I climbed out, shaking and vomiting up water. He looked at me in surprise and asked, 'Did you have a nice swim?'" Her new analyst commented that he suspected she had been drowning for a very long time, and she burst into tears. Her first therapist had related to her on the basis of her precocious and highly developed false self, her life accomplishments, and social position, but had never grasped the level of desperation she lived with as a constant companion.

Child, adolescent, and adult patients have reported to me the chill of being "forgotten" while waiting to be picked up at school or after-care, until slowly and agonizingly it dawned on them that no one was coming. The securely attached child "knows" that the car broke down or there was some communication problem, but that it will all be worked out in a little while. The avoidant and ambivalent attachment children all worry to varying degrees depending on their previous experience, but the disorganized attachment children panic. From worry to panic, each moment brings fresh opportunity for the silence of abandonment shock. "Waiting to be picked up" is, of course, only one of many possible landscapes of separation anxiety; abandonment shock can relate to repeated failures of reliability of the "*container/contained*" (Bion, 1957) relationship.

Somatic states of abandonment shock bring to mind the desolate and devastating poverty of post-war countries: freedom to choose, to rebuild, exists, but there is little infrastructure to support growth. Individuals who endured massive doses of abandonment shock while growing up are at a loss when it comes to forming deep, authentic connections with others. Theirs are not the lifelong friendships based on intimacy and mutual regard; often their friends are precious to them because they remind them that they exist, that they have shared history, at least with someone. We are really talking here about emotional deprivation. If a parent was never consistently "there," the infant and developing child have to endure a kind of primal absence of mind-to-mind resonance, a human variant on the wire or cloth monkeys of Harlow's (1958) research (see Chapter 2).

Even if you have read his article, "The Nature of Love" before, it's worth checking out again. In the context of abandonment shock and disorganized attachment, the pictures alone are enough to make you cringe in comprehension of the ravages of deprivation.

The infant who falls and falls into the annihilation anxiety of abandonment shock may grow into a person who is never really there, drained of vitality and juiciness. Let's look at a clinical example.

The White Abyss instead of the Black Hole: Lisa

Lisa was a 44-year-old woman in twice-weekly individual psychotherapy. She had a formidable false self. Her parents didn't really love each other and only married because Lisa's mother was pregnant with Lisa. She was treated like a doll rather than a person. After 6 years of individual work, she still found herself mostly blank. I tried everything I could think of to reach her, to no avail. In desperation one day I called her a "Stepford wife," referring to the movie about vapid, robotic women. She smiled, accepting my compliment that she was pretty. At a loss, I uncharacteristically shared my frustration with her Teflon wall: everything I had tried to reach her heart slid right off her. Nothing "stuck." She simply shrugged and smiled vacantly in appreciation of my efforts. At least I was paying attention to her, she said. She had adhesively pursued a series of unsuitable relationships with empty men, hoping that, in the child they might have, she could find the vitality missing in her life. I decided to try group therapy.

In group she had mostly been vague and empty over the many years. At first she was skeptical about whether anyone in group cared about her or her feelings. She worked through her painfully empty relationship with her parents in the group transference and then confronted her unhappiness as a businesswoman. She dropped out of twice-a-week individual therapy and group therapy to become a spiritual director. After completing her training and discovering that the life of a spiritual director was not for her, she returned to group, where she continued to explore her unsatisfactory dating relationships and lack of deep friendships. She was pleasant with other group members, asked a lot of questions, but remained largely superficial. Occasionally she would painfully and silently squeeze out a few tears, collapsing her face into her hands, horrified, humiliated, and saying she wished she could disappear into a hole so no one could see her. A few minutes later she would have completely reconstituted her defenses and was again vague and pleasant.

Finally, one night in group she said she was thinking of leaving because she could never figure out what it was she was supposed to be working on. After asking her permission, I "shadowed" (Moreno, 1991) her inner voice to her parents, standing behind her and giving voice to the abandonment shock I suspected was there. "You left me to fall and fall and never helped me understand what I was feeling; it was like I was a building collapsing into itself, nothing was left, just the dust and cells of my body, like the World Trade Center buildings, all destroyed inside my head. I never got to exist." Nodding vehemently,

Lisa broke down into the first loud sobs she had ever shed. She mused that she was always falling, and that no one had ever caught her before.

> It's like I was a silent movie that had no actors, just annoying music. There was no me to tie to the train tracks, and no one would have heard me if I could have screamed, anyway. The music just kept playing in my family while mother silently smoked her cigarettes; they hated each other and wished I had never been born to imprison them together. Mother was too young to have a family, and certainly didn't love him. I'm not even certain now that she even loved me. I don't think she loves anybody.

In the months after this session, Lisa began to come to life. She began seeing an art therapist, impressed by the way art therapy facilitated growth in other group members. She became deeply interested in other group members in a way that had "heart" instead of being primarily cerebral. She visited her idealized mother and confronted her mother's malignant narcissism and destructiveness to the rest of the family. She took up jogging and began to develop activities and interests with other women that were more genuine. She formed a circle of friends that went camping together, played board games together, cooked meals together, and the like. She bought a new house that she thoroughly enjoyed and adopted two kittens whom she adored. She took up oil painting and took many painting trips to Italy and Costa Rica. She broke off her desperate pursuit of men for the sake of "attachment to anyone" and became curious about the kind of man *she* might really be interested in, a novel perspective that she had never considered before. While in the midst of a triathlon she met a man who appears to be in love with *her*; she is taking it slowly with him. In short, it seems she is developing a self that had been largely short-circuited over the preceding 43 years.

As Lisa showed us, the forces bound in abandonment shock are fearsome. Like a drowning infant or toddler, she simply sank to the bottom and died inside, without dramatic and obvious struggle. The collapse into wordless, meaningless despair endured by Lisa and others like her is captured by Grotstein in his description of "black hole" experiences of cumulative trauma. He describes the paradoxical power of abandonment shock in terms of "surging powerlessness, of implosion, of disintegration, of disorganization into non-organization, in short, the decimating, annihilating power of nothingness;...tormenting nothingness paradoxically mixed with 'nameless dread,' the decathected chards or residues of abandoned meaning" (1990a, p. 267). Grotstein (1990a, 1990b) described this slow implosion into the silence of oblivion, of abandoned meaning: "A violent, implosive pull into a 'black hole,' one which is experienced as spaceless, bottomless, timeless and yet, paradoxically, condensed, compact, and immediate, yielding suffocation anxiety" (1990a, p. 281). Grotstein hypothesizes that the traumatic state itself dissolves the holding-containing matrix of the internal and external world with a dissolution of figure/ground distinction: "As the patient experiences descending into the 'black hole' there often is a 'white out,' a 'blank psychosis,' which corresponds to shock-induced frozenness of the whole sensory apparatus..." (1990a, p. 281). Like an avalanche descending a mountain face to obliterate all traces of its passing, Lisa's feelings would pass through her, leaving behind nothing but blankness until she finally faced the depths of her childhood distress.

Patients who have experienced this state early in childhood report a particular relationship with time that becomes accentuated during periods of chronic pain and abandonment, such as those following bereavement, a breakup, etc. Time appears to be unrelentingly persecutory. Suffering feels endless. Perhaps reminiscent of a containerless infancy, in which time unfolded to reach infinity itself, structureless time haunts patients who struggle with abandonment shock. Like the monkeys in a cage without a mother, there is nothing to hold onto. An altered sense of time stretches out, reality gets distorted. Most of us are familiar with the experience of waking at 2 in the morning, worrying about something. As the long night drags on, we toss and turn trying to stop thinking; our worries intensify and still we don't fall asleep—until we do. We touch the experience of abandonment shock. The next morning, most of us wonder why we made such a big deal out of a small worry.

Timeless Dread of Weekends: Amy

One patient, Amy, struggled with abandonment shock over weekends. If she had no good book, no plans, or if a friend canceled a plan at the last minute, Amy would disappear into nothingness. She tried to go to a movie by herself and fled the theater in tears, certain that the world could see that she was all by herself. She would call up in panic on Friday afternoon, unable to figure out what to do with herself over the long hours until her job started on Monday morning. The sound of the clock ticking drove her nearly mad, as it reminded her of weekends with her grandparents. Her parents were quite depressed and left her for long periods at her grandparents. A pioneer woman, her maternal grandmother had run away from Missouri at 14, lied about her age and taught at an Indian village in Alaska before meeting Amy's grand- father, a gruff timber captain who also was a runaway. Being neither conversationalists nor interested in Amy's inner life, her grandparents structured Amy's visits to their house with chores, the (for Amy) dreary sounds of golf and baseball tournaments, and long mandatory naps in a guest room that had only a Bible, a bed, and a ticking clock on the bedside table. There were never any toys, books, interactive games, or children's television shows to watch.

On the rare occasions Amy got to stay with her paternal grand- mother, it was a different story. Her paternal grandmother delighted in her granddaughter's presence. They had constant interaction, played all sorts of imaginary games, read books together; naps (which were optional) were spent cuddling up with two affectionate cats. Amy grew up dependent upon others to help her feel alive. Books were her con- stant friends, the more imaginative the better. As a young single adult, she was delighted when she finally bought her first decent television/ videotape machine and learned to rent videotapes to entertain herself. She was becoming self-reliant, and no longer dreaded empty spaces of unscheduled time. Time had changed from enemy to benefactor. Poet Charles Simic (1996) captures the essence of Amy's abandonment- shock-dominated passage of time,

> Squinting Suspiciously
> I was watching time crawl roachlike
> Shuddering and stopping
> As if some of its legs
> Had already been plucked.
>
> It still had the whole of infinity
> To climb like a kitchen wall.

The very thought of it,
In all likelihood,
Causing these jitters,
These teensy-weensy doubts.
It must be the chill, I told myself.
Neither one of us can get warm
Even on a hot night like this.
O cruel time, you need someone to throw
A blanket over you, and so do I.

> "Squinting Suspiciously" from *Walking the Black Cat*,
> by Charles Simic. Copyright © 1996 by Charles Simic.
> Reprinted by permission of Mariner Books, an
> imprint of HarperCollins Publishers LLC.

Love Thwarted: Gillian and Westin

Even individuals who grew up with secure attachment can experience abandonment shock in the severe grief of sudden bereavement. Gillian, whom we met in Chapter 3, was a 53-year-old woman of enormous emotional range, who had just been inexplicably deserted by her beloved partner Westin. She and Westin had been talking seriously about marriage. Westin, second generation descendant of a Holocaust survivor, was a long-term patient of mine. To avoid intensity, he had created a "bunker" to escape to. Bunkers were a favorite theme for him in his life and in his art. His intense terror of intimacy had surfaced in a couples session, over a discussion of how Gillian would like to be able to touch him more tenderly and make him feel less alone. He then broke off contact with her abruptly. He frequently disappeared into "the bunker" to process profound preverbal issues, but usually maintained some kind of contact with her during these periods of alienation. On this occasion he was traveling due to his work commitments and used the hiatus to avoid contact with me as well.

Usually during a "bunker" period Westin relied on his therapy to keep his alienation from becoming too ego-syntonic. This time he avoided calling me or his art therapist to set up a long-distance appointment. After three weeks of silence Gillian wrote him an email requesting some emotional contact, and he responded in chilly reminiscence: "I think fondly of your heart, but I cannot think of what to say right now." When he resumed his individual work, he could not seem to remember what it felt like to be in love with Gillian, only irritation that she was pushing him to tolerate tenderness in touch, and that he was relieved to be "away from" the relationship. He could not decide whether to contact her to break up, or to continue to avoid her until she handled things for the both of them. He had some vague fantasy that his love for her might return if he just waited long enough. His indifference to her welfare was quite uncharacteristic of his typical demeanor toward her, but he could not work his way out of this icy, protected stance toward her.

Several weeks later, still frozen by the abandonment shock of his abrupt departure from her life, Gillian went over to his house in grief, demanding some closure to his silence. He declined to work on the relationship further; he had too much terror, he said. (We examine this terror more deeply in the section to follow on potential shock: dread.) Writing about the shock of his decision to turn away from love and attachment in her journal, Gillian noted that he reminded her of Anthony Hopkins in the movie *The Remains of the Day* (Ivory, 1993). The character Anthony Hopkins played also turned away from the promise of love because it was just too overwhelming a possibility to contemplate. Gillian wrote about the shock of "ghosting" years before the term existed in popular culture.

From Gillian's journal:

> I'm just writing with the prayer and intention to release the pain...grief seems easy compared to the shock...it's really more than that...
>
> In all my life I've never felt this much trauma...I live such a rich life...filled to abundance with love and an amazing faith that saves me and nourishes me and always, leaves me grateful...but there is a shock around my heart that aches beyond measure, very much like a child's first experience of betrayal and visceral abuse....
>
> And although I am a woman and not a child, and I truly felt present and not naïve or wearing blinders, nothing prepared me for the way Wes treated my heart...I knew he was frightened, even at times terrified...but regardless of his injuries, I feel horrified. At times I think "this can't be real"...Wes could not have treated me with such cruelty...a complete disregard of the golden rule...for

my heart, it's recovering from shocking abuse from a soul I knew and loved....

At times it's excruciating to bear...it's been over a month...I connect in the heart to each person I see, both in my practice and my life. There is weight of it when I am alone...I cannot find the way out of the deepest and most shocking disappointment of my life...

And then the way opens and for a time, I feel my heart opening more with a strength that is more than I have ever known and a certainty of love beyond measure, always available.

I know already some of the learnings...they have come quickly and vividly to comfort and reassure me, that I continue to be very alive and fully committed to my path of the heart, there is no doubt...My spiritual director told me something cryptic the other day: beware of the wolf.

And then there are times, like now, when I remember him...and for a moment I wished he'd never come, never walked up to my door and I saw him...and recognized his soul immediately.

There were so many ways he could have left me—with dignity, love and respect for us both...I would have understood letting go...I would have been left with such a different memory...this memory of this last month is the harshest landscape to navigate...I know I will, and I know that choosing to love in every moment I can will become the compass. But at this very moment, regretting trusting him with the tenderness of my heart. I can't quite see the horizon, or the sun.

The Persian mystic poet Hafiz (c. 1320–1389) expresses Gillian's dismay and consternation at Westin's turning away from love:

A Great Need
Out
Of a great need
We are all holding hands
And climbing
Not loving is a letting go.
Listen,
The terrain around here

Is
Far too
Dangerous
For
That.

From the Penguin publication *The Gift: Poems by Hafiz* by
Daniel Ladinsky, copyright 1999 and used with permission.

Shattershock: Disorganized Torture, Black Holes, and the Fractured Container

Shattershock is the psycho-physiological sequela of a break or fracture of the child's emerging mind/body psyche after an inadvertent
experience of *near-torture* at the hands of a parent or other loved one.
Shattershock is attachment shock in the extreme, when the psyche
actually shatters under the impact, like the glass in a windshield
when a rock glances off it. Most of the time the windshield remains
outwardly intact, but tiny spider lines of shock fracture and radiate
throughout the glass pane. Meerlo (1961) coined the term "menticide"
to describe the breaking of the mind into capitulation and submis-
sion/surrender when the captive's or victim's psychological needs are
exploited by threatening and hostile caretakers from whom there is no
escape. At first, under conditions of torture, the needs for solace, rest,
and oblivion are evenly balanced by needs for defiant self-expression,
loyalty to others, and refusal to yield, surrender, or submit. Stover
and Nightingale assert that ultimately everyone can be broken down.
In the context of deliberate, organized political torture, the goal is to
break the will of the victims and ultimately dehumanize them (1985).

The conditions of torture, at least superficially, resemble the
childhoods of children with early childhood attachment disorganization: total dependence upon the captors; unpredictable switches
between harsh and lenient conditions; good cop/bad cop, as it were;
timelessness; rough handling; intrusiveness into the personhood of the
captee; unpredictable and random sensory assaults on the senses; per-
petration of meaninglessness. Suedfeld (1990) reviews the report of the
APA subcommittee on psychological concerns related to torture and
concludes that central characteristics of torture include: (1) an individual who is in the control and power of some group or individual;

(2) suffering that may be mental or physical; and (3) pain that is inflicted deliberately.

Disorganized attachment and the shattershock of childhood are not usually created deliberately by an intentional and organized perpetrator group or individual but by a *disorganized parenting figure with no particular motivation*. Unfortunately, a small group of children *do* grow up within malignant criminal families and are deliberately pimped out for child porn and other awful experiences. Nonetheless, even in relatively benign families, shattershock comprises a state of mind of "lived" torture "lite," unknowingly perpetrated by parents who are unable to contain or process intense affects when their children need emotional attachment. Much like those who grow up in a war zone, these children never know when a bomb blast is going to go off; they have to pick their way carefully through the land mines of their parents' emotions.

As a practicing child analyst, Dorothy Bloch (1978) studied the terror of children who believed their parents were bent upon killing them. This is a difficult thought to ponder, since we take parental love as a given, a backdrop. For example, commenting on the "ordinary" parent–child relationship, Bollas (1995) says of "basic trust,"

> ...it precedes reflective consideration, almost a thoughtless assumption, derived from parental care of a child. We know, don't we, that this is the infant's and child's trust in the mother and father who look after the child, who certainly withhold any violent or murderous response, and who bear the child's greed, omnipotence, empty-headedness, and jealousness.
>
> (p. 186)

Grotstein (1991) asserts that predator/prey anxiety exists as an inherent preconception in the human species and appears in young children from the beginning of life. Thus, it is not unusual that witnessing or experiencing violence would be terrifying at a biological as well as at a psychological level for an infant. Physical and emotional violence were not rarities in the homes of the children Bloch (1978) analyzed. She noted the bottomless feelings of humiliation and the unalterable sense of helplessness many of these children endured. Her conclusion was that in order to resolve the "parallel attachment systems" (my words) of terror and yearning, these patients embarked on a lifelong struggle to win their parents' love as a primary defense against their fear of infanticide:

> ...[they] attempted to explain and justify their perception of their parents' hostile and aggressive feelings by blaming themselves. Their implicit hope, since their worthlessness had provoked those feelings, that whenever they changed and became worthy they would be loved, can be found even among the children who attempted suicide and the abused children who later committed murder. This delusion both sustained them and perpetuated their suffering. My treatment of adult patients frequently revealed that it invested their entire lives and eclipsed time and reality. In its service, infancy remained the anchor of their being, life was made to seem eternal and age meaningless.... Their security demanded that they seek within themselves the causes of the parents' anger or hatred or their wish for infanticide.
>
> (p. 226)

Bloch goes on to share a patient's description of herself in a terror state after witnessing scenes of violence in her family: "When I let everything frighten me...I lose myself in a panic that comes out in wildness and screaming and laughing and feeling sick and empty, and everything looks like papier-mâché and I can't trust anything..." (p. 228). The shock zone of shattershock is the legacy of parents who were not themselves parented in a secure fashion. Lyons-Ruth et al. (1999) hypothesize that,

> If the caregiver has not experienced such comfort and soothing in relation to her own past losses or fear-evoking experiences...the infant's pain and fear will evoke her own unresolved fearful affects, as well as her helplessness to know how to find comfort and resolution in relation to them....
>
> (p. 38)

Lyons-Ruth quotes Egeland et al. (1988):

> Therefore a hostile–helpless infant–caregiver relationship should be viewed as a primary source of dysregulated fearful arousal for

the infant, one that holds little promise of resolution over time in the absence of significant changes in the caregiving environment or significant new relationships.

(p. 45)

Both the caregiver and the child are sucked up into a containerless spiral filled with the intensity of an emotional cyclone. The forces acting on and within a dyad caught in an attachment disorganization maelstrom meet no shock absorbers or brakes to slow momentum. When there is no container to hold the forces of terror, panic, desperation, raw need, hatred, dissolving and disappearing, eating and being eaten, and the other intense negative affect states that babies and young children sometimes generate in their parents, mayhem ensues.

Grotstein (1990a) describes this experience mayhem as the black hole state:

The disintegrative nature of the black hole is a chaotic state of turbulence and experience of the awesome force of powerlessness, of defect, of nothingness, of zeroness—expressed not just as a static emptiness but as an implosive, centripetal pull into the void..." (p. 257). Nothingness within a container...is healthy because the latter affords a meaningful context for the former, whereas "nothingness" without a container constitutes the "black hole"...and approximates chaos or randomness and may invoke the participation of "no-thingness" in order to fill it. Ultimately, I seek to nominate nothingness and meaninglessness as the most dreaded nadir of human experience. I believe that they constitute the fundamental traumatic state. Thus "space" is not an area within which human relationship might be allowed to develop but rather it is the presence of an inhuman and malevolent absence that must be blotted out of awareness at all costs. A manic variant of this "black hole" experience is that of explosive expansion or even of splintering....

(p. 281)

Meltzer (1975) reports that psychoanalyst Esther Bick described to him a mother/infant attachment pattern during which mother and infant were sharing and *amplifying* negative emotional states mind-to-mind, presumably because the mothers lacked the internal resources for self-regulation required to sooth self and infant in the face of distress. Bick elaborated that many individuals with this background are relatively high functioning (like analytic candidates) and do not seem terribly ill. She observed an escalating spiral of panic in mother/infant dyads that resulted in the temporary disintegration of both parties. In his discussion of Bick's work, Meltzer says:

> ...she had observed in her work of direct observation of mothers and infants, something that had to do with states of catastrophic anxiety in certain infants whose mothers seemed somehow unable to contain them. When these infants got anxious, their mothers got anxious too and then the infant got more anxious and a spiral of anxiety tended to develop which ended with the infant going into a state of some sort of quivering and a kind of disintegrated, disorganized state that was not even screaming, not a tantrum, just something that one would have to describe as disorganized. Mrs. Bick began to observe this phenomenon also in certain patients, generally patients who, on the whole, did not seem terribly ill, in candidates; in people who came because of things like poor work accomplishment, unsatisfactory social lives, vague pathological complaints; in people who are somehow on the periphery of the analytic community and wanted to have an analysis and couldn't quite say why. She began to observe that these patients in their dream life and in their waking life were subject to states of temporary disintegration very much like the infants.... She discovered...that they weren't properly held together by a good skin, but that they had other ways of holding themselves together.
> (1975, pp. 295–6)

These observations led to Bick's formulation of the concept of defensive "second skin formations" in people who weren't properly held together in early life by a good psychic skin (Anzieu, 1989). To cope, they developed "other ways" to hold themselves together with the infant's skin functioning as a boundary for the ego. Frances Tustin (1986, 1990) was a child therapist who studied autistic enclaves and defenses in both children and adults. Ogden (1989) further elaborates on Tustin's work, noting the "autistic-contiguous position" that helps overwhelmed infants, and the adults they develop into, to defend against annihilation anxiety by relying on sensations at the skin's surface as part of their defensive repertoire. Elaborations of these defenses throughout a lifetime result in either self-soothing by "comfort" sensations (a purring cat, the warmth of a fire, the weight of a blanket; in essence, containment via the body envelope); or by finding an "edge," lest one disappear entirely (the rhythmic pounding of jogging, procrastination, the sharp bite of hot tea, nail-biting, or trichotillomania).

One wonders how often therapeutic failures have been influenced by this type of uncanny and disconcerting negative limbic resonance, with panic spiraling out of control in the therapeutic dyad. The following clinical example illustrates the shattering of the self during attachment shock.

The Particle Accelerator: Mariah

A therapist patient, Mariah, brought to me the following written material (excerpted) to articulate her shattershock. Her mother had transitory psychotic episodes but functioned primarily as a high-level narcissist. Mariah describes shattershock as "the particle accelerator experience." When I read her the above paragraph about Bick's observations, she sighed with relief and said: "I thought I was the only one who had this experience."

> My mother and I and my husband and I share this awful pattern I call the particle accelerator experience. Neither one knows anything about emotional connection, so if I am upset at all, all hell breaks loose unless I just go away and dissociate, self soothe, whatever. There is a feeling that just keeps flying back and forth between us like a particle in a tube at an increasing acceleration, propelled by some force. A failure of maternal containment...it just keeps on escalating tension and speed in a visceral way until I explode. It's never the other person who explodes, at least on the outside, it's always me. This isn't a metaphor, or a mind-thing, it's in my body. I hear it as a steadily building whine, which climbs into a shriek, maybe me screaming in my head, I don't know. I remember "losing it" hundreds of times in the cupboard under our stairs,

Harry Potter style, during middle school and high school. I would scream and scream into the universe until I just ran out of screams, like Forrest Gump.

I experience the shattering as a visceral sensation; being hurled away violently, away from the tube against the wall, then fracturing into a thousand pieces like a large glass container would, I feel the impact, hear the shattering, then I feel a mess, all jagged pieces inside. In college I would throw glassware, glass ashtrays, anything like that as hard as I could into a garbage can or against the bathroom just to hear the sound of the glass shattering into fragments…somehow this weird enactment was satisfying to me, as if what was on the inside was transferring to the outside of me. Of course, I'd clean it all up, so no one was at risk from the glass shards.

I wonder if there was any real loud hitting or anything that I don't remember? I do have those unexplained healed hairline fractures on my pelvis, who knows? I've seen mother slam her head into the kitchen counter—maybe she got violent with me when I was little. She had so little patience with me when I was crying for her, she hated it; she couldn't bear it when I needed her. Like the time I was home from college with a 103-degree fever, something called Hong Kong Flu, late on Christmas Eve because I had to be bussed in for 200 miles, all the airports were closed. I couldn't eat dinner, and she got furious at me for not eating, even though she knew it was my favorite food in the world. She ended up screaming at me and I was crying and saying I'm sorry and it got so weird, I tried to leave her house, but I was too sick, the hotels were all full, there were no airplanes available. I eventually went dead, dorsal freeze maybe; I was stuck in that house with her for 10 days. It was horrid, making nice after that. There was no "talking about" in my family.

Somehow everything was always my fault. She never admitted to any issues. Sometimes it's like the particle accelerator with my husband. He hates it when I am crying and trying to tell him what I am feeling. He flips into his childhood, when his parents were going at each other shredding each other to bits. I'm not like that, I don't want to hurt him, I just want to tell him about my desperate feelings, I'm trying to help him understand me, but he can't listen.

Anyway, when he storms away from me and won't listen to me, I end up huddled onto the floor, grabbing on for something stable to hang onto and sobbing or screaming like a banshee.... I'm a total mess. It's embarrassing.

Mariah and her husband John worked hard to contain shattershock between them and to learn how to nurture each other when one of them shatters. Although Mariah had the more obvious meltdown, actually each of them shattered with escalation of tension. Mariah relied on her pets, exercising, reading, and warm baths to calm down. When she broke an ankle and was unable to walk for comfort, she became frantic with anxiety. Neither she nor her husband knew how to restore equilibrium to the relationship—what we call "co-regulation—once it spiraled out of control. As Mariah felt more desperate, her voice would grow louder and shriller, more closely approximating a distress cry. John, hearing the loudness, flashed back to his childhood experiences of listening to his parents tear at each other instead of communicating. If either one could get calm enough to observe that the other felt shattered, use active listening to each other's feelings, or become vulnerable enough to ask the other for patience, then the spiral would reverse. Mariah, hyperverbal, preferred that words be used to reconnect first; John, more nonverbal, preferred to try and reach out for safe, reassuring touch. The two of them slowly developed the tools they needed to resolve the terror each had of being in the presence of danger from the other.

"Blood Orange" was written by Charles Simic, the man who was blown out of his bed by a bomb explosion at age 3. He grew up on the streets, foraging for food, and immigrated to the United States as a teenager. In this poem he gets close and personal with the shattershock experience. The poem could be described as articulating shattershock.

Blood Orange
It looks so dark the end of the world may be near.
I believe it's going to rain.
The birds in the park are silent.
Nothing is what it seems to be.
Nor are we.

There's a tree on our street so big
We can all hide in its leaves.
We won't need any clothes either.
I feel as old as a cockroach, you said.
In my head, I'm a passenger on a ghost ship.

Not even a sigh outdoors now.
If a child was left on our doorstep,
It must be asleep.
Everything is teetering on the edge of everything
With a polite smile.

It's because there are things in this world
That just can't be helped, you said.
Right then, I heard the blood orange
Roll off the table and with a thud
Lie cracked open on the floor.

> "Blood Orange," p. 52, from *Walking the Black Cat* by
> Charles Simic. Copyright © 1996 by Charles Simic.
> Reprinted by permission of Mariner Books, an
> imprint of HarperCollins Publishers LLC.

Soulshock: The Structure of Evil

Siegel's focus on the nascent sense of self suggests that it is in mind-to-mind emotional limbic resonance that we learn who we are, how to feel, and how to regulate how we feel. What happens when an infant, a child, is in mind-to-mind resonance with malevolence, madness, deceit, corruption, and ruthlessness? The adult has superior available intelligence engaged in the service of cruelty, superior mobility and physical resources, superior reasoning and language skills, possibly superior street smart and people-reading skills, and the ability to deceive if he wishes to. The child has a trusting heart, an open innocence, and an engaging presence. I suggest that even casual everyday interactions between such an adult and a vulnerable child can, because of spiritual and emotional toxicity, at a minimum taint the child's open innocence and trusting heart, draining away some of his vitality; even this relatively benign outcome is predicated on the child not being a particularly attractive target for predatory violence on the part of the adult. Should the hapless child be the intended target, and survive the encounter physically, I believe his soul will be shocked away from his body for some time, his body trapped in traumatic processing, his heart constricted, his vitality squashed, and his innocence lost.

Terr (1990) discusses the uniqueness of this variety of traumatic fright. The fright from (soulshock) trauma is so unique that we don't even have a "right" word for it in English. Helplessness? Terror? Horror? One little boy, after being kidnapped for ransom, told Terr, "I already know what it's like to die—to be killed. You can't breathe." On a few rare occasions adults will give such eloquent words to their own terrors from childhood that we can better grasp how traumatized children feel. Terr quoted the words Naipaul had used to describe his childhood terror in a 1981 *Newsweek* piece:

> I have two very early childhood memories of my father being men-tally ill and of waking up in a hospital room and being strapped in a bed. ...I have always been fighting a hysteria that plagued me as a child, the old fear of extinction and I don't mean dying. I mean the fear of being reduced to nothing, of being crushed.
>
> (1990, pp. 36–7)

Terr notes that being psychologically overwhelmed, the sensation of being "reduced to nothing," is such a hideous feeling that the victim seeks never to experience that sensation again. Fear of further fear—the immobility response—keeps victims from trying to escape even when their chances seem good. Children and adults who have been kidnapped and held hostage have long puzzled FBI authorities because the authorities literally had to drag the protesting hostages to safety. In collaboration with Terr and other child trauma experts, the agents came to understand the role that terror of fear itself plays in the dynamics of shock paralysis.

Authors and movie directors have spent lifetimes trying to teach us about soulshock, about what it is like to be touched by darkness. Soulshock is the horror of nightmares come true, finding betrayal and malice in your bedtime story along with hot cocoa. Soulshock is telling your mother your father abused you and getting slapped in the face for disrespect. Soulshock is finding out that lies make up the threads of your family's tapestry. Soulshock is discovering that Alfred Hitchcock and Stephen King wrote the screenplay of your life.

I have never met a psychotherapist who has not been touched by evil in some way; even if we specialize in the "worried well," we are bound to run across the occasional unspeakable horror. We struggle to frame the concept of evil within familiar boundaries, to pin it down for further study by surrounding it with words that name its essence. As psychoanalyst Christopher Bollas put it:

> There is a place called nowhere, a country where [evil] lives and from which he strikes. We know this place. Even if it is beyond our perception, we know it exists. It is the place of the split-off unknown, where actions with unanticipated consequences originate, where sudden destructiveness against or from the self arises, a zone of darkness that weaves in and out of selves, preserving darkness and nowhere in the midst of vibrant mental life and human relations.
>
> (1995, p. 190)

Peck (1983) defines evil as that which kills spirit; Erich Fromm, as that which desires to control others, to foster dependency, to discourage capacity of others to think for themselves, to diminish spontaneity and originality, to keep others in line, to rob them of liveliness and humanity. Goldberg (2000) argues that to understand evil requires us to uncover the destructiveness bred within attachment relationships, especially the family: "People who are living destructive and/or disturbed lives...have a marked incapacity for intimacy and caring" (p. 204). Humiliation, contempt, neglect, "do what I say not what I do," and deception within the family structure itself are some of the familial corruptions he cites.

Lewin (1996), Peck (1983), Bollas (1995), and Grand (2002) have directly taken on the subject of evil by writing about it. While the topic of evil is almost too unnerving to think about, they urge us as therapists to open our minds and hearts to its effects. Lewin acknowledges,

> We often wish to close our eyes and close our minds and close our hearts so that we do not have to meet the challenge of evil. We

all too readily can be led down the dangerous path of trying to make the world a better place to live by pretending...intelligence in the service of cruelty is evil.... Each time we reduce a person to the status of a thing, ignoring the crucial dimension of the other's inner experience, hopes, strivings, and need for love and respect, we put ourselves in proximity to evil.... The horror of differences that we see as located outside ourselves bespeaks a horror of our inner diversity, our sense of the plenitude of our own potentials as a nightmare.... When we speak of evil, compassion knows that we speak of a process by which people misunderstand themselves, make themselves morally misshapen, and wreak havoc not only on the world around them but on the world within them; compassion knows that evil is a set of existential mistakes with dire consequences.

(1996, pp. 292–3)

Being reduced to the status of a thing by a person significant to you, such as your parent, spouse, or therapist, is one of the most horrid affect states possible to experience. Kristeva (1982) and Mitrani (1996) describe this state of feeling reduced to the status of a thing as being a state of the *abject*:

...[this is] felt as a totally catastrophic collapse or as a dreadful sensation of being ripped-off and thrown away. In a sense, the latter is an experience of total and irreversible dejection. It is not an experience of the loss of the object or even the presence of the absence. Instead, it is an experience of the presence of what Kristeva (1982) termed "the abject." She suggested that the "abject"—a jettisoned object—retains only one quality of the object it once was—that of being opposed to or separate from the subject.

(Mitrani, 1996, p. 170)

Abjectness is a visceral experience rather than a mental concept; I believe it is an essential aspect of what Balint (1952) termed "the basic fault." This essence of being treated as/seen as/felt to be utterly despicable or contemptible becomes installed as a neural map in the core sense of self when the child is violently repudiated and metaphorically jettisoned by the primary object, with resulting ruptures in the child's psychic skin. An awful enough circumstance this is indeed, when abjectification of the child occurs because of simple misfortune and ignorance in the parental dyad. We shall explore "abject" experience further in Chapter 7. How, then, do we expand our minds to encompass the fate of the youngster who encounters genuine evil—however we think of this—in another?

Bollas (1995) writes compellingly about the structure of predatory evil as a complex perversion, a transformation of early childhood trauma into a source of excitement. "The trauma is represented in transformed disguise, and it is continually enacted in dramatic space with the other as accomplice" (p. 210). This drama is presented to "show" elements of awful preverbal experience that eludes the realm of words, to somehow transcend the perpetrator's own early "soul death" and live again by passing that death on to some "other."

> The person who has been "killed" in his childhood is in unwilling identification with his own premature mortality, and by finding a victim whom he puts through the structure of evil, he transcends his own killing, psychically overcoming his own endless deaths by sacrificing to the malignant gods that overlooked his childhood.... The shocking harm erupting in the midst of a benign texture of the real (as opposed to our imaginary transformation of reality into something alarming) is deeply disturbing, and it preys upon a certain kind of fear we have that is so great we cannot even experience it as fear: a dread that reality will cease to support us in safety and will do us harm. Some people who were victims of a childhood trauma that occupied their subjectivity—in effect displacing the imaginary with a kind of theater of the real, capable of infinite repetitions but no creative variations—realize that even more shocking than the content of what happened to them is the trauma that the real in the first place actually did something profoundly consequential...something happened which never should have.
>
> (Bollas, 1995, pp. 291–3)

Although Bollas writes of serial killers engaged with the structure of evil, we do not have to look to the esoteric or diabolical to find applicable case material from our everyday psychotherapy practices. I am sharing the following example to illustrate how common everyday evil is in our clinical practice.

The Spaceship Adventure and the Psychedelic Menticide: Frank

I saw Frank twice a week in individual therapy—we meet him again in Chapters 5 and 6. When I first met him, he was wary and skeptical about how I could help him. He came to me at the urging of his wife, who knew some other men I had worked with. He told me his wife was worried about him because he had never felt anything about his childhood. He wanted to learn how to feel his feelings like other people did. A good-hearted man and doting parent, he stayed a bit distant, especially with his wife, whom he adored. However, he could not talk with her about how important she was to him. As it turned out, he had been raised by two wealthy but emotionally remote invalid parents. His mother had declining health all his life; in a wheelchair due to multiple sclerosis, she was addicted to morphine. He remembers her room as dark, silent, and scary. His father was away much of the time, so Frank was raised primarily by a succession of nannies and housekeepers. After his father had a stroke in front of Frank, the remaining family descended into chaos, drifting from relative to relative, household to household.

Deep-seated disturbances in identity, belonging, and security in the world rendered Frank vulnerable to being enticed by others who resonated with and countered his insecurity. Because of his early lack of groundedness, Frank felt helpless, fragile, and out of control. People with traumatic backgrounds tend to be extremely susceptible to anyone who can take control, who can stir up hope of gratifying unmet dependency needs, and who can elegantly counter their extreme sense of vulnerability and powerlessness (Herman, 2015). We shall see in the following clinical vignette how easily others can spot and exploit vulnerabilities like Frank's.

Frank's extreme wariness about therapy, as it turns out, was due in part to two intense soulshock experiences that occurred at age 10 and at age 20, which he had never processed with anyone. In his chapter "The Structure of Evil," Bollas (1995) talks about the process of transferring deadness from one person to another. This process involves six stages: (1) seduction—the promise of something good or desirable;

(2) the promise of a false potential space; (3) the development of a stupefying dependence that empties the mind; (4) shocking betrayal; (5) radical infantilization, dependence for existence on the whim of incarnated madness; and (6) the transfer of psychic death (p. 211). Although Bollas writes of serial killers, I have witnessed these stages in multiple arenas, including the organized abuse of children and in trafficking.

Frank endured two such ordeals which obliterated his capacity for trust and optimism. When he was 10, some older boys lured Frank and a friend into their basement to play "spaceship," with an unfortunate outcome. At age 20, a close acquaintance took him out into the country to take some kind of hallucinogen with him and, purportedly, to guide him safely on his first "trip." I call this second experience "the psychogenic menticide"—the breaking of the mind into submission.

Frank's Spaceship Adventure

1. *Presentation of good to the other.* Two older boys said they had cool spaceships in their basement and were somehow interested enough in Frank and his buddy to offer them an interesting opportunity. What a compliment!
2. *Creation of a false potential space.* Spaceships in the basement and two older boys, too—it sounded almost too good to be true.
3. *Malignant dependence.* Once Frank and his friend followed the boys to their home, it was a done deal. Frank was asked to sit in this odd chair with straps and wires, which they were told was just part of the spaceship apparatus. The other boy was told to watch. Once strapped in, there was no way out.
4. *Shocking betrayal.* The wires hooked up to an old wall phone and the older boys sent 220 watts jolting through Frank, terrifying him and making him sick. The idea that boys could/would do that to other boys was not a possibility until it happened, and Frank's world view shattered and cracked. Cruelty and betrayal had entered his world.
5. *Radical infantilization.* Now Frank couldn't have run away if he wanted to. The fear of the fear was more frightening than anything. He was unstrapped and told to watch while they strapped in and shocked the other boy. All he could think of was how glad he was it wasn't him again.

6. *Psychic death.* As the older boys whooped and hollered in glee, Frank experienced "the murder of his being." The self that was in need, that trusted the world, that believed in a good fate, was suddenly killed.

Frank does not remember if he and his friend discussed what had happened. His own mother being "absent" on morphine, his father away on an oil rig, he believes he never told anyone about this terrifying experience. He never saw those older boys again. While we discussed Bollas's structure of evil, Frank's eyes got wide and he cried. While telling me about the shock experience he said the hair on his arms raised up as he "felt" the shock again course through his body.

Ten years later, a new friend who he had been smoking marijuana with at the frat house offered to let him try something more fun than mundane partying. It was called "acid."

The Psychedelic Menticide

1. *Presentation of good to the other.* A man in his middle 20s, a regular at the frat house, pretended to be a friend to gain Frank's confidence and supplied him with marijuana, forming a drug buddy relationship and meeting him at parties.
2. *Creation of a false potential space.* The "friend" offered a special experience that would be really fun, different, and special: a guided trip on "acid." Like before, Frank felt really special that an older guy would show an interest in him.
3. *Malignant dependency.* Once Frank swallowed the pill (the friend did not, so he could "be there for Frank") and agreed to go out in the country alone with his "friend," he would be totally dependent upon him for the next 12–24 hours for a safe "trip."
4. *Shocking betrayal.* On the drive out to the country the "friend" began to make contradictory orders: drive slower, no I said drive faster, no I said drive slower. At first Frank thought the drug he had taken was blurring his judgment. But he gradually became aware that his "friend" was intentionally playing with his mind to terrorize him. The "friend" told him that God said that Frank was going to hell and proceeded to quote from Dante's "Inferno" about the different circles of hell.

5. *Radical infantilization.* His companion proceeded to pretend to read his mind, suggested frightening hallucinations to him, laughed at his terror, and suggested even more frightening hallucinations that to Frank's horror would actually seem to begin to happen. He told Frank that he had a direct link to Frank's mind and could do anything to him and with him that he wanted. Somehow the experience ended, and back at the fraternity house Frank saw him one more time, confronting him. He just shrugged and laughed and disappeared forever. In therapy we processed this excruciating experience as a mind-rape experience. It lasted for somewhere between 12 and 16 hours, with violent flashbacks for years afterwards.

6. *Psychic death.* Frank lost his faith in heaven after this incident. In an odd trick of the mind, Frank "knew" with certainty that he had been to hell already during the drug experience, and that all life after death had to offer was more of the same. On several occasions while single, he broke down when alone in his apartment and thought he was going mad. He thought he was in hell, and called his mother insisting that she repeat the words "I love you Frank." She did so, and Frank collapsed to the floor, relieved because the flashbacks stopped.

Frank discovered that he had avoided therapy all his life because he had vowed "no one will ever mess with my head again." When we first processed the shock and horror of these two soulshock experiences and how they understandably made him fearful of therapy, he broke down and wept in relief at things making sense. The shock and confusion had been in his body all these years and had blocked him from really being intimate, from taking the kinds of chances he needed to take in order to be who he really could be. In actuality he took to therapy like a duck to water once he understood that it is not about mind control. He made rapid strides in intimacy with his wife and children and began to establish friendships. After we untangled his traumatic thinking about hell during the flashback experiences, he rediscovered the possibility of faith and began enjoying church on Sundays with his family.

Soulshock comes in all sizes and shapes. Frankl (1959) once compared suffering to the noxious gas of the Holocaust chambers: it fills the room no matter the size, so there's no point in comparing sufferings. From the wife who discovers her spouse has been embezzling her money by getting her to sign it over to him, free and clear, to the son who discovers his father has been cheating on his mother, soulshock rocks the soul and shatters assumptions about who we are and who our loved ones are. Soulshock is part of coming to terms with life, disappointment, and mourning in adult life; but what are the consequences of soulshock in infancy and later childhood? Certainly, deep confusion will result about questions such as real/unreal, safe/unsafe, truth/lie, solid ice/thin ice. A psychic house will be built on a foundation of a floor lined with psychotic tile, 2 by 4s with shock holes throughout, meaninglessness blown into the walls as insulation, with a rooftop of suspicion and cynicism. The psychic envelopes of traumatized children are fated to be torn, ripped, damaged, or obliterated. As Jeremy Holmes (1996) explains,

> …Traumatized children lack a theory of mind in the sense that they have difficulty in seeing others as having feelings, intentions and desires, any more than they can accurately define their own inner world. Faced with aggressive or sexually intrusive parents, the normal process of secondary intersubjectivity, in which a child shares her experiences of the world with her caregivers via visual cueing, imitation, and so on, is inhibited. …To perpetrate his cruelty, the abuser has to remove from his consciousness the knowledge that the child can experience fear, pain, disgust, and so on. The child grows up in a world in which his feelings—and meanings—are discounted or obliterated.
>
> (pp. 15–16)

We have looked at cephalic shock, abandonment shock, shattershock, and soulshock, No matter what dimension of shock experience is involved, shock states are devastating to our past, our present, and our futures. Terr (1990) discovered that traumatized children have an altered sense of time. Their time sense had gone awry after profound physical trauma; in a sense, they had already "died" in their past. These traumatized children "knew" that they were going to die young, say, in their 20s. Like Winnicott's "fear of breakdown" (1974), what is anticipated in the future is actually something that has already been survived in the past.

Kalsched (1996) speaks movingly of the animating spirit at the center of healthy living, which is compromised in traumatic stress. While never annihilated completely because this would mean literal death, he makes room for the possibility that the spirit may be shocked into cold storage and fail to re-root naturally in the embodied person without the tending of a devoted gardener, like a bulb that has been harshly uprooted and then needs to be tenderly replanted when the ground is ripe, fertile, and no longer quite frozen solid. Solomon (2003) calls this "earned" secure attachment: it takes many years of a consistent, reliable relationship for the hypervigilance of disorganized attachment to fade within a secure relationship. This hypervigilance contributes to brief paranoid states, meltdowns, and difficulties fully engaging in relationships because of the amount of dread involved. The human capacity for dread creates a heavy burden, even though its counterpart—anticipation—is a delight. Remember, Siegel (1999) called the brain an "anticipation machine," one that constantly scans the environment to determine what will come next (Siegel, 1999, p. 30). Let us turn now to examine the role that dread plays in relationships.

Potential Shock: Dread

Dread is a complex feeling; it collapses the space between past, present, and future and the space between reality and fantasy. If Winnicott is right, and the "fear of breakdown" is a fear about something we have already endured, then the examination of our dreads about the future illuminates our understanding of the self from long ago. Dread is a visceral experience: the body braces, the musculature tenses, and the stomach registers queasiness. I believe dread is the psychological equivalent of the body's memories about and preparation for inescapable shock. As we explore our patients' experiences of their dreads, we may have a temptation to urge them to change their attitude, their expectations, in order to avert a self-fulfilling prophecy: "Quit being such a pessimist and give things a chance. Focus on the positive, not on your negative predictions about what *may* happen." However appropriate such a cognitive/behavioral intervention may be for some people who wallow neurotically with doom and gloom, the thoughtful examination of dreads may prove to be a passkey out of kingdoms of unvoiced anguish.

Dread of Invasion: Cherie

Consider, for example, the dreads of Cherie, an oncology patient who also experienced a back problem for a number of years. Cherie dreads check-ups with her oncologist, bone scans, physical pain, meeting new doctors, asking for help, medical and dental procedures, and above all, going to the hospital. How does she characterize her dreads?

> Every time I go in for a yearly checkup, I dread hearing the news that the cancer's back, that it's spread after all. I can't help but remember the shock of that first diagnosis, when there was a distinct "before" and "after." My world as I knew it crumpled in an instant, never to be the same again. When I go in for that bone scan, my body is on high alert, poised to run from catastrophe. Whenever I notice a new pain or tenderness somewhere in my body, I literally shake with fear that it's metastasis.

Her dreads about doctors and physical pain are re-creations of her period of absolute dependency upon an unattuned, unempathic mother, and the shocks of being dropped, rejected, and in unbearable circumstances.

> When I'm in pain I begin to feel desperate, like it will never end, and I can't get away. I hoard pain medication because it's so awful to risk asking for more; what if the doctor says no? I'm so totally dependent on him to understand what I'm going through; he has the absolute power to grant me relief or withhold it. I am so ashamed when I need to ask someone to help me carry something; I should be able to do things for myself and only finding out the hard way that my physical therapist was right about me not trying to do some things on my own was able to get me past my dread of asking for help. I'm afraid they'll look askance at me, think I'm weird or disgusting.

It comes as no surprise to learn that Cherie's mother treated her neediness with contempt and disparagement, even on such occasions as asking for help with her homework, or when she was in the throes of stomach flu. When Cherie reports to me about medical procedures she has to endure, such as radiation, chemotherapy, IVs, and the like, she evaluates the experience based on how she was treated by the medical professionals.

> I am so afraid they will be brusque and just treat me like a piece of meat to be shoved around, sometimes they don't even act like they know I'm a human being with fears and vulnerabilities. It's like I'm having to brace against being handled roughly, and I'm always startled that there isn't more compassion in their manner. Tears leak out of my eyes involuntarily on those occasions. I just hate showing how vulnerable I am to someone who doesn't honor my experience. Sometimes I luck out and get someone who has lots of warmth and empathy, and then I don't have to brace and can relax; then it's like being held instead of being handled.

Indeed, Cherie's parents spoke frankly with her about not having held her during her infancy. "Oh, we picked you up for feeding and changing and bathing, but Dr. Spock said not to coddle babies with excessive holding." It became evident that Cherie had been handled as a child, not held in such a way that she could relax.

> My mother told me that I came into this world a prude, that it was an ordeal to pry my legs apart to clean and change me. She didn't seem to realize that she was revealing to me how roughly she was handling me; the tension in my little body had nothing to do with prudishness but everything to do with feeling unsafe.

How does Cherie understand her dread of hospitals?

> I'm trapped, unable to get away. The only times I ever feel emotionally safe are when I can go out for a walk, a row in my kayak, a bicycle ride, or a hike. Nature makes me feel calm. When I'm in a hospital, there's no getting away from the people who have absolute

control over me and my needs. The environment is so inhospitable, almost antithetical to healing. All those interruptions, intrusions, lights and noises make it almost impossible to relax or get any sleep. There's nothing familiar to hold onto.

Cherie was born 4 weeks premature. She was rushed to a neonatal unit and spent her first 2 months in an incubator, with intubations, frequent heel pricks and all the noises and intrusions of a neonatal unit. She had to have a heart valve repair before she was allowed to go home. Her parents visited a few times but were told that she was too fragile to hold yet. She was not held by her parents until the day she came home from the hospital. Thus, she was separated abruptly at birth from everything familiar to her: her mother's voice, rhythms, and body. No wonder Cherie detests hospitals.

Indeed, when Cherie was told she needed to have an endoscopy evaluation, she became hysterical and panic-stricken even though she knew she would be asleep during the procedure. She couldn't figure out why she was so terrified of the endoscopy, but she spent the week leading up to the procedure in a state of heightened anxiety and dread. Years later during a body therapy session, she began to cough in an unusual way and felt frightened for no apparent reason. Her body therapist had previously been an obstetrics nurse and recognized the sounds as the peculiar coughs that intubated preemies make. Her body relaxed instantly upon hearing this information, and she felt she understood her dread of the endoscopy.

Dread of Intimacy: Westin and Gillian

Adult patients have described a variant of frozen body experience, what L. E. Hedges (1994, 2000) terms "organizing experience," a visceral, "let me out of here" reaction to the presence of too much love. We read earlier about cephalic shock (Lewis, 1981, 1983/2004, 2006) that stems from awkward parenting and marks the musculature with frozen tenseness. As cephalic shock gets structured into the brain, I wonder if that frozen "stunned" feeling doesn't manifest also in our adult patients who are frightened of the mind-to-mind contact involved in tenderness and intimacy. Whereas most of us fear abandonment, abrupt severing of attachment ties, and the sense of lack of safety that ensues, a certain group of patients, possibly those who suffered from extreme cephalic shock as infants, seem to have developed hard wiring that runs counter to "mother as protector from predator." Instead, mother "is" predator. Thus, aloneness has somehow become hard wired as the ultimate safety, and it is the continuous presence of the "other, the I–Thou relationship" (Buber, 1957) that shocks, summoning up images of mother/predator. Thus, the relaxation of "being alone in the presence of the mother" (Winnicott, 1958) never can occur, except paradoxically, in the presence of silence and solitude and the Older Self who ministers to the child within. The relentless dread that suffuses the qualitative experience of "being together with another" in deep intimacy, is suffocating; nothing less than survival anxiety is at stake during this panic state. At this level of vigilance, getting away is the highest priority and supplants any memory of the good times in the relationship.

In my experience, this transference is more likely to be enacted with a lover than with the therapist because getting away from the therapist is so much easier, and the focus in the therapy room is more on the patient's needs. The intensity of the death spiral of the panic state cannot be overstated. I have seen relationships destroyed at all costs, no matter how precious and life affirming, because they threaten to upset the applecart of homeostasis (Mitrani, 1996) that has kept the patient reasonably high functioning. In the early days of a romantic relationship, Westin, whom we met earlier in this chapter, found himself longing for sexual contact with Gillian, the woman he was falling in love with. He had been celibate by choice for a number of years prior to meeting her. As they made love and she cried out his name in joy during the moments of orgasm, he found himself afraid he would die on the spot. He rapidly developed a mysterious proctitis that rendered him fortuitously impotent for a number of months. When he tried to re-institute sexual relations with Gillian, the woman he believed he was destined to marry, he found he could not do so unless he got high. His anxiety was too great.

He began to dread even the possibility of a lovemaking session with her. As he became increasingly phobic about physical and emotional intimacy with his partner, he found himself entering paranoid states to break off contact. After a particularly moving couples session in which she professed abiding love for him and longing to touch and be touched by him, he found himself compelled to break off the relationship altogether, without knowing why. For months he was unable to mourn the loss of his love, to whom only weeks earlier he was considering proposing. Indeed, he was unable to even recall the good moments in their relationship; he felt he had narrowly escaped a dangerous situation by escaping the threat of intimacy. "She was too much for me; I felt that I would die in her presence." Only a year later was he able to comprehend the depth of his fear of vulnerability; he then began for the first time to mourn the loss of the love of his life. At core, there was a terror that could not be withstood.

> It is too much for my brain; this is in my body, not in my mind. This is not a thing of choice but of survival, I am shaking with terror. I know I wanted to marry her three weeks ago, but I cannot. She wants me to surrender my heart to her; to make love to her, not just make sex; to see her and be seen. You say my face grimaces oddly in ways I do not even know when I think about this. I know surrender is not really dying, but it is like dying. It is the most frightening word in the English language. I am terrified, terrified, terrified. I cannot do this thing; it is too much.
>
> (personal communication)

> When the person that stands between me and danger—
> is the danger
> Her well-intentioned reach towards me
> has clumsy fingers of ice
> Her gaily wrapped surprise
> of terrible loneliness
> Tickles me with freedom
>
> (Westin, personal communication, 2003)

Westin's early history helped us understand his complicated feelings about "surrender." He had grown up in affluence but without attachment. His father forced Westin to bend to his will every night at dinner. Westin learned to dread dinnertimes with a passion. If he didn't clean his plate his father would sit nearby watching him like a hawk lest he slip his food to the family hounds. "Chew, swallow" he would chant repeatedly. Westin had been a sickly boy and was slight in build; his father justified this eating ritual with concerns for Westin's health. He wasn't allowed to run and play with other boys or go to camp, lest he waste away. Instead, his parents dragged him on interminable culinary vacations throughout Europe, stopping at every Michelin-rated restaurant they could find. There, the ordeal would be replayed endlessly.

In therapy with me, Westin learned to tolerate contemplative eye contact, during which we gazed into each other's eyes with the intent of establishing an intimate connection. Early on it made him weep with both inconsolable longing and an unbearable franticness to escape. He entered a period of deep mourning for all the lost goodness he had evacuated because it "hurt too much to keep." He noticed that he would break moments of intimacy with me, in group, and with his friends: "love burns," he said. However, another part of him was vibrantly alive and danced in relationship with the other like a flower garden blooming in spring. Unlike a conflicted neurotic, Westin developed two different, parallel relationships with love: one based on the deepest of contact; the other, a vertically split relationship, was dangerously immature and phobic. He realized that a young emotional part of him believed that risking the love of another was terribly dangerous. Surrender to the power of merger kills, this part of him believed, and he was ready to fight to the death to preserve the little corner of heaven his younger self called the bliss of solitude.

When he thought about dating again, he shuddered with dread, recognizing that he had grown too much to have empty, unconnected sexual relations, but as yet lacked the ability to sustain sufficient emotional and sensual intimacy for a real emotional relationship with a woman. He also wept with the longing to partner, to rejoice with a soulmate. In his art therapy he learned that he alternately repudiated and treasured the feminine aspects of his heart: his sensuality, his capacity for tenderness and nurture, his ability to meet others at any depth and hold them safe, his boundless container for joy and beauty. An "old soul," he instinctively recognized the other at the soul or spirit level, although he dared not linger in a soulful plane for fear of getting lost. Our thrice-weekly connection was all he could handle, but he was determined to grow past this point of stuckness. He worked actively to build a tolerance for intimacy so that he could partner someday. He knew he would forever regret destroying the love of Gillian his soul mate, the woman who said she "would have loved him forever." After a particularly moving session, Westin disappeared from my life forever, saying he was too "busy" to do therapy.

Dread of Future Horror: The Long Watch

Constant vigilance is exhausting to the nervous system. I have worked with many youngsters who are constantly on the lookout for bullies waiting to pounce on them, trying to find a route home from school that won't make them easy "prey." Others speak of having had to learn to "read the weather" of their parent's moods: would they be manic, or angry, or drunk today? One woman grew up anxiously in her small town, watching the clock with her mother in the evenings…as the minutes ticked by, neither knew when, or if, her father would find his way home safely from the bars. Sometimes the police would come by, directing them to the nearest hospital where he lay recovering from a car accident. Other evenings the cops would half-carry him home with his wry apology around midnight. Sometimes he collapsed on the front lawn in a drunken stupor. And of course, there are scores of sexual abuse survivors who grew up listening for creaks in the hallway that portended a bad evening.

How do we keep alive our own vitality and sense of connection to loved ones when we walk in the shadows of death and torment? Keeping the home fires burning for a family member who is seriously ill is a unique landscape of anguish, all its own. So many dreads creep into the emotional landscape of doctor's offices, into ICU waiting rooms, and into the halls of nursing homes: dread that the loved one won't get better again, dread that they will, dread that the pain will worsen, dread that their loved one will be incoherent again, dread that the doctors won't provide pain relief, dread that insurance won't pay, dread that the mean-spirited nurse will be on duty tonight, dread that the doctor won't return frantic phone calls, dread that the surgeon will bring more bad news, dread of a relapse. Families who have lived through countless "this is it!" phone calls develop an exhausted numbness; adrenaline fails to command their attention the way it used to. Yet the dread of past and future shocks floats throughout waking and sleep, implacable and tormenting. Chronic illness in a family member creates its own private circle of hell, tainting our hopes and dreams of the future, ever threatening to rupture the ongoing nature of daily life with shocking intrusions into the rhythm of relationship. The following excerpt from *Blinded* (2004) a murder mystery by Stephen White (psychologist-turned novelist), captures the exquisite dance with dread that a couple and their child endure when they must wrestle with the ravages of relapse from multiple sclerosis:

> "Tough day?" I finally asked. "You feeling all right?" The second question was a back door way of wondering out loud about the current status of her struggle with multiple sclerosis...I hated asking. She hated answering. ...Last time I checked, the living room was devoid of elephants. ...interferon wasn't intended to deal with a rogue elephant that had snuck into our living room anyway. And that's what we had right now: a rogue elephant. ...I wanted to take the damn disease she had by the throat and tighten my grip on it until it died. ...I didn't know if my wife wanted me to say that I wouldn't leave her, to reassure her that the latest permutation of her illness hadn't changed a single facet on the surface of my heart, but I feared that the very mention of her vulnerability might make the circumstances too real for her. ...Neither of us mentioned the bull elephant that had pitched a tent in our living room. ...Going home that evening, I faced the more daunting task of trying to be an effective husband and father in a home that was quaking from the aftershock of illness and treatment.
>
> (White, 2004, pp. 55–413)

Shock can serve as a doorway, a portal to soul-searching and depth of experience. Although shock carries the weight of an imperative, in that we are forced to confront circumstances beyond our capacity, we always have a choice about whether, and how, we allow shock to serve us in our growth.

References

Anzieu, D. (1989). *The skin ego.* Yale University Press.
Balint, M. (1952). *Primary love and psycho-analytic technique.* Hogarth.
Bion, W. R. (1957). Differentiation of the psychotic from the non-psychotic part of the personality. *International Journal of Psychoanalysis,* 38, 266–75.
Bloch, D. (1978). *So the witch won't eat me.* Grove Press.

Bollas, C. (1995). *Cracking up.* Hill and Wang.

Bowlby, J. (1980). *Attachment and loss: Vol. 3. Loss.* Basic Books.

Brody, S., & Axelrod, S. (Producers). (1968). *Mother–Infant Interactions* [Videotaped series].

Buber, M. (1957). *I and thou.* (R. G. Smith, Trans.). Charles Scribner's Sons.

Carroll, L. (1865). *Alice in wonderland.* Macmillan & Co.

Damasio, A. (2003). *Looking for Spinoza: Joy, sorrow, and the feeling brain.* Harcourt, Inc.

Damasio, A. R. (1994). *Descartes' error: Emotion, reason, and the human brain.* Grosset/Putnam.

Egeland, B., Jacobvitz, D., & Sroufe, L. (1988). Breaking the cycle of abuse. *Child Development, 59,* 1080–8.

Ferenczi, S. (1931/1980). Child analysis in the analysis of adults. In M. Balint (Ed.), E. Mosbacher (Trans.), *Final contributions to the problems and methods of psychoanalysis* (pp. 126–42). Brunner/Mazel, Publishers.

Frankl, V. E. (1959). *Man's search for meaning.* Simon & Schuster.

George, C., West, M., & Pettem, O. (1999). The adult attachment projective: Disorganization of adult attachment at the level of representation. In J. Solomon & C. George (Eds.), Attachment disorganization (pp. 318–46). The Guilford Press.

Goldberg, C. (2000). *The evil we do: The psychoanalysis of destructive people.* Prometheus Books.

Grand, S. (2002). *The reproduction of evil: A clinical and cultural perspective.* Routledge.

Grotstein, J. (1990a). Nothingness, meaninglessness, chaos, and the "black hole" 1: The importance of nothingness, meaninglessness, and chaos in psychoanalysis. *Contemporary Psychoanalysis, 26*(2), 257–90.

Grotstein, J. (1990b). Nothingness, meaninglessness, chaos, and the "black hole" II: The black hole. *Contemporary Psychoanalysis, 26*(3), 377–407.

Grotstein, J. (1991). Self-regulation and the background presence of primary identification. *Contemporary Psychoanalysis, 27*(1), 1–33.

Hafiz. (1999). A great need. In *The Gift* (D. Ladinsky, Trans., p. 165). Penguin Compass.

Hall, B. (Creator). (2014–2018). *Madam secretary* [TV Series]. CBS.

Hedges, L. E. (1994). *Working the organizing experience.* Jason Aronson.

Hedges, L. E. (2000). *Terrifying transferences.* Jason Aronson.

Herman, J. (2015). *Trauma and recovery: The aftermath of violence.* Basic Books.

Holmes, J. (1996). *Attachment, intimacy, autonomy.* Jason Aronson.

Ivory, J. (Director). (1993). *The remains of the day* [Film]. Columbia Pictures.

Kalsched, D. (1996). *The inner world of trauma.* Routledge.

Koehler, B. (2003). Interview with Gaetano Benedetti, M.D. *Journal of the American Academy of Psychoanalysis and Dynamic Psychiatry, 31*(1), 75–87.

Kristeva, J. (1982). *The powers of horror: An essay on abjection.* Columbia University Press.

Levine, P. A. (1997). *Waking the tiger.* North Atlantic Books.

Lewin, R. (1996). *Compassion.* Jason Aronson.

Lewis, R. A. (1981). A psychosomatic basis of premature ego development. *Comprehensive Psychotherapy, 3,* 91–102.

Lewis, R. A. (1983/2004). Cephalic shock as a somatic link to the false self-personality. Available at: www.yumpu.com/en/document/read/11428826/cephalic-shock-as-a-somatic-link-to-the-false-self-personality.

Lewis, R. A. (2006). Frozen transference: Early traumatization and the body-psychotherapeutic relationship. *USA Body Psychotherapy Journal, 5*(2), 18–25.

Lyons-Ruth, K., Bronfman, E., & Atwood, G. (1999). A relational diathesis model of hostile-helpless states of mind: Expressions in mother-infant interaction. In J. Solomon & C. George (Eds.), *Attachment disorganization* (pp. 33–70). Guilford Press.

Main, M., & Hesse E. (1990). Is fear the link between infant disorganized attachment status and maternal unresolved loss? In M. Greenberg, D. Cicchetti, & M. Cummings (Eds.), *Attachment in the preschool years: Theory, research, and intervention* (pp. 161–82). University of Chicago Press.

Main, M., & Solomon, J. (1986). Discovery of a new insecure-disorganized/disoriented attachment pattern. In T. B. Brazelton & M. E. Yogman (Eds.), Affective development in infancy (pp. 95–124). Ablex Publishing.

Matter, C. (2016). *Poetry analysis of Marin Sorescu.* Prezi.com.

Meerlo, J. (1961). *The rape of the mind: The psychology of thought control, menticide and brainwashing.* Grosset and Dunlap.

Meltzer, D. (1975). Adhesive identification. *Contemporary Psychoanalysis, 11*(3), 289–310.

Mitrani, J. L. (1996). *A framework for the imaginary,* Jason Aronson.

Moore, M. S. (1992). *Attachment: mothers and infants* [unpublished doctoral dissertation]. University of Texas.

Moreno, A. J. (1991). *Psychodrama* (7th ed.). Beacon House.

Naipaul, V. S. (1981). The storyteller's art. *Newsweek,* November 16.

Ogden, T. H. (1989). *The primitive edge of experience.* Jason Aronson.

Peck, M. S. (1983). *People of the lie.* Touchstone.

Perry, B. D. (1997). Memories of fear. In J. Goodwin & R. Attias (Eds.), *Images of the body in trauma.* Basic Books.

Pizer, S. A. (1998). *Building bridges: The negotiation of paradox in psychoanalysis.* The Analytic Press.

Schuengel, C., Bakermans-Kranenburg, M. J., van Ijzendoorn, M. H., & Blom, M. (1999). Unresolved loss and infant disorganization: Links to frightening maternal behavior. In J. Solomon & C. George (Eds.), *Attachment disorganization* (pp. 71–94). Guilford Press.

Serling, R. (1962). Little girl lost. *Twilight Zone collector's set, Episode 91* [TV series].

Siegel, D. J. (1999). *The developing mind.* Guilford Press.

Simic, C. (1996). *Walking the black cat.* Harcourt Brace & Company.

Solomon, J., & George, C. (1999). The place of disorganization in attachment theory: Linking classic observations with contemporary findings. In J. Solomon & C. George (Eds.), *Attachment disorganization* (pp. 3–32). Guilford Press.

Solomon, M. F. (2003). Connection, disruption, repair, treating the effects of attachment trauma on intimate relationships. In D. J. Siegel & M. F. Solomon (Eds.), *Healing trauma: Attachment, mind, body, and brain* (pp. 322–46). W. W. Norton & Co.

Stern, D. B. (2003). *Unformulated experience: From dissociation to imagination in psychoanalysis.* Analytic Press.

Stover, E., & Nightingale, E. O. (Eds.). (1985). *The breaking of minds and bodies: Torture, psychiatric abuse, and the health professions.* W H Freeman/Times Books/Henry Holt & Co.

Suedfeld, P. (1990). *Psychology and torture.* Hemisphere Publishing Corporation.

Terr, L. (1990). *Too scared to cry.* Harper & Row.

Tronick, E. Z. (1989). Emotions and emotional communication in infants. *American Psychologist, 44,* 112–19.

Tronick, E. Z. (2007). *The neurobehavioral and social-emotional development of infants and children.* Norton Series on Interpersonal Neurobiology.

Tustin, F. (1986). *Autistic barriers in neurotic patients.* Karnac.

Tustin, F. (1990). *The protective shell in children and adults.* Karnac.

van Sweden, R. C. (1977). *Regression to dependence: A second opportunity for ego integration and developmental progression.* Jason Aronson.

White, S. (2004). *Blinded.* Bantam Dell.

Winnicott, D. W. (1958). The capacity to be alone. *The maturational processes and the facilitation environment* (pp. 29–36). International Universities Press.

Winnicott, D. W. (1974). Fear of breakdown. *International Review of Psycho-Analysis, 1,* 103–7.

Chapter 5

Sometimes It Takes a Village
Treating Developmental Trauma in Combined Therapy

You may have noticed that many of the patients you encounter in this book were treated in a combination of group, individual, and art therapy. Sometimes I was both individual therapist and group therapist for the same person. On other occasions, a therapist who knew my style (attachment-oriented, infinitely patient, and relational) and believed that my groups would allow their patients to learn about themselves and thrive, referred their patients to work in my groups. For example, shame (especially shame about who one is) is an issue that really needs to be healed with other people going through the same awful experiences: it is difficult to heal such shame in one-to-one therapy (see Chapter 7 for a thorough exploration of this topic). One gets an entirely different sense of a person in group therapy than in individual therapy. Issues such as mistrust, paranoia, hyper-competitiveness, false self, merger with others, envy, and inability to articulate oneself in front of other people—these are but a few of the issues that arise more naturally in a group setting. I also was privileged to train with and learn from some of the best art therapists in the nation, and worked elbow to elbow with art therapists during my many years in inpatient settings. Art therapy can resolve impasses between patient and therapist. And it is impossible to bluff or fake in art therapy because the conscious mind is entirely bypassed in art, no matter what the intention of the patient is.

Liotti (2018) recommends the benefits of combined therapy (two or more modalities or individual therapists) in the repair of the shattered states inherent to disorganized attachment, noting that having two or

DOI: 10.4324/9781003262367-7

more therapists (individual therapists, psyschopharmacologists, group therapists, art therapists, body therapists, or couples therapists) operating in two or more parallel systems in team treatment "…might prove superior to any single setting in coping successfully with the relational strains characterizing the therapeutic relationship with these severely traumatized patients" (p. 147). Although the treatment team of two individual therapists is rarely used in outpatient psychotherapy, Liotti highlights the benefits of combined treatment in parallel systems with complex patients, as long as the therapists are functioning as a coordinated treatment team. He points out that "having two therapists operating in two parallel settings is held as useful by the guidelines of the American Psychiatric Association (2001)" in the treatment of complex trauma (p. 147).

Although combined therapy and a treatment team are commonplace interventions in inpatient settings, little has been written about their ability to aid the outpatient treatment of challenging patients by:

1. Slowing down defensive enactments and mitigating extreme separation anxiety.
2. Allowing more self-reflection and mirroring of the self while learning about the self in relation to others.
3. Allowing the therapists to feel more secure and less caught up in countertransference enactments, by providing a container within which the therapists feel less besieged and dysregulated by their patient's shattering.

Two or more therapists involved in a therapy must stay in close touch with each other as they work to unravel complex defensive structures. Just as in inpatient treatment, therapists can be played off against each other by a good manipulator. One of the therapies explored below will reveal the unfortunate circumstance of all parties concerned failing their patient (Bernie) because of his extraordinary ability to manipulate. The more challenging and complex the patient, the more helpful it can be to work in a treatment team if trust among the therapists is high. Chapters 6 and 7 will bring the group therapy setting alive to you in a way that case vignettes from complex treatment team experiences cannot, yet there is much to learn from the following brave patients.

Jennifer

Jennifer was referred to me by her art therapist when she was about 30 to work in group on her defenses against intimacy. She presented as superficial and sarcastic but was deeply sensitive underneath. Both a therapist herself and a fine arts degree major, she was self-reflective and easy to work with. She came to our initial session wearing heavy boots and a leather coat (it was hot outside). She laughingly explained to me that she used clothing as a pretend barrier to protect herself; she advised me to check out what she was wearing to determine how safe she was feeling and how vulnerable she was willing to be. I brought up the notion of "second-skin formations" (see Chapter 2) with her, which fascinated her; it made sense of something she had always known intuitively but not really understood. Within a few weeks she began wearing sandals to her sessions, but over the course of 6 years giggled whenever I referred to our first session, and she said I had made up the Doc Martin boots (although she admitted having a pair).

She was raised by narcissistic parents. Her mother and father had divorced when she was quite young after a tumultuous marriage. Her father had a penchant for dating younger women close to Jennifer's age. Her challenge in group was to open her heart and learn to allow others to care about her. Her mother leaned on her for support, and she had grown up bouncing back and forth between rejection and merger. She fended off all overtures with sarcasm or deft humor. Her personal goal was to "get the hell out of group," but her art therapist supported her staying in the group until she had learned how to love. She must have threatened to quit group 40 times before she finally was ready to leave. She imagined I either loathed her or needed her to prop me up: both versions of her mother.

Jennifer scoffed at the notion of love. Both her parents spent money freely on themselves but were inconsistently stingy with her. She had difficulty remembering much about her childhood. She knew she had been raped in college but had never really processed this experience. She thrived in graduate school but was reviled by her father for wasting her degrees on useless pursuits such as fine arts. For graduation he gave her a diamond ring because, he sneered, she was not pretty or accomplished enough to ever catch a man on her own. The group raged with her about how hurtful and inappropriate this was, and she ended up throwing the ring in his face. He offered her countless opportunities to travel with him and his new step-wife. He threatened to cut her out of his will if she did not accommodate his wishes. Fearing his rejection, she accompanied him on a couple of trips—one on safari with him in Africa. At age 33 she met a loving man, married him, and left group (most reluctantly) while she was carrying twins. Not only had she learned how to love, she became a superb mother. She laughed ruefully that she hated leaving group once she had learned how to belong.

Jennifer was a relatively easy person to work with. Her therapy was straightforward and uncomplicated. Let's turn now to see how team treatment works with people who experienced considerable neglect and confusion early in life.

The Interface of Deprivation, Neglect, and Familial Breakdown

In families with limited emotional resources, the nurture of children frequently suffers. In non-nurturing families that face medical challenges, the emotional development of the children takes a back seat to the management of the illness, especially when it is the parents who are incapacitated. The impacts of chronic shock and deprivation combine with the horror of disease or mental illness, tending to wreak havoc with children's emotional development and creating a tendency to dissociate as a last-resort coping strategy. One of the most devastating aspects of these families is the inability to ask questions and otherwise discuss tragic events. Even in families with plenty of nurturing, the adults sometimes get so caught up in managing crises that children's questions go unaddressed. In nurturing families, young children tend to persist with their questions until someone takes them seriously. This principle is exemplified in a 1940 movie called *Five Little Peppers at Home*. When a financial crisis necessitated a sudden move to a smaller house, no one was willing to answer 3-year-old Phronsie's questions, snapping "Don't ask so many questions," or "because," to her queries. The charming young actress persisted with her questions in realistic fashion, undaunted by rebuffs, until she finally understood what was going on. Refusing to give up on her quest for answers, she engaged her mother directly by interviewing her doll in front of her mother while they were packing. In all seriousness she then turned to her mother and said something like: "I realize *I* ask too many questions, but [Dolly] is confused and upset. She doesn't understand why we have to leave this home we all love. Grandpa is happy here and so are we. She doesn't want to leave him and neither do I." This young actress accurately captured the determination of a normal 3-year-old to understand what is happening to her.

In the following two examples, neither Frank nor Bernie was able to get answers to their questions; they finally turned off their distress through dissociation. Both were intellectually gifted, so they were able to escape into the world of school and ideas, pursuing advanced degrees. Both had experienced profound deprivation as a consequence of parental illness. Frank's mother developed rapidly progressing multiple sclerosis when he was 6 months old; his father suffered a massive stroke when he was 8. No one explained anything about what was happening to him. Finally Frank stopped asking questions, even when the family moved away from their home. The household was so caught up in managing illness that, despite the family's affluence, Frank didn't even have a bedroom of his own. He was raised by a succession of nurses and nannies, one of whom took the time to read to him on at least one occasion. Frank cries whenever he remembers his wondrous delight at this kindness. Bernie's mother was addicted to both barbiturates and alcohol. She was in and out of rehabilitation hospitals throughout his life. He essentially raised himself, learning to dissociate as a toddler and taking over the administration of her medications by age 11. Till the end of his life, Bernie questioned nothing, even when it would have been in his interest to do so.

A Hamster in a Cage: Frank

Frank came to me at the urging of his wife. When I first met him, he was wary and skeptical about how I could help him. (We explored the causes for this wariness in Chapter 4.) He told me his wife was worried about him because he had never felt anything about his childhood, which had been haunted by illness and breakdown. Not only did he lose his mother to the neurological dysfunction of multiple sclerosis, but he had also lost his father—first to an emotional breakdown, next to the ravages of a serious stroke. Frank wanted to learn how to feel his feelings like other people did. A good-hearted man and doting parent, he stayed a bit distant, especially with his wife, whom, he told me, he secretly adored. However, he could not talk with her about how important she was to him.

His mother had suffered declining health all his life; in a wheelchair due to multiple sclerosis, she was addicted to morphine. He remembers her room as dark, silent, and scary, with creepy medical equipment everywhere. A constantly filling catheter bag particularly bothered him. His mother never complained; indeed, she barely existed as a person as far as he was concerned. He really didn't experience having a mother, except in the literal sense. He bonded more with his father, who had more pizzazz and emotional presence, but was out working on oil rigs much of the time. Frank was thus raised primarily by a succession of nurses, nannies, and housekeepers. His father was hospitalized for a mental breakdown when Frank was around 3 years old. The breakdown was one of many sources of family shame.

Frank had never had a room of his own. He either shared a bedroom with his father or, when he got older, slept in the TV room. When Frank was 8, his father fell to the floor from their shared bed: he was having a stroke. Frank remembers the sheer horror of knowing that something terrible was happening; his father was writhing, making scary noises, but couldn't talk. Frank remembers being pushed out of the way when the nurses attended to the emergency. No one explained what was happening. Frank was rigid with terror. The next few years are mostly a blank. He knows he and his mother had to move in with her parents while his father was in a rehab hospital.

When the father eventually returned to the family, he was seriously brain injured. The mild-mannered father Frank remembered had transformed from Clark Kent to Godzilla. After the stroke, he was prone to rages and angry outbursts. The man who had always joked had become someone whose face contorted in bizarre rages. One afternoon Frank was playing baseball when, to his delight, his father showed up to watch. After the coach called Frank back to the bench in rotation, Frank's father went ballistic. He ran down onto the field shouting and swearing at the coach. Frank was mortified, but his coach understood what was happening and reassured him.

Frank and his father were still able to share a love of books and traveling. When Frank graduated from high school, he and his Dad traveled to as many of the national parks as they could in one summer. He remembers this trip with fondness, yet when his father died years later, he felt as empty of feeling as when his mother had died.

Frank revealed a recurring dream about standing facing a blank wall. He would wake up from this dream in absolute terror. We finally reconstructed the meaning of this dream as his experience of losing his mother to multiple sclerosis at about age 6 months, the age when stranger anxiety begins to set in. At about this time, she had lost all ability to move her facial muscles in normal ways. She could speak, but in a remote, expressionless fashion. As Frank and I discussed the nature of terror for young children forced to confront lack of facial expressiveness in a beloved parent (Tronick, 1989, 2007), he broke down for one of the first times and wept with me. Dreams like this represent one way in which we preserve sensory aspects of traumatic preverbal experience.

The metaphor Frank developed for his childhood is that he was treated much like a pet hamster: he was fed regularly, his cage was cleaned out, and whenever the family moved, he was dragged along in his cage. He refers to his caretakers as "keepers" and likens his childhood to living in zoo. Mostly he was left to entertain himself. No one ever talked with him about what had happened to his mother or father, why they moved so often, or what his parents' many and lengthy hospitalizations were about. He was just carried along like a family pet. As Frank worked on himself, he came to grieve deeply about the sadness of his life. Waves of feelings would suddenly come over him and he would tear up with me for one or two minutes, then flash me a cherubic smile and quip: "I so love therapy! I can feel!" One weekend night shortly thereafter he threw himself on his bedroom floor and just sobbed and raged with his wife about how nobody was ever there for him. He forbade her to talk to him like a grown-up and insisted she just listen to him as the child he had never gotten to be.

He was highly avoidant of family meals, preferring to eat alone in front of the television despite otherwise deep, loving feelings for his wife and children. Only after we explored the dreadful state of dinnertime in his family of origin (his mother rigid in a wheelchair, his father drooling or ranting nonsense) did he begin to experiment with attempting to enjoy mealtimes with his family. In a similar vein, when we explored his distaste for conversation with his wife and family, he realized that he hated to talk while seated or standing up. He had been interrogated formally on a daily basis by his incapacitated parents who were anxious to escape their dreary lives by partaking in his youthful experiences. He had never experienced a sense that they were genuinely interested in his internal self. Therapy sessions stimulated a similar dread.

In my office we used to sit face to face, and he was usually uneasy, formal, sterile, and robotic with me. One day I suggested he lie on my couch facing me, because his back was "out," and he was in evident physical pain. He relaxed unbelievably, and we never returned to the face-to-face chairs. When we were exploring his discomfort relating to his children, I suggested he try an experiment of "floor time" with them. He was to lie on the floor, inviting his three young children and wife to join him. To my surprise he took to this suggestion gleefully, exclaiming that he wished someone had sat on the floor with him when he was little. To this day the family enjoys some variant of "floor time" together. He discovered he felt his most comfortable, most like himself, when reclining.

Frank was not at all in touch with his body. When others talked about feeling fear in their "gut," he couldn't relate at all. He only knew fear as it presented in his mind. Frank encountered so much fear on a daily basis while growing up that he learned to insulate himself from the experience. When his wife discovered a lump in her breast, he realized that he had noticed it himself the week before during their lovemaking, and then promptly "forgotten it." As they faced the round of tests, biopsies, and the like, he was a desperate wreck. His first thought was "what will happen to me if she dies?" His immediate reaction was that group would become much more important to him if he were to lose her. He came to realize that he used his wife as a "second skin" to shield himself from the horrors of his early life. As he imagined losing her, he could not contemplate how he and his children could survive. Only after finding out that his wife was okay was he able to make the imaginative leap back into his past where he indeed had lost both parents and all capacity for joy. He began to feel compassion for the boy who had never really existed except as a shell. To learn more about Frank's therapy experiences, see Chapters 4 and 6.

Faulty Neuroception and Relentless Hope: Bernie

Neuroception (Porges, 2018) is our nervous system's ability to tell whether we are safe or in danger. Like Frank, Bernie suffered severe neglect in an upper-middle-class family. The only part of his life that worked was school, where Bernie excelled, eventually becoming a well-respected surgeon.

Bernie's father was the town pharmacist; his mother was the town's most notorious drunk. His earliest memory was the taste of alum, the central element of antiperspirant. He presumes he must have rooted around hunting for her breast while she was passed out and found her armpit instead. She was addicted to morphine, other pain killers, and sedatives. His brother became a serious drug addict and died in his early 40s. Bernie self-medicated his despair, confusion, and panic with alcohol and Xanax, but was highly responsible about his substance use. He was refractory to all antidepressants, developing serious adverse reactions, but did well on benzodiazepines. Interestingly, trauma researchers have noted that the benzodiazepines are uniquely effective at calming the nervous system of those suffering debilitating pain as well as acute separation distress and protest upon separation from a mother. It's also possible that Bernie had developed an early addiction to sedatives through nursing with an addicted mother.

Bernie remembers a childhood filled with chaos and uncertainty. Sometimes his mother would leave the house for hours on end. When he would return from kindergarten or first grade, he would sit on the front lawn sobbing, fearing she was gone for good, but waiting for her nonetheless. She never took him to school or made breakfast, but every now and then after school she would make him steak and French fries. On one such occasion when Bernie was 10, she caught herself on fire at the stove because she was so loopy. Bernie had to figure out how to put out the fire and called his Dad to get her help.

The same year he came home to a horrifying sight. His family kept chickens, and, because he wasn't allowed any other pets, Bernie became quite attached to the chickens, naming them and loving hunting for their eggs. One day he returned home to find them plucked and in the freezer. His mother thought his distress was amusing. "What did you think they were for? They'll make a fine dinner someday."

On more than one occasion, his mother would drive while she was raving mad and drunk, her children cowering in the car. During one such nighttime episode, she tore off all her clothes, threw them out the window, and eventually threw the keys out the window too, ordering the kids to find them.

When he had his 11th birthday, his father turned over to Bernie the task of giving his mother her twice daily shots of sedatives, which were administered in her buttocks. For the rest of his life Bernie developed a bizarre attachment, one might call a fetish, to the sight and feel of his mother's buttocks, the only part of his mother he had ever had access to. This fetish was to draw him to various unsuitable women over his lifetime. Never once did he question his safety with them. Bernie was so desperately looking for a replacement for his mother, that he developed almost no sense of self-preservation: all he cared about was being with a mother substitute. His nervous system was wired to ignore all contradictions and inconsistencies, a form of trance logic unique to those with severe early dysregulation.

Predictably, Bernie was drawn to alcoholic psychopaths as mates. I met Bernie during a period of anguish with his third wife. Only after being confronted with incontrovertible evidence of her ruthlessness, lying, stealing, and sociopathy, did he eventually file for divorce. This action left him a shattered man. The only respite from panic attacks he could find was in his home, which he loved. The house was ultra-secure and surrounded by a forest, an enclave of serenity within the busy city. Any independent action he considered, such as looking for a new house to live in, rendered him hysterical with anxiety and terror that "she" would get mad at him. I saw Bernie in tandem with an art therapist several times a week and also saw him once a week in group therapy. His art therapist and I encouraged him to use our office phones as a container when he was feeling in crisis. Despite this level of therapeutic support, his attorney called me, concerned that Bernie was racking up an enormous legal bill using her staff for supportive psychotherapy, calling them 15 or 20 times a week to shore up his ego strength and calm his panic. Gradually over the 2 years following the divorce, his nightmares and panic attacks abated, and he became more able to self-soothe and accept soothing from his two therapists. He became highly committed to his weekly group session and learned to open his heart to others besides the "wife of the week." His dating adventures were plagued with agonizing panic states, desperation, and separation distress as he slowly matured.

Bernie had many different side-by-side states: the sensitive poet, the cynic, the ruthless aggressor, the desperate little boy, the dedicated and brilliant physician, the fisherman. He had periodic amnesia episodes, especially after any warm and caring exchanges. The desperate little boy was bound and determined to belong to a family. He liked dating women who had young children of their own, so he had someone to play with. The presenting ANP (apparently normal personality; Van der Hart et al., 2006), Bernie, was a successful, charming, educated, poetic, and insightful surgeon; only after 2 years of bizarre dating fiascos did I realize I was dealing also with an EP (emotional personality). I tended to "see" more different Bernies than did his art therapist. I saw the ANP, the brilliant, insightful doctor, and the cynic; she saw the EP, a panicked and disintegrated boy/man who was sneaky, lied by omission, and had bad judgment.

Bernie had a 34-year-old son who was a crack addict and tended to rant and rave at Bernie for not giving him money. Part of Bernie's therapy centered on "tough love," since his son had stolen from him repeatedly, brought a crack dealer girlfriend into his father's house to live, and subsequently wrecked the house. We made deals that he would not give money to his son, only to find a week later that he had somehow reneged on his promise. In group therapy Bernie learned that he did not question inconsistencies, so it was with a bemused confusion that he would report that he had somehow written a check to his son without exactly understanding why he was doing so. His son once visited him in an agitated, hostile, obviously altered state. Bernie called up a neurologist friend of his to get some medication for his son's attention deficit disorder (ADD), but neglected to warn his friend that his son was an addict. When I confronted him about this omission, Bernie realized that he had been so upset by his son's tantrums and rages that all he could think of was getting him his drugs and getting him to return to the city where he used to live. Bernie's EP was feeling traumatized and wanted to pacify his son so that he would love him again, or at least stop yelling at him.

Early Neglect Due to Parental Addiction

The only way Bernie could cope with the severe neglect he endured was to dissociate. Part of him simply waited until he could eventually find a good mother. Bernie's EP thought nothing of "buying" love, from either his son or from women, and he would spend thousands of dollars on presents for women he barely knew. On one occasion a month before Christmas, we had actually discussed reining in the dollar amount of his presents for the women in his life. A couple of weeks later, I asked him about what he was planning on giving one of the women. He literally cackled in delight and chortled "Too late; you're too late, I gave it to her last night. It was only $300, though. I was good." Later that week he confessed to his art therapist, "Actually it was $800, I don't know why I lied to Kathleen about it. I guess I was afraid I'd get in trouble. But she forgot to bring up presents and ask me about it on time, so I got away with spending lots of money, hah hah." This kind of thinking is concrete, childlike, and typical of the EPs with DDNOS (dissociative disorder not otherwise specified). Until my co-therapist and I figured out we were dealing with "little Bernie," an EP, Bernie's erratic relationship behavior had simply not made much sense in terms of his overall character and level of psychological sophistication. Once we were able to work directly with little Bernie as well as adult Bernie, his life began to settle down. After kicking his son out of his house and repairing the damage his son had wrought on the house, he began to scrutinize the women he dated more carefully before bringing up marriage.

Because he was so used to a neglectful environment, Bernie was unable to buy anything comforting for himself. Eventually it became clear that an immature self-state thought it was acceptable to buy things for others, but not for himself, because once when he was little, he had broken into his piggy bank of silver dollars and bought himself a model airplane kit. His mother punished him severely for this transgression. Once we figured this out, Bernie began to be able to shop for himself. He gleefully bought himself an X-box so that he could self-soothe in ways other than chasing women. The X-box was a purchase he had been dithering about for 8 months: he loved video games but didn't feel he deserved to spend the money on himself.

Impact of Parental Dysfunction on Bernie's Dating

When a mother is entirely unavailable and the father does not compensate for her absence, the children grow up at risk for developmental trauma and developmental stress disorder (Schore, 2002, pp. 9–30), a neurological condition characterized by an inability of the brain to regulate feelings, an inability to manage stress without falling apart, and a tendency to dissociate. Bernie's dating life could be characterized as mayhem. If a woman bore even the most superficial physical resemblance to his mother, he would fixate on her and pursue a relationship with her. Before I knew him, he had caught sight of a nurse in a hospital bending over. Her buttocks were shaped like his mother's, he exclaimed, and he "knew" instantly that he wanted to marry her. His analyst warned him against marrying her ("Be careful what you wish for, you might get it"). Bernie's EP heard this statement literally, and gleefully rushed out to ask her to become his third wife. By the time I met him, the marriage was a divorce in process and his soon-to-be ex-wife was acting like a severe sociopath.

Both his other therapist and I struggled to keep Bernie's EP in check. He secretly courted a woman named Krista who was in group with him, buying flowers for her and then canceling the order. They exchanged furtive emails with each other proclaiming their mutual fondness. Eventually she got "busted" by her individual therapist, who told me about what was going on in the group. As we processed this relationship, Bernie realized that his attraction to Krista was only partly due to her fine character. When he sheepishly brought in a photograph of his mother, we could all see that Krista was a dead ringer for her. Krista left the group ostensibly for financial reasons, and Bernie rapidly discovered he was not in love with her after all, even suspecting that she might be slightly exploitive with him because he was so financially successful. He befriended her and got her a job where he worked.

One night during his therapy, he repeatedly called a different woman he was pursuing, leaving increasingly insistent messages that she call him right away. When she confronted him in irritation: "Why did you call me so many times tonight," Bernie absolutely broke down, leaving me and his other therapist 20 messages which he didn't remember leaving. The next day when he saw his art therapist, he was distraught, frantic, and hysterical. "I'm a bad, bad, bad boy," he sobbed. When she asked him if he would like her to sit near him on the sofa, he shook in terror and said, "No! You're scary."

As he and I began to talk about "little Bernie," Bernie quizzed me on why I hadn't told him about little Bernie sooner. I replied that I hadn't known he was somewhat separate from adult Bernie. Bernie looked at me in consternation and said, "But I thought you knew everything," and then chuckled at himself. "I guess that's little Bernie talking, I know you're just human like me." Despite his sophistication and professional accomplishments, he was astonished that it had taken his art therapist and me several years to figure out that he had an internal "self-state."

Bernie finally figured out the dating pattern that had saddled him with three unfortunate marriages and innumerable unsuitable girlfriends. Little Bernie would find a woman who was just heartless enough to feel "like mommy" and pursue her until he caught her. He then would be "a good boy" and do anything she required of him until she moved on. He was flabbergasted to realize that his search for a mother replacement was the problem in all his relationships with women, not being essentially unlovable. He created a T-shirt to wear with the slogan "It's not me!" on it. Once picking heartless women became ego-dystonic[1] as a result of therapy, little Bernie would chase a woman (sometimes three or four at the same time) until she was caught and then skedaddle, leaving adult Bernie to puzzle about what he was doing discussing marriage with a woman he barely knew. In group, he listened closely to disclosures and feedback from others who had "self-states." (See Part 2 for more about group work.)

Denying the Emptiness of Neglect When a Parent Cannot Parent: Relentless Hope

Relentless hope is a term coined by Martha Stark (1994) to describe the transference enactments manifested when patients refuse to grieve early deprivation and insist on finding a replacement in either therapy or in a romantic relationship. Bernie had always pooh-poohed the utility of art, refusing to draw with his art therapist and deriding the drawings of others in group, until he finally let himself try a drawing.

He had meant to draw an adult person but ended up drawing a terrified little boy in the midst of chaos. This drawing was followed in rapid succession by pictures depicting him clinging to the ground at the edge of a cliff; little Bernie in an electrified "pen" where he was kept most of the time; little Bernie pushing me away; little Bernie living in an igloo; me as a witch; and me as a queen. His group was helpful for him in validating the power of his drawings to reveal split-off aspects of himself that were not readily available.

Next, he made the discovery that this "transference" of feelings from childhood to therapist that everybody talked about was a vital presence in his relationship with me. He couldn't believe that other group members were upset that I would go on vacation—one therapist was as good as another, and he was satisfied with the substitute therapist's presence. When he drew pictures of me as a witch and as an arrogant queen, he began to realize that little Bernie had an altogether different opinion of me than he did. Then one day he wrote me a check with his ex-wife's first and last names on it instead of mine. We shared the same first name, Kathleen (as did Bernie's mother). He then mentioned that his art therapist called me "Kate," and in glee announced that little Bernie would call me Kate from now on to differentiate me from his ex-wife and mother. "I don't have to call you Kathleen anymore! I'm free of the witch and the queen!" he exclaimed. Utilizing concrete and magical thinking, Bernie was working out the transference with me.

Bernie became strong enough to begin wrestling with his relentless hope about finding a mother. His younger self continued to be a mastermind seducer, who determinedly pursued woman after unavailable woman in a desperate effort to fend off grieving for his childhood emptiness. Bernie became enraged in group when the topic of "wire mothers"[2] came up. He couldn't abide it when Harlow's woefully neglected monkeys came into the conversation, because they too closely mirrored his own barren childhood. He came close to quitting group in order to escape sadness. He continued to resist deep attachment to other group members, as well as to his therapists, as he began to "let in" their fondness and warmth even the tiniest bit. Although he mocked the idea of "mirroring" as important developmentally, he secretly devoured every crumb of positive feedback he received. He kicked his addict son out of the house, stopped supporting him, and embarked upon a remodeling project to undo the damage his son had done. He never could relate to the idea of self-soothing.

Sadly, his son died in a one-vehicle accident at 3 in the morning, high on crack. Bernie began having car wrecks too and generally fell apart over the next year. He began lying to me and his other therapist about his dating and money habits, and we finally banished him from individual therapy but allowed him to stay in group. He appeared to work hard on himself in group but was lying to us there, as well. Several ex-alcoholics in the group asked him about a possible link between his accidents and drinking. He flat-out denied any association, pointing out that he was on call during these periods and would never jeopardize his medical license. Shortly thereafter, we received a phone call that his newest lady had found him unconscious at the bottom of the stairs in his house. My co-therapist visited him in the hospital (she was a hospice worker and a hospital chaplain in addition to her other degrees). We were shocked to discover that he was in formal detox with the DTs (*delirium tremens*, severe alcohol withdrawal accompanied by rapid onset of confusion, shaking, irregular heart rate, and hallucinating), which only occurs with serious withdrawal from long-term alcoholism. He did not recognize her despite having worked with her for more than 20 years. How had we missed the signs? He had vehemently denied drinking to all of us. He never left the hospital or got to say goodbye.

Developmental Trauma from Maternal Emptiness and Despair: The Dead Mother

Andre Green was a French psychoanalyst who introduced the concept of the "dead mother" as a way to understand children's responses to a depressed or unavailable caretaker (Kohon, 1999). Over time the concept has evolved to differentiate between two syndromes: first, those involving people whose "mothers" (caretakers) were previously available and then gradually faded away, and secondly, syndromes involving "mothers" who were never there at all. Famous literary figures exhibiting this despair include Sylvia Plath who wrote "*The Bell Jar.*" Green considered this oeuvre to be a *roman à clef*, based as it is on a protagonist's descent into depression and despair that was partly autobiographical, paralleling Plath's life. She committed suicide just after her novel was first published in 1963.

Green saw the dead mother complex as involving a caretaker who was initially involved with the child but who then "switched off" from emotional resonance to emotional detachment, possibly from mourning. The impact on the child, when she or he cannot restore or even experience a feeling connection, is the internalization of a hard, unresponsive emotional core which resists trust and reconnection. Plath's father died when she was 8, after struggling with anxiety and despair following the amputation of a foot due to untreated diabetes. A close friend had died of lung cancer, and Mr. Plath's fear that he, too, was dying of lung cancer prevented him from seeking treatment until it was too late.

Chefetz (2015) further elaborates on the dead mother as a presence of the absence, the opposite of Winnicott's "going on being":

> …an internalization of emotional deadness and emptiness. So, the child has reflected back from the parent a great emptiness that is representative of the vacantly lived and unformulated interior of the mother. Emptiness in a child grown to adulthood may reflect this as an attachment to the presence of absence.
>
> (p. 298)

How challenging it is to find a way into an existence of vitality when the parent fails to mirror accurately who the child is. "The dead mother refuses her own moods, killing off contact with her inner life" (Bollas, 1999, p. 100). I have had patients who struggled to feel that they "existed" at all as people. Indeed, it would have been preferable to have been treated as a pet or a doll than to be unseen, unrecognized, unknown, unvalidated, and presented with unending blankness.

"How Do I Know I Exist?": Fred

I worked with Fred three times a week in individual therapy and once weekly in group therapy, for more than 20 years. We first met Fred in Chapter 2. His parents were affluent enough to place him and his brother in the care of rotating nannies and to seek weekly individual and family therapy for themselves throughout their lifetimes. The parents were highly anxious people who found the challenges of child-rearing overwhelming. Although Fred's birth was medically uncomplicated, he grew up hearing how terrifying childbirth had been for his mother. Both parents were a bit withdrawn and morose, using tranquilizers for self-soothing. His mother was attacked, possibly raped, while he was still in diapers. The family story was that she had loved Fred as best she could until this attack, and had then fallen apart for decades. What memories Fred had of his parents from childhood was about *their* internal states.

Fred was desperately anxious and awkward. Upon meeting me he shook my hand formally and had difficulty relaxing in my presence. His dream life was preoccupied with themes of existence/non-existence. He had recurring nightmares of gazing into a pond looking for his reflection and seeing only dead fish floating belly up and bloated. Another recurrent dream involved starving at a banquet buffet resplendent with every imaginable appetizer, main dish, and dessert, all of which he was allergic to. If he ate, he knew the food would poison him. If he didn't eat, he was condemned to watch others eat, feeling invisible and envious. In a moment of introspection, he noted that the buffet mimicked his life—he was condemned to be a perpetual observer who could never partake.

In yet a third recurrent dream he again wrestled with themes of isolation and existence. Just as a snowman in the backyard of a large family, he gazed though the window at their family dinners. The children had carelessly created him during a snowstorm and then abandoned him. He longed for a hat but was left only with stone eyes and a carrot for a nose, staring wistfully into the children's dining room. Parents, full of laughter and warmth, smiled fondly at their children in this dream. They dined sumptuously and hugged their children while he melted away slowly in the sun. He mused aloud that this dream captured the essence of his struggles to exist: he always battled being on the outside looking in, disappearing inch by inch as others thrived.

Fred had no "personal" memories of his life before he was about 8 years old. He reported being aware of a constant state of agitation that only faded during school classes. He could not tell me about any interests or hobbies, nor describe what he liked to read or watch on TV. Fred was teased mercilessly by his peers growing up. Not only was he awkward to begin with, but everyone knew that his brother had committed suicide in middle school by hanging himself. Kids veer away from peers touched by death. High school was also difficult: he had no athletic talent and was rejected even by the other "geeks" for his oddness. He worried constantly about his mother: would she also commit suicide? Would his parents break up? His parents' therapist described them as somewhat "on the spectrum" with histories of sexual abuse (Fred's mother) and suicide (Fred's father's father). Highly intelligent, Fred was an academic at a nearby university. He had never had a close friend or romantic relationship and was barely tolerated by his academic colleagues. He decided to take a year's absence from academic life to immerse himself in therapy.

In individual therapy Fred felt extremely young to me although he was nearing forty. I was his second therapist. He had given therapy a go when he was a junior in college at Cornell University, but felt particularly misunderstood and shaken by that experience. His therapist had been in private practice in Ithaca. When he tried to express his lack of existence to his therapist with the metaphor "I feel like leaves without a tree," and shared his mounting despair about whether he existed or not, his therapist diagnosed him as schizophrenic and put him in a hospital for several months.

Fred didn't mind the hospital experience because he enjoyed being around others who struggled to find meaning in life. One day in the hospital he mused aloud in his group session that he just might feel like breaking some windows someday. In his mind he was playing with "existence" by making some big noises such as shattered glass. That would make people notice he was alive! However, the staff took him literally and threw him into four-point restraints. In four-point restraint, Fred could finally sense his body as he struggled against the leather bindings on his wrists and ankles. Getting thrown into restraints became his favorite new game. Like a toddler throwing food from the highchair for the parents to recover, Fred would muse aloud in the hospital about imagining aggressive actions only to land for hours in the restraint room. While being restrained he was comforted by the physicality of the experience, as the process involved physical touch (being taken down physically), as well as mechanical four-point restraint.

As the staff caught on to Fred's antics, he began to be placed in a locked "time-out room" when he got verbally rambunctious. He hated the isolation of sitting listlessly in the time-out room and felt profoundly misunderstood. He had never so much as thrown a toy across the room in his life and knew he was no danger to others. He believed the diagnosis of schizophrenia was terribly inaccurate: he had no real thought disorder, no hallucinations, and no ideas of reference. It took him months to convince the staff of his sanity and lack of dangerousness.

Hence, he was a bit reluctant to engage a therapist again, but since a colleague of his recommended me highly, he decided to give me a trial run, as long as I promised not to hospitalize him for no good reason. It didn't hurt that he spotted my diploma from Cornell. This diploma gave him some hope that I might just possibly understand him because we had something in common. I promised him I would not hospitalize him without good cause, and we embarked on a 20-year exploration into the meaning of his life.

His primary exploration was: How do I know I exist? Fred couldn't identify any likes or dislikes. For example, he had no idea what flavor of ice cream he preferred. He struggled to figure out whether he was warm or chilly. He had almost zero sense of self and even less sense of his body. Whenever the "attach" or "connect" words came up, Fred wigged out because the syllables disappeared into meaninglessness. Ogden (1989) describes this experience as a primitive state called "the autistic-contiguous position," a pre-symbolic sensation-dominated organization that manages extreme annihilation anxiety and provides the beginnings of a sense of the place where one's experience occurs. Anxiety in this mode consists of an unspeakable terror of the dissolution of boundedness resulting in feelings of falling or dissolving into endless, shapeless space, as manifest in the snowman dream.

Despite his discomfort with these concepts, Fred had taken this year away from his academic life to work intensely on "attachment" and "connection." We embarked on a bizarre form of play therapy. We played games such as "Hide and Seek," and "Marco Polo" (without the pool), both of which delighted him because he could sense my searching for him. I had a large office with a waiting room, a playroom, a kitchen, a bathroom, and a back office full of windows containing a salt-water aquarium and areas dedicated to individual therapy and group psychotherapy. There were lots of places to hide or call each other from. When he tired of these games he upped the ante by bringing in a long rope which he used to "attach" us together during our sessions by tying an end to each of us.

Physically Fred was pudgy and clammy. In ritualistic fashion he ended every individual session with a hug that made my skin crawl. I tolerated this enactment for years until I sensed he was ready to explore what it meant. When I finally summoned the courage to ask about his insistence on these hugs, he was a bit stung and affronted by my interruption of our ritual. He told me I had "broken things that were working" and thought briefly about leaving therapy. I persevered, telling him the hugs felt like he was "copping a feel" of my breast. After some silent thought, he admitted that the purpose of the hugs was partly to "experience me experiencing him," and partly to feel the softness of my breasts and body so that he could relax. I gently suggested we suspend the ritual for a bit to see what happened. Without these hugs he became increasingly desolate and lonely, aware of both his longing for and dread of intimacy. He began to imagine dating for the first time. When I suggested taking small steps like adopting a cat, he changed the subject.

In group, whenever anything of any intensity was being explored he fell instantly asleep, snoring loudly. The group members understood that he was not yet capable of tolerating strong feelings. They attempted to be compassionate despite the revulsion that Fred inspired within them. He asked inappropriate questions and made inappropriate comments. For example, when a group member's distant aunt died, Fred inquired about the funeral: How did the corpse look? Did it smell weird? Did she touch the body? An ongoing issue was his inability to "connect" with anybody in the group. He wanted to be in a relationship like everybody else, but the complexity of romance eluded him entirely. A couple of trial dating relationships ended badly. Gradually he became fond of other group members and was able to describe why. The group pleaded with him to be patient with himself and to start with small steps, suggesting, as I had, that he adopt a cat to discover companionship and affection. He scoffed at the notion and claimed it would be marriage or nothing.

Fred stayed in both group and individual therapy for many years. Gradually he developed a greater sense of self, weathered the death of his parents, and began to explore the world of online dating. One day to my astonishment, he announced that he was leaving therapy very soon because he had planned a trip to Europe—this would be a first for him—and wouldn't be able to make his appointments regularly for quite some time. He thoroughly planned an exit ritual involving poetry, candles, a symbolic "toast" with a bottle of wine, cake, and a farewell card thanking me and chronicling his accomplishments during therapy. He left me in triumph. Periodically he sent me postcards from various countries. A year later, he phoned me to let me know he had acquired a cat.

The Dead Mother in Group Therapy

Five patients currently in group together have found the dead mother concept life-changing. All five had had some individual therapy either before or during group. Doug's father committed suicide in a mental hospital when Doug was still *in utero*: his mother understandably retreated into shocked numbness. Tessa's father died when she was just 3 months old, and her world collapsed. Kinsey's mother was beset by a vicious seizure disorder when Kinsey was 3 years old and was never really herself again. As Kinsey got older, her mother, an equestrian, fell off her horse while jumping and became incapacitated by chronic pain. Addicted to pain medicine, she lay in bed much of the time. Kinsey's father had a touch of Asperger's disorder and left his wife; visitations were sterile and disappointing. Ginger had two non-functional parents. Her father was incapable of telling her he loved her when she insistently asked, chiding her for asking: "I put a roof over our head and food on the table don't I?" He had a paranoid streak and covered all the windows with sheets and butcher paper so no one could peek in. When he would leave town on business, her mother would grab Ginger and her sister and hole up in a tiny windowless bedroom, terrified. Eliot was adept at creating personas and hiding his real self—even from himself.

"The World Will Be OK If I Make More Money": Doug

Doug was referred to me for group therapy by his individual therapist. Although Doug was an entrepreneur and successful businessman with a loving wife, he was terribly anxious, to the point that he vomited when he ate. He dreaded each workday, dreaded eating, dreaded being overwhelmed by shame and anxiety, and dreaded being at his house. He strove to master his feelings by attending self-talk inspirational seminars and talked endlessly about work pressures. The external was easier for him to grasp than his internal self. He measured himself by how much money his business generated and drove himself ruthlessly to make more money, ostensibly so that he could take care of his family.

Doug's mother, devastated by her husband's suicide and emotionally unable to connect with her son, soon brought a man into the house to fill the void. She went through the motions of being a mother, but Doug was a frantic baby. His grandmother said his colicky screams were the most heart-rending screams she had ever heard from an infant. He was close to being a failure-to-thrive baby. His father's suicide was a family secret, never to be spoken of. His stepfather was crude and abusive, a drug addict, and an alcoholic, scattering pornography around the house.

Doug's childhood and adolescence were a nightmare; his mother threw the stepfather out of their house repeatedly but always caved in when he demanded to return. They lived in a neighborhood dominated by gangs; drive-by shootings were common. Doug's stepfather so resented Doug (he kept telling him he couldn't wait for him to be old enough to move out) that, during an argument, he hurled at Doug the information that his Dad had killed himself. Doug searched for information about his father, to no avail.

Although Doug knew he was fortunate to have married his wife, he didn't really appreciate her when I first knew him. He was terrified he would end up killing himself as his father had. He could not stand feeling sick, anxious, and depressed all the time. After a breakdown, he consulted a psychiatrist for medication and saw an individual therapist, who referred him to group with me. He did well on the medication but got confused when the psychiatrist scoffed at what he was working on with me. She stated emphatically that there was no such thing as pre-verbal trauma, that his conditions were purely biological in origin. He just knew his obsessive preoccupation with killing himself was linked to his father's demise and his mother's breakdown afterwards. He was frustrated that his psychiatrist was so dismissive and certain that pre-verbal trauma was nonsense. He finally spent one weekend dedicated to yelling at his father's picture about abandoning him and his mother and coming to terms with the tragedy of the suicide. He then left individual therapy and pursued his growth in group alone.

Before the above breakthrough, he had lived in his mind and was nearly phobic about his body, nausea, eating, and health. Afterwards, he came to terms with his emotional deprivation in childhood, acknowledged his identification with his father, and grieved his mother's inability to connect emotionally. He gradually learned to trust group members, his wife, and me. However, what really opened his heart was the birth of his three children. He knew he could not abandon them the way his father abandoned him. During the first two births he was not emotionally present. He "knew" he loved them but guiltily confessed that he couldn't "feel" love for them. He pushed himself to "act" like a real father as much as he could, until his 2-year-old son had a meltdown trying to get him to watch him and said, "Daddy likes his phone better than me." Eventually he came to treasure his children and wife as the precious individuals they were. Work stresses faded as a therapy topic and his emotional presence intensified. He began to fall in love with his children and his wife.

"I'm Dead Inside": Tessa

Tessa was a happy 3-month-old baby when her father, a doctor, was in a fatal car wreck coming home from the hospital. Tessa's mother descended into shock and despair, going through the motions of being a mother in numbness. Tessa has some good early memories of her mother, enough to enable her to parent her own sons later in life, but her mother lost her zest for life and invited a scary, alcoholic man into the family. The stepfather violently abused the boys in the family and threw Tessa against a wall. He left pornography lying around the house and occasionally masturbated openly, but did not touch Tessa sexually. The family descended into poverty and squalor; Tessa was held together primarily by her favorite older brother, who became an anchor in her life. Tessa remembers "faking it" at school but never daring to bring anyone home. Unfortunately, when Tessa was 15, her older brother was also killed in a car wreck, and her world collapsed again. She hid her despair from the world and somehow made it through high school with stellar grades.

Because she was brilliant, she got a scholarship to college where she met her future husband. The marriage lasted 15 years but was not a happy union. He seriously abused her physically, but she hung in there with him, trying to get the light to come back in his eyes, like she had done with her mother. She came to me for individual therapy because her husband had left her for another woman and defrauded her of custody rights. She was in terrible despair and believed that a part of her was "dead," just as a part of her mother had died when she had lost Tessa's father. We worked on her dead self for 3 years until she was ready to join group, to work with others who were familiar with dissociation, abject despair, and "the dead mother." She gradually came alive again and revealed herself to be a talented musician, artist, and chef who spoke many languages. She remarried happily to a kind, gentle man. Although she remained cut off from her own sons through her ex-husband's efforts, she "parented" upcoming talented young men and women who had potential in the music industry, neighbor children, and her beloved nieces.

Tessa's primary work in group was de-idealizing her mother and giving up the role of "cheerleader." Her family role was that of trying to wake up her mother's dead eyes and bring a smile to her face. Tessa learned to join others in their sadness instead of trying to cheer them up by looking on the bright side. She poured herself into her music as an alt-country singer, using music to revive her dead self, mourn her brother and other relatives who had taken her under their wing, and embrace life. As she developed more self-awareness and capacity for connection, she became beloved by the group. She no longer felt dead inside.

Dorsal Shutdown and Co-regulation: Kinsey

Kinsey has good memories of her early childhood. Her mother was artistic, playful, and creative. Her father actually played with her. Then Kinsey's mother had a series of seizures and was never quite the same. Making matters worse, she developed a chronic pain condition after an equestrian accident and became addicted to pain pills and benzos. During these years Kinsey remembers throwing herself on the floor and playing dead, hoping her parents would bring her back to life. They would step over her "dead body," and go on with their day;

Kinsey's emotional pain, indeed Kinsey herself, was invisible to them. Kinsey's father became exhausted and, fed up, left the family.

Kinsey remembers using fantasy to self-soothe. "When I grow up things will be better." She developed a complex, rich inner life and created rituals of arranging her stuffed animals and her room that were comforting. When I met her, she was about 26, partnered with Adam, a brilliant computer guy who became affluent quickly. She was sensitive, had enormous emotional depth, and I fell in love with her quick wit, infectious smile, and self-awareness. She had been in analysis with a therapist whom she fired for being cold and unresponsive. Kinsey felt unseen by her and even more frustrated when the analyst wouldn't try to connect with her at all. According to Kinsey, the therapist had "dead eyes that could not be warmed."

I was captivated by Kinsey from our first session. Although we had our "moments" of her disintegrating when I made a therapeutic error of some kind, she forgave readily when I tried to repair the mis-attunement. Kinsey and Adam went through a series of couples therapists who all found Kinsey to be difficult to work with because she retreated when she was hurt. Adam had a confident false self who was easy to relate to. No matter how often I co-consulted with this couple's therapists, they believed Kinsey to be nothing more than a pain and couldn't figure out what to do with her when she would shut down. They could not sense her extraordinary emotional depth, sensitivity, and vitality. All they saw was a difficult, withdrawn woman who was mistrustful and hard to get to know. Kinsey herself was invisible to them. They did not understand that what they were encountering, and co-experiencing, was dorsal shutdown (Porges, 2018), a freeze state in reaction to perceived threat or intense shame that can be full collapse (see examples of "going to the floor" in Chapter 6), an inability to think clearly or access words or emotions, or even an inability to move the body. In Kinsey's case, she could sense that the therapists did not like her particularly and, losing her characteristic animation and insightfulness, she descended into shame and despair. Porges (2018) describes possible warning signs of dorsal shutdown as "an absence of the client. The therapist can feel the amorphous sense of reaching out and not finding anything solid to connect with. The client experience I have heard over and over is the sense of being alone, lost, and unreachable. This is where despair lives" (p. 24).

Kinsey and I had our "moments" of impasse when I had been inadvertently mis-attuned, but we weathered these storms and learned how to co-regulate. Co-regulation involves recognizing cycles of rupture and repair and *learning to soothe at the appropriate level* to reinstate social engagement. During these brief impasses (which always felt dreadful, as if I had destroyed us and our potential), I learned to ask her what she noticed inside. Physically she would slump into dorsal collapse; she would lose the ability to think, lose all vitality, and drown in shame. Eye contact, which normally flowed easily between us, became impossible. When we worked our way out of these dorsal freezes, sometimes with humor or curiosity or feisty sarcasm, we would both feel relieved and reconnected. During these impasses I, like her other therapists, would freeze inside and search frantically for resolution. Unlike her other therapists, I never gave up and doggedly pursued the Kinsey I knew was hiding behind her shadow. We learned to identify what she termed "twisty thinking" that sabotaged our work and her growth, imprisoning her in the awful doom of worthlessness. Kinsey joined group in addition to continuing in individual therapy with me. Group allowed her to work on her dismay when people failed to understand her properly.

Porges (2018) teaches that the way out of dorsal freeze and shutdown is ventral vagal engagement. This social engagement system allows us to experience variety in our emotions—feel excited, sad, or feisty—and brings a grounded presence to emotional experience; it is also called "upregulation." Levine (2010, 2015) further helped me understand that one way people emerge out of a freeze state is with aggression. My favorite memory of this phenomenon with Kinsey was early in our relationship. I was trying to engage her with tenderness, and she snapped "That train has left the station. Too late."

I learned to intervene in several ways with Kinsey when we fell into a dorsal hole. Notice my use of "we." When re-enactments are involved, both therapist and patient are swept up in chaos. Sometimes I could engage her curiosity; other times when she was stuck in invisibility, I asked permission to remind her who she was in my eyes. As I told her that I knew her as a feisty, gorgeous, brilliant, tender, feminine, "hip," mystical, and generous woman whom it was an honor to work with, we would move her out of the dorsal slump, and she would re-animate. I am known for my authenticity, so Kinsey never found me disingenuous.

Kinsey left Adam when she realized that he was too self-absorbed and enmeshed with his complicated family to actually co-parent with her when they had children. They stayed friends, however, being each other's first loves. Kinsey and I continued to work together in both individual and group therapy. Kinsey struggled for a long time with abject despair, worthlessness, and a deep-seated belief that she was unlovable (see Chapter 7 on abject despair). Her new home, chosen carefully while she was leaving Adam, had initially entranced her with possibility, but became a container for all that she secretly believed to be true about herself: it had a rotting foundation and was a perpetual mess.

A pattern emerged of Kinsey's investing in whomever she was dating (she was strikingly beautiful and had no trouble attracting suitors) with elements of fantasy, no matter how obviously unsuitable the man was as a long-term partner. They were boy-men who were never going to grow up. Then when "his" attention would stray in a narcissistic moment, she would "collapse" again, re-enacting the ultimate truth that she was completely unlovable. She would turn somersaults trying to re-ignite the spark of their early dating, to no avail. Then she would descend into a protracted despair and bewail the disappearance of their early excitement, blaming herself. These proxy "mothers" stayed permanently dead because they had no partner potential, they were just "cool, hip" dudes. She played out the same scenario in work situations that were unsuitable to her intelligence and creativity. A techie, she landed positions in start-up companies run by boy-men in their 20s who devalued her intelligence and contributions. Consequently, she felt worthless most of the time.

Finally, she took a year off both bad work situations and bad dating and resolved to go deep inside with me and in group to resolve her feelings of unworthiness. This was a terrifying year for her as it involved a leap of faith in herself.

Kinsey discovered many internal strengths during this period. She explored her sexuality, her femininity, her powerful intellect, and uncovered her deep intuition and mystic sensibilities. She had a keen appreciation of nature and beauty and was adopted by a cat who enchanted her. At the end of about a year, as she was going about her life, reinvesting in her home and her potential, she was "discovered" by a Real Man whom she is going to marry and have children with. He tended to collapse, too, into dorsal shame during their arguments, but she knew how to re-engage him. During the same period of time, she was "discovered" by a group of savvy businesswomen who hired her on the spot to be their creative consultant. Kinsey was no longer invisible.

"I Have to Be Perfect": Ginger

Ginger grew up in a family atmosphere of terror and collapse. Her job was to take care of her mother and not be a burden. She imagined that if she could be just perfect, her mother would smile and relax. Because her mother was so anxious, Ginger refused to go to school and stayed home for several years to look after her. She would periodically ask her father plaintively if he loved her, and he was unable to find any reassuring words or sense her need for affirmation. In group, Ginger adopted the persona of a wise woman who was periodically supplanted by very young self-states. An accomplished artist, married to another successful artist who adored her, she had tried art therapy on and off for decades. Because she made a living doing art, she always rejected the idea of art therapy contemptuously as "beneath her."

Finally, her individual therapist (also an art therapist) threatened to stop working with her if she didn't do art; her perfectionist posturing was stalemating the therapy. She embarked on a courageous journey of doing art about her truest inner feelings and did a year-long series about the darkness she grew up in. When she shared a series of paintings and drawings about the darkness, we were awed by their depth, their raw vulnerability, and their honesty. Ginger transformed into a true wise woman. The veneer of a childlike narcissistic perfectionist fell away, and she became one of the group's most powerful voices. Her husband was so moved by her vulnerability, he wrote her a love letter telling her that marrying her had been the best decision of his life. The circle complete, she finally had the "words of affirmation" that she had always craved. She no longer needed to be perfect.

"I'm Whoever You Want Me To Be": Eliot

Eliot was referred to me because he had had a profound group experience in a church retreat and asked his pastor where he could keep working in a group setting. Eliot was one of the most "slippery" people I have ever worked with. He declined individual therapy but wanted to learn more about himself in a long-term group. His mother had tried to commit suicide on several occasions, and she still struggled with bouts of depression, so Eliot flinched every time the phone rang in case it was bad news from home. In the first 4 years, his work in group centered on his business problems: Why had he needed to be so perfect as a child? Was he doomed to be a trickster or a fraud? Why did he keep getting himself into consulting positions that always backfired on him with criticism and lack of appreciation of his gifts? Why did it always feel that he was about to get into trouble? Eliot grew up in a military family in which he was expected to get As in school. So Eliot did; he was a consummate hacker and tinkered with his report cards throughout middle and high school until his father at graduation made a toast to him about being in the top 10 percent of students in the state (and therefore would have been eligible for a scholarship). The jig was up.

Eliot was the strong silent type in group, but he thought about group every day—like practicing the piano between lessons. His comments to others were always thoughtful, meaningful, and on target. On the rare occasions that he got angry, he fought extremely fairly. By the time Eliot finally figured out how to create a professional life that was meaningful to him, his work in group shifted to focus on his family problems. Eliot was married and had elementary school-aged children. His wife and he were committed parents, agreeing on most parenting decisions but divided about whether their son had serious emotional problems. The boy had gone through a period of episodic violence and school refusal that lasted for more than a year. So, in group Eliot talked mostly about family issues. Then the family's life was threatened twice in a week—once by a vindictive crazy driver and once by an unhinged neighbor who had a reputation for being a crystal meth-head. The entire family took a year-long course in Krav Maga (serious self-defense), and Eliot brought in plenty of terror from these experiences that helped him bridge to his terror about his mother's depression and his fear of being inadequate to keep her alive or make her smile. Accessing his fury about threatening incidents and learning to channel his helpless rage into martial arts helped him feel empowered. After all this admittedly good work, Eliot announced that he felt ready to graduate.

Our "deal" in group is that leaving must be a collaborative decision. Although Eliot was adamant about leaving, I just had a feeling that all was not well, and told him I had no idea what his marriage was like or whether he loved his wife. He ignored me for a few weeks trying to wiggle out of thinking about this, and then, over 6 months of really paying attention to the interactions between his wife and himself, he realized that he hadn't loved his wife in a long time. He was profoundly disappointed that, despite her traumatic past, his wife was unwilling to do couples or individual therapy in order to save their relationship. Another 2 years went by as the couple dealt with an ugly divorce, and Eliot was once more ready to quit. Again I had a feeling I couldn't quite put my finger on, and brought that confusion into the group. "I know who you are as an employee, as a husband, as a father, as a neighbor to friends in need, as a philanthropist, but I don't have any sense of who you are as a man. Who are you anyway outside of your roles? You have enormous emotional depth and range and yet I can't get a sense of *you* at all. What are you like sexually? What do you like about yourself? Who do you want to become?"

He chuckled and said that I was getting in the way of his faking his way through life. He broke down eventually to confess that he had always worn a mask and then confused the masks as his identity. He had no idea who he was. He had thought he loved his wife, yet had been unhappy for 10 years, unwilling to face it. He had just shoved that worry aside like he had the worry about his mother, and tried to keep both of them happy. Over the next 8 months, he really took up the challenge of figuring out who he was deep inside, and then left the group with our blessing. He remarried someone he was really in love with and whom his children adored, and while finishing this book I got an announcement of the birth of their child.

We turn now to explore two chapters devoted to the analysis of developmental trauma in two long-term group therapy settings from 1982 to 2007. Admission to these groups was strictly controlled: with rare exceptions, one had to have had individual therapy either before or during the group period, and had to understand that group therapy was a multi-year project. A few of the patients you will remember from earlier chapters, but most will be delightful newcomers.

Notes

1 Ego-syntonic and ego-dystonic are two terms of art that I have found useful to people trying to change their lives. In order to change a way of thinking or behaving, the codified beliefs and habits have to begin to feel "off" or strange to the individual trying to change, rather than seeming normal. For example, one patient who used to be heavy always bought clothes that were several sizes too large. His belief that he was still "fat" influenced his choice of clothes. This belief seemed normal to him despite its irrationality; it was ego-syntonic, at one with the self. Once he began to see himself as the lean, muscled man that he had become, his impulses to buy "big clothes" began to seem weird to him; these impulses had become ego-dystonic, or not fitting with the self.
2 See Harlow's "The Nature of Love," described in Chapter 2.

References

Bollas, C. (1999). Dead mother, dead child. In G. Kohon (Ed.), *The dead mother: The work of Andre Green* (pp. 87–108). Routledge.

Chefetz, R. A. (2015). *Intensive psychotherapy for persistent dissociative processes*. W. W. Norton & Co.

Kohon, G. (Ed.). (1999). *The dead mother: The work of Andre Green*. Routledge.

Levine, P. A. (2010). *In an unspoken voice*. North Atlantic Books.

Levine, P. A. (2015). *Trauma and memory*. North Atlantic Books.

Liotti, G. (2018). Disorganized attachment and the therapeutic relationship with people in shattered states. In J. Yellin & K. White (Eds.), *Shattered states: Disorganized attachment and its repair* (pp. 127–56). Routledge.

Ogden, T. H. (1989). *The primitive edge of experience*. Jason Aronson.

Plath, S. (1963). *The bell jar*. Harper & Row.

Porges, S. W. (2018). *Clinical applications of the Polyvagal Theory*. W. W. Norton & Co.

Schore, A. N. (2002). Dysregulation of the right brain: A fundamental mechanism of traumatic attachment and the psychopathogenesis of post-traumatic stress disorder. *Australian and New Zealand Journal of Psychiatry, 36*, 9–30.

Stark, M. D. (1994). *Working with resistance*. Jason Aronson, Inc.

Tronick, E. Z. (1989). Emotions and emotional communication in infants. *American Psychologist, 44*, 112–19.

Tronick, E. Z. (2007). *The neurobehavioral and social-emotional development of infants and children.* Norton Series on Interpersonal Neurobiology.

Van der Hart, O., Nijenhuis, E., & Steele, M. (2006). The *h*aunted *s*elf: Structural *d*issociation and the *t*reatment of *c*hronic *t*raumatization. Norton Press.

Part II

Group Therapy with Developmental Stress and Trauma

Chapter 6

Falling Forever
The Price of Chronic Shock

Marilyn was a 30-year-old company CEO who loathed her group therapy session every Tuesday night. She insisted that I ignored her and gave preferential treatment to all the other group members, as her mother always did with her sisters. Worse yet, she could hardly stand to look at me because I resembled the Wicked Witch of the West. For 4 years, she had been game-playing, sulky, and non-communicative in group. I knew from her individual therapist that she desperately longed for my eyes and my warmth. Yet whenever I tried to engage her on a verbal level, I felt rebuffed, inadequate, and incompetent. If I would catch her eyes and smile at her the moment she walked into the group room, she would briefly light up, only to descend into haughty frozenness once group began. She spoke in a rote, distant, intellectualized manner that was perplexing, given the consistent vulnerability she brought to her individual therapy. She confided to her therapist that she had fantasies of throwing herself down my stairs to compel my concern but would become blank and dismissive when I asked her about these fantasies, acting like she had no idea what I was talking about. She knew that her therapist and I discussed her progress on a weekly basis, but whenever I brought up any content from those sessions, she acted confused.

Since she was working actively in individual therapy about the agony she experienced with me but was "playing hard to get" with me in group, I allowed her to wrestle silently with her ambivalence, inviting her to share her disappointments in me but not pressing the point when she chose to be dismissive. I thought of her as an entrenched "help-rejecting complainer," a quiet borderline who was stuck in a re-enactment of her early childhood. A bit of background: Marilyn's

DOI: 10.4324/9781003262367-9

mother was abandoned to an orphanage at an early age and tended to be eerily silent. Marilyn's father was a combat veteran who was unable to talk about his feelings. When Marilyn was 1 year old, her mother had another baby. Simultaneously, the mother became gravely ill and was bed-bound for 2 years. During Marilyn's toddlerhood she had to gaze distraughtly from the floor at her mother holding the new baby; she was not big enough to crawl up on the bed nor could her mother reach down and pick her up. And to make matters worse, Marilyn was so nearsighted that she could not rely on maternal eye contact for emotional connection or reassurance.

Marilyn gradually began to thaw toward other group members and interact warmly, but she maintained the "ice queen" façade with me. One evening she shared a dream in group: A botanical garden had a rare and beautiful species of tree, lush with multicolored flowers and delicious fruit. The tree was slowly dying, however; unbeknownst to the caretakers, the ground beneath the apparently healthy tree was frozen. The roots beneath the tree were rotting, starving, and desperate for nurturing attention. This dream heralded a major shift in our work together. As I listened to this dream, I developed a new understanding that Marilyn was not so much characterologically disturbed, as she was quietly and subtly dissociative (dissociative disorders not otherwise specified [DDNOS]). She struggled with vertical splits ("side-by side, conscious existence of otherwise incompatible psychological attitudes in depth" (Kohut, 1971). While part of her was an over-intellectualized executive, another part of her was a frantic toddler, with fractured affects and concrete thinking. I thanked her for her dream and told her that I suddenly understood that I had been torturing the "baby" in her all these years, and that I was deeply sorry. She burst into a heart-wrenching, undefended wailing of rage, terror, and tears. In vulnerability and confusion, she asked why I was being nice to her *now* when I used to watch her fall and fall without trying to catch her. She turned to the group to ask why they hadn't said something all those times she obviously shattered into pieces in group. The group members explained that they were startled to find out that she was suffering, that she always looked quite "together," if somewhat irritated by my incompetence. She was flabbergasted by the group's response. How could all of us have so missed the obvious: *she was in shock all the time in group, just like she had been in shock all her life; she might as well have been left on a mountain to die, for all the help she had received trying to connect with me.* She thought group was supposed to help her learn how to connect; instead, I had helped her do what she did best: survive nothingness. I told her that if I had *known* there was a frantic 2-year-old inside of her trying to beg for help, I would never have left her to die in the cold, frozen ground; that I had presumed she had the skills to come to me since she was so sophisticated in many other respects. She was fascinated to learn that she looked so different on the outside than she felt on the inside and resolved to learn to take better care of her needs for emotional attunement. She had buried her emotional self behind a wall of impenetrability, which even she had difficulty accessing.

The Tuesday Night Group

For the past 9 years, this group was composed of middle-aged individuals who manifested vulnerability to disintegration, in conjunction with a high level of functioning, considerable ego strength, and a demonstrated commitment to personal growth. Most individuals were in at least twice a week individual therapy, some with the author, others with various other primary therapists. I collaborated weekly with these primary therapists. The group had slightly more men than women, totaling 12 in all, most with some history of a difficult childhood but not outright abuse. None carried a PTSD diagnosis or presented with amnesias, "lost time," or other formal signs of dissociation. All the patients in the Tuesday group had experienced extensive cumulative trauma (Khan, 1974) due to failed dependency and/or neglect. None of the patients carried a dissociative diagnosis, but eight of the patients demonstrated chaotic and alternating attachment patterns consistent with the construct of disorganized attachment (by clinical observation and history). Of the other four, two appeared to be avoidantly attached, and two displayed preoccupied/anxious attachment. Three of the group members were in stable marriages; most had been married and divorced long before entering group. Two group members had never married. Only four group members had any substantial or enduring friendships before entering group.

Reverberations of Marilyn's Work in the Group Process

After Marilyn revealed her dream and introduced the notion of chronic shock into the group, group themes increasingly depicted shock, deprivation, terror, shame about needs, and yearning. Although Marilyn's dream had served as a gateway to her inner world of fragmentation, she remained unconvinced that she had done the right thing (bringing her dependency needs into group). She guardedly asked me how I felt about the last session, confessing that she was terribly mortified to have acted like such a baby. I told her that I thought her dream had powerfully captured her inner reality to help me finally understand her, and thought her rage appropriate, not babyish. I added that I looked forward to many such interactions with her and other group members who felt let down by me, because the only way to find out if you could really be yourself in a relationship was to test the waters and find out if the other could survive your rage. Marilyn was startled to notice that she was already feeling closer to me, and said so. On the other hand, she admonished me; although her "little girl" was happy that I had finally apologized for being so mean to her, my apology had not let me off the hook. While she would continue to work in individual therapy with the "little girl" self to enable her to talk with me at some future time, she didn't know if this little girl could ever learn to trust me. Marilyn herself trusted me, but she said the little girl still believed I hated her.

The group went on to explore the meaning of apology in their lives. Several members expressed their surprise that I would admit having made a mistake, much less be willing to apologize. John shared how meaningful it was to him that his father admitted that he had not been the greatest father. Others wept at the futility of wishing that their parents might ever realize or acknowledge their mistakes. Raine talked about how loving both her parents were and complained that the group seemed to be into parent-bashing. Group members told her that while her parents had been loving, she would eventually have to face the reasons she had so much anxiety and terror, which she kept locked up in a metaphorical closet. Paul scoffed at the idea that apologies from parents could be meaningful, as his father whined constantly about being a bad father, while simultaneously asking for reassurance and continuing to be abusive. Yet he was intrigued that I had offered no excuses and simply focused on Marilyn's pain, without asking her to forgive me or take care of me emotionally. He asked me why.

I talked for a few moments about secure and insecure attachment, explaining that two experiences seem to facilitate attachment security: the experience of someone trying to understand what is going on inside us (Siegel & Hartzell, 2003) and emotional repair when something distressing has happened within the relationship (Tronick & Weinberg, 1997). By assuming that Marilyn was playing hard to get during her early years of group, I failed to understand her or resonate with her struggles. My apology, given in the context of my empathic failures, had specifically addressed her frantic helplessness when I turned *away* from what she thought were desperate cries for help, leaving her to stew in a sulk.

Split-off Affects

As accretions of chronic shock accumulate without emotional repair, children develop defensive strategies to wall off unbearable anxiety. Similar to the numbing/flooding cycles of chronic PTSD, the cycles of chronic shock manifest in a paradox: patients oscillate between feeling just fine and then inexplicably falling apart. Frank, a high-powered attorney you met in Chapter 5, who was cool as a cucumber in his manner, provides an apt example of this oscillation in process. He had experienced occasional short-lived periods of breakdown throughout his life, which he usually attributed to a "bad trip" on psychedelics. Although during the previous group he had said that he couldn't really relate to Marilyn' sense of chronic shock and abandonment, he reported that Marilyn's work last week had led to a breakthrough for him into the world of feelings. A dramatic encounter with disavowed feelings had opened him up to his own experiences of massive childhood deprivation. His wife had been telling him for years that he had had an awful childhood, but he had insisted to her, and to himself, that his childhood had been "normal." Marilyn's work in the group last week had catalyzed an emergence of primitive feelings he did not know were inside him. One day last week, his wife and children had been fairly demanding. When his wife snapped at him, Frank had dropped to the floor of his bedroom, sobbing that he just wanted *her* to take care of *him* right now. He remembered hanging onto the floor until she joined him there, and he clung to her for the first time in their long marriage. He had grown up in a house dominated by illness. His mother had contracted severe MS when he was less than a year old, and his father had had a massive stroke in front of him while Frank was in a shared bedroom with him. Chronically unaware of any internal experience (alexithymia), Frank had never been able to feel anything about his life before he "went to the floor." Five other group members reported that they also went to the floor (like toddlers do) when overwhelmed; they described a sense of needing secure ground to hold them together.

Over the next months, Frank's frozen self began to thaw, always in bursts of raw, unexpected affect, remnants of an unprocessed life. He re-experienced a recurring nightmare he had had all his life that conveyed early horror (Tronick, 1989) about his inability to find himself in his mother's face. His mother had gradually lost her ability to smile or achieve facial expression after he was born; by the time he was 6 months old, she had no capacity for facial mirroring. In the dream, he was frozen, inches away from a blank wall directly in front of his face. He would always wake up from this dream screaming, wondering why he couldn't just turn away from the wall.

Other group members also brought in repetitive dreams reflecting annihilation anxiety and dissociation consonant with their life histories: hiding; digging up the bones of someone they had killed and buried long ago; falling from an airplane; sliding uncontrollably on roller skates; raving, psychotic attackers; and chaos. Allowing themselves to fully acknowledge the devastating havoc that debilitating childhood anxiety had wreaked on their lives, group members began to work seriously on identifying needs, wishes, and self-soothing. Waves of grief swept through the group: grief for stuckness, lost time, barren childhoods, missed opportunities, investment in destructive relationships, developmental delays, and lives with unfulfilled potential. The toll of chronic shock, they discovered, was the walling off of unbearable experience through disavowal and encapsulation.

The Balloon as Metaphor for Encapsulation

The following vignette demonstrates the inner contents of an encapsulation in a powerful moment of projective identification: Paul communicated his inner experiences of violence, shock, and terror to all of us in the group by "acting in" with a balloon. In group Paul seemed to float among extremes of bitter cynicism, paranoia, insightful and touching warmth, and hopelessness. A gifted artist, he used black humor to deflect the intensity of his feelings and to avoid vulnerability. His parents had both been emotionally volatile, bursting into rages and disparagement at the least provocation. Up to now, he had kept his own rage and terror tightly under wraps in group, but frequently had episodes of frantic weeping, raging tantrums, and desperate pleas for help in his individual therapy. He, along with the rest of the group, had been highly supportive of Marilyn's risk-taking, as well as openly envious of the progress she was making. Some weeks after Marilyn's confrontation of me, he came into the group uncharacteristically late, exploding a balloon aloud as he opened the door.

This group meeting occurred the week after the Washington snipers incident. Because of seating arrangements, I and one other group member (John) jumped in our seats at the sudden loud noise; we could not see Paul coming through the door, balloon and pin in hand. My first thought was that a gun had gone off. Paul and several others laughed uproariously at my discomposure. My adrenaline was so high from being startled so severely, I momentarily entertained a fantasy of kicking him out of group for the night. For a while the group tossed around the issue of whether the joke was hilarious or just a cruel and tasteless acting out of aggression, given the snipers at large. John joined in the general hilarity (being first and foremost a prankster himself) but then brought the group to order, asking if Paul couldn't see how he had scared me. Besides, the snipers were a big deal, someone else added, nothing to laugh about. The group fell silent and stared at me with consternation. Before I could think clearly enough to comment with any clinical acumen, I quietly asked Paul not to bring any more balloons to group, but said that his angry feelings were welcome anytime if he brought them *in words*. I was secretly embarrassed and furious that my well-hidden PTSD had been exposed.

Paul of course felt shamed by me and said so angrily. He talked about how he had handled his feelings through delinquency and vandalism as a teenager, and that he could relate to the snipers' thirst for vengeance and mayhem. He confessed he wanted to talk about his rage but was afraid the other group members and I would be afraid of him, or shame him as I had just now. Marilyn gently suggested that perhaps

Paul's baby-self didn't know how to talk to me in words yet, but that she at least admired him for his courage and creativity in bringing his rage into group with the balloon. The shock inside him, she said, was now something we could all relate to; he had found a way to make us, on the outside, feel what he often felt on the inside. A chorus of agreement murmured through the room. Westin added that it was Paul's parents that more resembled the snipers, with their chaos and violence, and not Paul.

I puzzled inwardly about what was going on with Paul, me, and the balloon, and realized that Paul was envious of Marilyn's articulate self-expression, as he himself was close to exploding with bottled up rage and sadness. I commented that his balloon was kind of like Raine's bulging closet of disavowed feelings. I wondered if he was afraid of exploding in the group like the balloon did; at least with the balloon he could feel in control, and choose the time of the explosion. He angrily responded that he did occasionally explode just like the balloon out in the world, and that he always felt ashamed afterwards. He worried that the group couldn't hold all his feelings; that its skin was as thin as the balloon's. My skin was certainly pretty thin, he pointed out, as I couldn't even take a joke without retaliating. Several group members chuckled anxiously, watching to see what I would say next. Marilyn said that she understood, that she too was afraid that if she continued to open the door to her feelings, that she would go crazy or have a breakdown, exploding all over the group like Paul's balloon. Westin and John joined the fracas: how could I expect people to share their feelings if I just humiliated them when they did? The group rallied around Paul and Marilyn: was I eventually going to shame everyone like I had just shamed Paul?

I was torn; I had always held that putting things into words, not actions, was the meat and potatoes of group work. I also realized that I had inappropriately shifted my embarrassment about being so nakedly vulnerable into Paul. I needed to find a way to acknowledge my inappropriate affect if I expected to teach group members to be accountable. Having difficulties with sensory-motor integration due to premature birth, I have always been overreactive to loud sounds and prone to manifesting exaggerated alarm reactions. I admitted to the group that I had been embarrassed by my obvious startle reaction, and told Paul I was considerably better at handling anger than I was sudden sounds. I asked him if he would trust me and the group enough to continue exploring the part of himself that was trapped inside the balloon, doing his best to use words whenever he could. He grudgingly agreed, with the proviso that I try to remember his sensitivity to humiliation. I invited the group to keep a watchful eye on me. If the group had stood up to their bad mother once, I pointed out, perhaps they could count on each other to do so again.

The group encouraged Paul to take the risk of opening his heart to the possibility of being understood. He talked for the first time about the part of him that could understand serial killers and murderous rage. Paul was touched by their concern, but still expressed worry that everyone would be afraid of him now that they knew the truth about him. His mother had identified him as "The Devil" throughout his childhood and called him by that name. He had always been a devout Catholic and had worried obsessively since childhood that he was already condemned to hell because his mother said so. This level of concrete thinking stood in sharp contrast with his philosopher/Renaissance man persona. John immediately jumped in with reminders of his own brushes with homicidal rage, urging Paul to stay with exploration instead of bottling it up again: "This group is big enough to hold all of our feelings, no matter how awful." The group-as-a-whole was preparing to undo dissociative defenses against chronic shock.

Encapsulation and Dissociation as Group Themes

Marilyn's dream, Paul's exploding balloon, and Frank's identification of going to the floor as an emergence of dissociated affect heralded a watershed epoch of growth in the group. From the outset, group members were astonishingly facile at identifying and working with dissociative encapsulation processes in themselves and each other, as if they had discovered all by themselves a new language that opened up entirely new therapy vistas for pursuit. The level of risk-taking, authenticity, empathic confrontation of destructive defenses and interpersonal exploration increased as the group explored a common ground of terror of vulnerability. I was continually surprised and startled with what the group and its members were teaching me. By a year's end, five of twelve group members had incorporated work on split-off self-states into their group and individual therapy; of the other seven group members, five had made significant breakthroughs in self-understanding as they began to comprehend the impact of defenses against annihilation anxiety on their inner and outer lives.

Despite my familiarity with more florid dissociative defenses, each new revelation of severe encapsulation surprised and shocked me a little as if I were encountering dissociation for the first time; I never saw it coming, not anticipating to see such severe vertical splits within a non-abused population. (One patient had a paranoid state that spoke only in French, his native language; another had an immature needy state that compulsively pursued unavailable women and insisted he was a "bad, bad boy" whenever rejection inevitably occurred.) Moreover, after Marilyn's group work I had expected the group-as-a-whole to organize defenses against deepening primitive themes such as terror, mortification, and annihilation anxiety, instead of dropping with quiet profundity into the blackness of the abyss.

Theoretical Underpinnings of Chronic Shock and Sub-clinical Dissociative States

Chronic shock is a construct with applications well beyond the attachment relationship. Chronic shock and ensuing encapsulated self-states can accrue from repetitive pain syndromes and medical procedures during infancy and childhood (Attias & Goodwin, 1999; Goodwin & Attias, 1999a, 1999b; Schore, 2003a); accidents of impact (Scaer, 2001); and physiological disfigurement and subsequent peer ridicule due to congenital impairment, developmental disorder, disease process or traumatic occurrence (Sinason, 1999). However, examination of chronic shock due to non-attachment etiologies, and its impact on body image and somatoform dissociation (Goodwin & Attias, 1999b; Nijenhuis, 2004), is outside the scope of this chapter, as is the exploration of dissociative states due to abuse.

Here, we will be looking at the devastating ripple effects of early neglect and deprivation on the nervous system and patients' capacity to feel safe with others, to tolerate and manage feelings, to envision a better life, and to self-soothe. We will examine the crucial roles of attunement and repair in developing secure attachments with others and a sturdy sense of self. I hope to build a platform for understanding the profound role that failed dependency plays in the build-up of unbearable affects. I propose that repeated shock states within attachment relationships and unrepaired distress during the formative years contribute to an inherent vulnerability to psychic shattering and abrupt fragmentation, which I characterize as "attachment shock." In the face of these unbearable affects, children cope by encapsulating the affects in autistic enclaves or covert dissociative self-states. These walled-off affects of attachment trauma are intransigent to change and difficult to access. I will interweave recent developments in post-Kleinian psychoanalysis and traumatology with interpersonal neurobiology and attachment theory to help us begin to think about how to reach these deeply protected psychic structures of shock, despair, meaninglessness, and terror embedded within many of our high-functioning patients.

Relational chronic shock is the embodied imprint of attachment traumata, persisting from early childhood flooding from uncontained, unrepaired distress, what Neborsky (2003) terms "the pain of trauma." "[E]ffective psychotherapeutic treatment can only occur if the patient faces the complex feelings that are 'inside the insecure attachment'" (pp. 292–3). We are not surprised when shock states stemming from disaster, war, or torture manifest in severe dissociation PTSD or disorder of extreme stress not otherwise specified (DESNOS). Nor are we surprised when sexual and criminal abuse result in dissociative identity disorder (DID), other specified dissociative disorders (OSDD), and insecure or disorganized attachment patterns. Only recently did the international clinical/academic community formally posit the existence of a sub-clinical variant of dissociative process related to attachment trauma (Liotti, 2004). Like the Tuesday group members, many high-functioning patients without a history of overt trauma, abuse, or blatant character pathology develop dissociative traits, encapsulations of annihilation anxiety, autistic enclaves (Mitrani, 1996, 2001; Mitrani & Mitrani, 1997) and vulnerability to disintegration and addictions. Why do these patients live in the chill of chronic apprehension, to the detriment of their ability to truly relax into peacefulness, play, and the pursuit of deep contentment? These are the compulsive caregivers and high achievers whose success masks clinical or sub-clinical dissociative states and chaotic relationships. In the course of depth therapy these individuals sometimes reveal covert primitive ego states existing in parallel with sophisticated, mature functioning.

Perplexed by a bewildering blend of strength and vulnerability, the Tuesday group members were quite relieved when they came to understand that some of their more problematic behaviors and decisions had been driven by primitive states of mind they were unaware of. Encapsulated ego states oscillate reflexively between terror of intimacy and desperate need for human contact, striving to insulate the patient from the vulnerability and vagaries of being human (Mitrani, 1996). Myers (1940) first described these alternating states as the "emotional personality" (EP) and the "apparently normal personality" (ANP). A topic once considered controversial, revolutionary, and exotic, clinical discussion about segregated self-states has now become commonplace among attachment theorists, interpersonal neurobiologists, traumatologists, many relational analysts, and many post-Kleinians. Nijenhuis and van der Hart (1999), Siegel (1999), Blizard (2003), and Liotti (2004) have integrated Myers' concepts with cutting edge breakthroughs and innovation from the fields of neuroscience and traumatology to provide a powerful model for current-day understanding of subtle dissociative processes such as those presented in clinical and sub-clinical manifestations of DDNOS.

> Repeated experiences of terror and fear can be engrained within the circuits of the brain as states of mind. With chronic occurrence, these states can be more readily activated (retrieved) in the future, such that they become characteristic of the individual. In this way our lives can become shaped by reactivations of implicit memory, which lack a sense that something is being recalled. We simply enter these engrained states, and experience them as the reality of our present experience.
>
> (Siegel, 1999, p. 32)

The "emotional memories" of the EP tend to be experienced as intense waves of feelings accompanied by visceral and kinesthetic sensations such as sinking, falling, exploding, and the like. Lacking the internal shock absorbers of securely attached individuals, the covert dissociative patient is vulnerable to emotional flooding and disrupted functioning under conditions of stress. Catastrophic anxiety states encoded in preverbal, implicit memory surface without any sense of being from the past, and underlie behavioral choices and strategies. Marilyn's shattering, and other high-functioning members' desperate panics, whimpering, paranoid episodes, ego-dystonic keening, and primitive raging are typical examples of EP presentations in clinical work. The defining characteristics of an EP state are the patient's utter conviction of clear and present danger in the here and now, mixed with a strong somatic experience and concrete thinking. Marilyn's EP was attachment based, but it is important to note that many traumatized EP's are defense-based (Steele et al., 2001), as was the case with the French-speaking paranoid ego state. So deep was his need to disavow needing anything from another, this patient would find himself savaging important relationships and discarding them, as if in the throes of mortal danger, without questioning why or exhibiting the slightest curiosity about the extremity of his actions. He was content to repudiate all need for people, creating an illusion of self-sufficiency by hiding in an internally constructed "bunker" that humans could not penetrate and where he had absolute control.

Encapsulated Self-states

Group psychotherapists are well acquainted with the differing character structures and typical clinical presentations of individuals whose character is organized around fears of rejection and abandonment; anger, resentment, and fears of non-recognition; shame and humiliation; or sorrow and melancholy. However, the character structure of many high-functioning individuals struggling with chronic shock, terror, dread, and overwhelm is typically organized around some variant of encapsulated self-states which function silently in the background until activated by the environment. Hopper (2003) considers that failed dependency, prolonged helplessness, cumulative strains, and a childhood atmosphere of dread, chaos, or oppression are crucial etiologic factors that have largely been overlooked by the clinical community of group psychotherapists. Prolonged hospitalization and physical distress in a child, spouse, or aging parent, bereavements, medical crises, the anxiety of parental unemployment or financial reversals, the chaos of divorce, the intrusion of horror affects which accompany disaster and criminal assaults, all contribute to exhausted and depleted parenting. Disavowal, dissociation, and splits within the child's developing self may ensue. "Basically, in order for life to continue and psychic paralysis [to be] avoided, the entire experience [of annihilation anxiety] is encysted or encapsulated, producing autistic islands of experience" (p. 59). We need a wider lens than those provided by terms such as trauma or abuse to capture the gamut of overwhelming challenges to infant development that distort character in hidden ways and interfere with patients' mobilization of their internal resources. Hopper describes encapsulation

> as a defence against an annihilation anxiety more basic than "paranoid-schizoid anxiety" in which feelings of persecution and feelings of primal depression are completely intertwined and undifferentiated.... [A] person attempts to enclose, encase and to seal-off the sensations, affects and representations associated with it...a sense of "having enclosed" and of "being enclosed."
>
> (2003, pp. 199–200)

Berenstein (1995) underscores the enduring nature of defenses against annihilation in patients who were poorly nurtured:

> It is impossible to live with such anxiety. The mind springs into action to save the child; the defense mechanisms are born. Inevitably, however, the defense mechanisms outlive their value. The child grows older and more competent. He is no longer realistically on the brink of destruction, yet the defenses refuse to die. Not in touch clearly with the real world, the defenses insist that if they are abandoned death will follow. The terror of this possibility gives them continued life at a terrible price; little by little they get in the way of a child's development, isolating him from reality and the warmth of other human beings.
>
> (p. xvii)

Hopper (2003) likens the selves of encapsulated patients to sets of nested Russian dolls that develop in parallel, but not without a price. The encapsulated selves never mature without grotesque distortions and can't help but impoverish life by their limited priorities and overemphasis on safety at any cost. They are, by and large, "ontologically insecure" (Laing, 1959), concerned mainly with survival and preserving the self rather than with fulfillment. These patients are bewildered by the ease with which others develop hobbies, marry well, and spend a fair portion of their leisure time in pursuit of peace, pleasure, and contentment.

Clinicians as a group are largely unaware that vulnerability to fragmentation, shattering, and accumulations of chronic shock disrupt one's capacity for the experience of pleasure across neurological, developmental, and cognitive dimensions (Migdow, 2003). Marilyn, for example, has been preoccupied all her life with themes of survival. She is fascinated by articles, movies, and books about people who have been shipwrecked, set adrift in a lifeboat, left for dead, or lost in the wilderness. The metaphor which best describes her life is one of endlessly treading water, enduring rather than living, hoping against hope that someone would find her before it was too late but not knowing how to ask for help. Ideas of pursuing hobbies and pleasurable offtime are merely quaint notions that don't apply, in the same camp with "wouldn't it be nice if I were a millionaire."

Kinston and Cohen (1986) propose that people who can conceive of wishing for things in the future have experienced need fulfillment in childhood. Patients who have experienced chaotic or impoverished attachment relationships may not only live less fully in the present, but may have difficulty envisioning a better future for themselves (Siegel, 2003). For these individuals, anxiety and a vague sense of dread are omnipresent in the best of times; at the worst of times they are struggling to overcome shock: shocking disappointments, shocking abandonments, shocking betrayals, shocking reversals in health and fortune. The substrate of shock lives in their brains and bodies as a shadow imprint of their earliest experience. Many of the Tuesday group members struggled with meaninglessness and a sense of having come into this world missing something essential. Each of them functioned publicly in the world as if he or she had exceptionally high ego strength, brilliance, generosity of heart, and exceptional self-awareness. Each was privately vulnerable to shattering into mind-freezing terror, social awkwardness, disintegration/fragmentation, catastrophic anxiety, and the desperate question, "What on earth is wrong with me?" What was missing was the psychic skin provided by good-enough mothering.

Omnipotent Protections

The most prominent leitmotif in the Tuesday group pertained to omnipotence: "No one has ever held me all my life. Everything is so much harder for me than for others. I have had to figure out some way to hold myself together, by myself." Bick (1968) first proposed the notion of a "psychic skin" as a projection of, or corresponding to, the bodily skin, which would hold and bind the fragmented mental and emotional components of the personality together:

> [T]he need for a containing object would seem in the infantile unintegrated state to produce a frantic search for an object…which can hold the attention and thereby be experienced, momentarily at least, as holding the parts of the personality together.
>
> (p. 484)

The bodily ego provided by the skin was further described by Anzieu (1989, 1990) as a skin ego and psychic envelope. When parenting is not "good enough," the inchoate psyche experiences insufficient containment, which creates metaphorical holes in the psychic envelope and renders the individual more vulnerable to shattering and fragmentation. Under conditions of failed dependency, disturbances develop in the domain of the psychic skin, and "second skin formations" develop (Bick, 1968) through which dependence on the mother is replaced by pseudo-independence (edgedness) or adhesive relating (Tustin, 1981, 1986, 1990) to create an illusion of omnipotence (Mitrani, 1996, 2001; Mitrani & Mitrani, 1997). Kinston and Cohen (1986) maintain that the failure of need mediation during infancy leads to a "persistent wound," a "gap" in emotional understanding, a "hole" in the fabric of experience: "Hole repair is what psychoanalytic therapy is about" (p. 337).

Mitrani (1996) represents the post-Kleinian perspective that the purpose of second skin formations, encapsulations of vulnerability (like Marilyn's little girl-self), and autistic enclaves (encapsulated self-states which contain not excess vulnerability, but excessive omnipotence), is to provide the vulnerable baby-self with an "omnipotent, omnipresent, and therefore thoroughly reliable mode of safe passage—'bruise-free'—through life, that is, free from madness, psychic pain, and overwhelming anxiety" (p. 96). To escape facing the depth of their vulnerability, contact shunning patients (Hopper, 2003) may paper over the holes in their psychic skin with encrustments such as toughness or gruffness, "crustacean" character armor (Tustin, 1981), intellectuality, over-reliance on rhythmic muscularity such as compulsive weight-lifting and exercise, or addictions. Merger-hungry or "amoeboid" patients (Tustin, 1981) cling onto the surface of another person in a style of pseudo-relating (Mitrani, 1996), using people as interchangeable band aids for as long as they are available to plug the holes within. The cultural phenomenon referred to as serial monogamy by savvy singles is often revealed, in depth psychotherapy, to be more of an attempt to staunch the flow of uncontrollable psychic bleeding with at least someone, however unsuitable, than it is a genuine search for a compatible partner.

Efforts to "hold oneself together" by skin-related self-soothing, called "the autistic/contiguous position" (Ogden, 1989), is a dialectical (transformative) mode of being-in-the-world which complements and interpenetrates with the depressive and paranoid/schizoid modes of being-in-the-world. When operating from the autistic/contiguous position, sensations and other nonverbal dimensions of self–other experience predominate: feelings of enclosure, of moldedness, of rhythm, of edgedness. As the infant develops into an adult capable of thinking about his sensations, terms like soothing, safety, being glued together, able to relax, peaceful, connectedness, cuddling, and merger may eventually become attached to the experiences of enclosure, moldedness, and rhythm. Words like shell, armor, crust, attack, invasion, impenetrability, bunker, and danger relate to sought after experiences of edgedness.

Psychoanalyst Symington (1985) highlights the survival function of omnipotent protections as an effort to plug gaps in the psychic skin through which the self risks spilling out into space, and underscores the dread of endless falling:

> The primitive fear of the state of disintegration underlies the fear of being dependent; that to experience infantile feelings of helplessness brings back echoes of that very early unheld precariousness, and this in turn motivates the patient to hold himself

together...at first a desperate survival measure...gradually...built into the character...the basis on which other omnipotent defense mechanisms are superimposed.

(p. 486)

Mitrani (1996) warns that these omnipotent defense structures are easily mistaken for intentionally destructive resistance and a turning away from the therapist. In actuality, they may be motivated by a will to survive the treatment, but to do so they activate omnipotent defenses to balance their acute vulnerability. Whereas some children of neglect turn to skin-related defenses for insulation and omnipotence, others learn to retreat into their own minds rather than rely on the vagaries of human relationship.

The Mind Object

In the wake of failed dependency, six non-abused members of the Tuesday group turned to their own minds to hold themselves together and ward off the abyss of chronic shock: "I think, therefore I am." Unlike skin-related defenses, the psychic skin of the "mind object" gains omnipotence by repudiating the body and its signals, replacing reliance on the mother with precocious self-reliance (Corrigan & Gordon, 1995). Unfortunately, opportunities for attachment and its vitality affects (spontaneity, sensuality, and pleasure) disappear in the process. "The baby compensates for who is not there by enclosing himself in a mental relationship with himself" (Shabad & Selinger, 1995, p. 228).

Raine, despite the continuous presence of two loving parents throughout her childhood, was chronically overwhelmed at age 2 by their affects of dread and horror as they struggled to parent her desperately ill newborn brother who was not expected to live past three. She remembers trying to make as few demands as possible on them. Her parents, both professors, attempted to master this ordeal by dint of their superior intellectual firepower, and Raine followed their lead. She constricted her emotions, as they did, trying to think her way out of the nightmare. In childhood she suffered from obsessive preoccupations, which manifested in group through perfectionism and a search for answers to an interminable list of questions.

Raine struggled to tolerate "feeling anything"; it seemed to her that everyone else in group was able to open and close the floodgates at will. She desperately feared losing her mind, the only barrier to chaos she had ever known. She spoke breathlessly and rapidly, making frequent jokes about her dread of learning about her inner life. The group was very gentle with Raine, recognizing the extreme vulnerability underlying her apparent self-sufficiency and intellectual aplomb. Her looming abyss of chronic shock was created not by insensitive parenting, but by the inadvertent flooding of her immature neurological system by parental turmoil and dread. She began vehemently rejecting being held after her brother was born, dreading the price of toxic shock she would pick up by osmosis. Her attachment style is anxious/preoccupied, with the tentativeness of a wild fox poised to flee. She and her spouse share an asexual marriage by choice.

Westin, the French-speaker with a bunker, remembers a childhood filled with rage, panic, and confusion as he tried to make sense of his bizarre parents. Once he discovered the soothing logic and predictability of mathematics, he turned permanently away from people, replacing the uncertainty of relationship with the quest for scientific certainty. Like the high-functioning paranoid characters described by McWilliams (1994), he would spend hours after an upsetting group or individual session trying to figure out "what was *really* going on."

Inside the Insecure Attachment

Failures in parental attunement result in shock affects being stored in the body/mind as working models of how to relate to others, resulting in insecure attachment (Solomon & George, 1999). Insecure and, especially, disorganized/disoriented attachment are the characteristic attachment styles of children who experienced chronically mis-attuned, unpredictable, and/or frightening/frightened parenting, along with little or no emotional repair of distress. Trauma doesn't just overload the circuits in some mysterious neurological fashion, but is related to meaning making (Krystal, 1988; Neborsky, 2003; Siegel, 1999). Group therapy is an ideal matrix for the working through of the cumulative trauma that manifests later in life as "fear of breakdown" (Winnicott, 1974). In individuals with no conscious remembered experience of breakdown or abuse, vulnerability to dread and horror affects may point to intergenerational perpetuation of anxiety states (Hesse & Main, 1999), as Raine's group work demonstrates. Repeated entrance into disorganized/disoriented states in infancy, what Hesse and Main term "fright without a solution" (1999, p. 484), may then increase the risk of catastrophic anxiety states, paranoid states, DDNOS, and other manifestations of fear of breakdown in the adult patient, even in the absence of overt trauma history.

Neuroscience now supports Winnicott's long-standing tenet that fear of breakdown may be terror of something that has already been experienced in the past. Hebb (1949) says, "Neurons that fire together, wire together" (cited in Siegel, 1999, p. 26) to form states of mind (Perry, 1999; Siegel, 1999). Fear experiences, especially, are practically indelible (LeDoux, 1994, 1996). *Attachment shock is the implicit memory of chronically uncontained and unrepaired distress in attachment relationships, which accumulates during childhood and manifests throughout life in the form of insecure attachment.* As shock states become increasingly engrained and dissociated, they may evolve from transitory states of mind into encapsulated, specialized sub-selves (Siegel, 1999) *whose purpose is to assist in insulation and recovery from shock.* Even in the absence of overt maltreatment, when parents have unresolved, partially dissociated traumatic anxiety that they transfer to their infants through subtle behavioral and emotional cues, their infants are seemingly unable to develop an organized attachment strategy (Hesse & Main, 1999). Instead, these children develop disorganized internal working models of attachment with multiple, contradictory, and alternating dimensions, along with a vulnerability to catastrophic anxiety states. The simultaneous need for the caregiver, along with fear of the caregiver's own internal states or reactions, disorganizes the infant's ability to seek and accept soothing from the parent as a solution to stress and fear. Thus, even some children who had loving parents (like Raine) may grow up into adults who isolate or insulate, fearing to turn toward others when distressed. In a recent study of children of mothers suffering from anxiety disorders, 65 percent of offspring had disorganized attachment (Manassis et al., 1994). Both terror and shame mechanisms may be involved in these children's developmental trajectories. Raine was so acutely aware of her parents' internal distress that she developed intense shame about her dependency needs as well as chronic dread of impending doom and fragmentation, all of which she camouflaged behind a veneer of jocular intellectuality.

Fragmented Self-esteem and the Fractured Self

I believe Kohut (1971, 1977; Kohut & Wolf, 1978) was approaching the threshold of terror trauma in his observations of traumatized patients who experienced early self–object catastrophe and narcissistic fragmentation. The self disorders that Kohut delineated, involving a central focus on shame and self–object dynamics, represent a slightly different population than the dissociative spectrum autistic/contiguous disorders described in this chapter, whose issues of fracture require a central focus on attachment dynamics and utter terror (with shame dynamics playing an important, but secondary role). Kohut relegated skin-based defenses to the domain of auto-erotic perversion, but his concepts of self–object functioning, narcissistic injury, vertical splitting and emphasis on shame were revolutionary.

Unlike most narcissistic patients, the high-functioning dissociative patient struggling with annihilation anxiety generally does not establish a stable self–object transference, and struggles with encapsulated terror of emotional contact regardless of any apparent idealizing transference. The transference resembles disorganized attachment rather than anxious or avoidant attachment. In addition to craving admiration or emotional connection, dissociative patients also overtly and/or covertly mistrust any situation that requires involving another human being. Empathic connection and interpretation of fragmentation subsequent to empathic failure is a necessary technical intervention, but is nowhere near sufficient for the development of a cohesive self in dissociative patients. Cognitive restructuring of dependency fears (Steele et al., 2001), explicit acknowledgement of vertical splits/ dissociated states and their attendant working models of attachment (Liotti, 2004), and a recognition of the survival function of the dissociated state (Mitrani, 1996) are prerequisites for growth, along with efforts to make sense of emotional turbulence and somatic flashbacks. Dissociative patients learn to work empathically with their own internal self-states, repudiating disavowal and learning to tolerate vulnerability. Interaction in the group supplants interpretation as the medium for change. The potential for multiple transferences within the fertile group environment increases the likelihood of the emergence of self-states that specialize in handling the dangerous and unpredictable.

Kohut recognized two different kinds of self-states: the "fragmented self" and the "depleted self" (1977, p. 243). In so doing, he foreshadowed advances in developmental neurobiology which have identified two phases of traumatization experience: winding up to explosive fragmentation, and shutting down into dissociation. Schore (2004) charges psychoanalytic theoreticians with overlooking and undervaluing the impact of early helplessness, annihilation anxiety, and dissociation in developmental psychopathology. Both overstimulation (prolonged protest) and understimulation (detachment and despair) wreak havoc on the development of right brain structures that underlie the emotional self. He describes two types of disintegration: *explosive* disintegration, characterized by dysregulated sympathetic hyperarousal, a shock-like paralysis in the right brain core self, which I liken to group members' paranoid states and panic attacks and episodic rages; and *implosive* collapse, which manifests in dysregulated parasympathetic hypoarousal, dissociation, withdrawal, and abject depression as manifested in group members' severe anaclitic depressions.

Especially in this latter state, helplessness, hopelessness, and meaninglessness prevail, what Grotstein (1990a, 1990b) calls "the black hole." Black hole despair, which we explore in Chapters 2, 4, and 7, is linked etiologically to the fundamental psychic damage and structural deficits of the "basic fault" (Balint, 1979) due to insufficient parental response to the infant's needs. Splits within the self and a subjective experience of something essential missing inside are characteristic, as are failures in self-regulation and affect integration. The something missing may well be psychic skin. It is probably no accident that Balint was Esther Bick's training analyst, sensitizing her to the prominence of fragmentation and disintegration experience in infants with inadequate parenting. Overstimulation, understimulation and dissociation stemming from failed dependency create an impoverished psychic organization characterized by feelings of "emptiness, being lost, deadness and futility" (Balint, 1979, p. 19): the black hole of chronic shock.

Black Holes and the Basic Fault

Most dissociative defenses encountered in group therapy are attempts to avoid entering the essence of the black hole experience, "an infinite cauldron of pain which annihilates all that enters it" (Hopper, 2003, p. 201). Many patients report that no matter how hard they tried to communicate what they needed to their families, they felt responded to as if they had never tried to communicate at all. Their universe felt arbitrary and randomized. Their efforts to connect meaningfully around their inner experiences failed. Grotstein (1990a) links black hole affect to failed dependency experience: "[T]he experience of randomness *is* [italics added] the traumatic state (the black hole) which can otherwise be thought of as the experience of psychical meaninglessness...ultimate terror of falling into a cosmic abyss" (p. 274). People traumatized by chronic shock speak of randomness and meaninglessness as devastating signifiers of their overwhelming powerlessness.

Proposing a deficit model of psychopathology underscoring the role of environmental failure, Balint (1979) developed the construct of the basic fault to describe an emerging new type of patient, one who could not find his or her place in life due to early failed dependency and excessive helplessness. Balint described the basic fault in the personality very carefully:

> not as a situation, position, conflict or complex.... [I]n geology and crystallography the word fault is used to describe a sudden irregularity in the overall structure, an irregularity which in normal circumstances might lie hidden but, if strains and stresses occur, may lead to a break, disrupting the overall structure.
>
> (p. 21)

As chronic shock accumulates, so do experiences of meaninglessness. The more a youngster experiences himself as unable to forge a meaningful bond with his parents wherein he feels understood and responded to emotionally, the more desperate, alienated, and bereft he feels. Meaninglessness is the link-breaker of connection (Grotstein, 1990a, 1990b) and the doorway to the black hole experience indigenous to the basic fault.

The disintegrative nature of the black hole is a chaotic state of turbulence, an experience of the awesome force of powerlessness, of
defect, of nothingness, of zeroness—expressed not just as a static
emptiness but as an implosive, centripetal pull into the void....

(Grotstein, 1990a, p. 257)

Krista tumbled into the abyss during her first group-as-a-whole silence
(a rare phenomenon in this group). She was the first to break the
silence after about two minutes, by asking some question of another
group member. As the group members explored their reactions to the
silence, she was surprised to hear that others could experience it as a
time to deepen, to self-reflect, to be curious. The silence had followed
an especially profound moment between two group members, which
had stirred up longing and attachment hunger in the rest of the group.
Krista said that any silence was filled with bleak dread and horror,
along with a sinking feeling in her stomach, a consequence of many
silent hours waiting for the police to knock on her door, either bringing
her drunk father home, or announcing his death. She and her mother
had sat in mute apprehension, listening to the clock tick, as another
catastrophe loomed nearer and nearer. Her mother had had no capacity to distract Krista by playing games, talking about her life, or the
like. An only child, Krista's job was to break the silence during the
(almost nightly) long watch, staying up with her mother until dawn,
when her drunken father, the police, or her father's buddies showed up
(with her father slung over their shoulder).

The black hole experience indigenous to the basic fault thus results
from a lifetime of being abandoned, unprotected, confused, oppressed,
or overwhelmed by significant others who cannot relate helpfully to
signals of internal distress. Raine's driven search for answers, Marilyn's
icy detachment, Westin's self-sustaining enclave of omnipotence and
paranoia, Frank's going to the floor, all represent determined efforts to
ward off, or climb out of, the black hole. A colleague once talked about
the basic fault in the following way:

You can tell who came into the world with his parents' blessing,
and who did not. The worst part is, everyone else can tell, too.
No matter how successful someone is, if they are struggling with

the basic fault, they will be certain anything that goes wrong in a relationship is their doing, and they will telegraph this certainty to others, who according to human nature, will almost certainly agree. The abyss is likely at any moment to swallow them up and eradicate their existence.

(S. Sikes, personal communication, 1995)

Chronic shock is the visceral knowing of structural instability and the ever-present danger of fragmentation, the lived experience of the basic fault in patients who had sub-optimal parenting. Chronic shock silently telegraphs its presence via facial expression, postural patterns, gait, voice, muscular rigidity, and other nonverbal communications. Therapy groups provide an invaluable opportunity to connect meaningfully around experiences of black hole despair, chronic shock, and terror of vulnerability, but such topics seldom arise spontaneously (outside of crises) due to dissociative defenses. The high-functioning patient has spent a lifetime containing and concealing disintegration and shattering shock experience, waiting for the safety of solitude to sort out all the feelings. The one exception to this rule is the paranoid state, which may either explode into the group in a rush of sudden consternation, or slip unnoticed into the group initiated by silent shock. Stoeri (2005) speculates that moments of shock and dread erupting into the transference demonstrate the dissociation of the positive transference from the negative. When the positive transference is dissociated, affects inside the insecure attachment can emerge, illuminating the other side of disorganized attachment which is usually inaccessible:

> when ingrained pathological dissociation is operating, each self-state exists in isolation from others and is incompatible with others, so that for any one self-state to express itself, it is as though the others do not exist.

(p. 187)

Such eruptions are quite disconcerting for therapist and group members alike, as they don't make any sense from a historical vantage point, and make all the participants feel crazy. Dissociative patients seldom tumble into the abyss because they put so much energy into preventing trauma from occurring by always anticipating it (Bromberg, 1998). Yet such moments represent a highly sensitive fulcrum for change: either impasse or progress may result. Any previously hard-earned therapeutic insights and self-awareness are temporarily AWOL, as the patient and therapist become caught up in a powerful physio-logical current of shock and dread. The therapist withdraws from the emotional abyss, preferring to "manage" the patient by finding a solu-tion: "It is at such times that an analyst is most inclined to bolster his protective system by selecting his favorite version of the different ways [to] convey to a patient 'it's your problem'" (Bromberg, 1998, p. 24).

Yet the abyss of the treatment crisis creates the therapeutic space to forge new ground. No compromises stand in the way of the patient finally making himself understood in all his vulnerability. The life and death nature of his existence becomes apparent as the patient risks all pretense of safety by coming out into the open. Because he does so against all his better instincts, he believes he is fighting for his life, for its dignity and meaning, even with his back up against the wall and fangs bared. This is the low road of neurological functioning: a road paved with chronic shock.

The "High Road" and the "Low Road"

In group therapy, the multiple, contradictory, and alternating working models of attachment disorganization present clinically as patients capable of swinging rapidly from "high road" to "low road" modes of functioning (LeDoux, 1994, 1996; Siegel & Hartzell, 2003). Low road functioning is initiated by the fear center of the brain, the amyg-dala, and may account for transient paranoid states. The amygdala has limited pattern-assessment skills, and if sensitized by previous trau-matization, it will over-assess innocuous stimuli resembling a previous threat as a current threat. Flooding and an automatic trauma cascade follow in the here and now, triggering dissociated affects, perceptions, behavioral impulses, and bodily sensations with no sense of being recalled from the past:

> Low-mode processing involves the shutting down of the higher processes of the mind and leaves the individual in a state of intense emotions, impulsive reactions, rigid and repetitive responses, and

lacking in self-reflection and the consideration of another's point of view. Involvement of the prefrontal cortex is shut off when one is on the low road.

(Siegel & Hartzell, 2003, p. 156)

It is the prefrontal cortex that supports self-reflection, mindfulness, self-awareness, and intentionality in our communication, even in the face of alarm.

High-functioning dissociative patients like Marilyn, Westin, Frank, Raine, and Krista easily confuse therapists by presenting initially with high ego strength, apparent observing ego, and a solid therapeutic alliance. All were perceptive, psychologically sophisticated, self-reflective, and unusually active group participants, even as new members. Their vulnerability to tumbling precipitously off the high road onto the low road was in no way apparent. The first time Krista tried to share about her life, she began a long fact-laden chronicle of her failed marriage and early childhood. I and other group members attempted to slow her down so that we and she could feel the emotional impact of what she was sharing. She burst into furious tears, and said she wouldn't risk sharing anything for the next several months until she learned to do it "right." I asked about her pain, and again crying, she threatened to quit group if the group couldn't let her share at her own pace. "I'm not ready to trust you—or myself—with feelings yet. I feel like I'm a therapy kindergartner and you are all running a therapy graduate school. You're not respecting my rhythm. I don't know if I can stay in this group." I talked about emotional attunement in infancy, and how babies need to look away sometimes, to be the ones in control of eye contact, else they end up feeling overpowered. She recovered her balance, became animated, and agreed that, yes, I had failed to understand her need to be in control. When she had tried to "look away" by continuing to tell her story in her own way, it felt like I had grabbed her by the chin and forced her to look at me, and herself.

Shock States: Of the Body, Not the Mind

By definition, shock is a jolt, a scare, a startle, a fall, a sudden drop, or a terror reaction; shock can daze, paralyze, stun, or stupefy us. We draw a sharp, deep breath inward and almost stop breathing. The shock of the sudden, the random, in an attachment relationship can have staggering impact. Bollas (1995) describes the devastating impact of the random and unexpected attachment shock that can be triggered by the relatively innocuous occurrence of a parental blowup, *even on the mind psyche of a child with secure attachment*:

> Every child will now and then be shocked by the failure of parental love.... But when a parent is unexpectedly angry with the child...the child's shock may result in what seems like a temporary migration of his soul from his body. This is not a willed action. It feels to the child like a consequent fate, as if the parent has blown the child's soul right out of his body. Each of us has received such an apprenticeship experience in the art of dying. We know what it is like for the soul to depart the body even though we have as yet no knowledge of actual death.... Each adult who has had "good enough parenting" will have a psychic sense of a kind of migration of the soul, sometimes shocked out of the body but always returning. This cycle of shocking exit, emptiness, and return gives us our confidence, so that even when we are deeply disturbed by traumatic events...we feel that somehow "it will turn out all right in the end."
>
> (p. 215)

In his metaphor "migration of the soul," Bollas pays homage to the dense physicality of shock experience, what mind/body therapists refer to as disembodiment and traumatologists as dissociation. Chronic shock response takes its toll on the nervous system and musculature of infants who are stressed, leading eventually to dissociation (Aposhyan, 2004; Porges, 1997). We now know from neurobiology that dissociation "is a consequence of a 'psychological shock' or prolonged high arousal," according to Meares (as cited in Schore, 2003a, p. 214). If even occasional shock states under conditions of secure attachment are shattering, what impact might repetitive shock states have even on the non-abused developing child who grows up with less than optimal parenting? What happens when attempts to soothe are non-existent, and experience teaches that things will not turn out all right in the end? Schore's 2003 two-volume opus on affect dysregulation makes the case for the cumulative trauma of neglect and early relational stress within caregiving relationships being powerful variants of childhood PTSD (Schore, 2003a, 2003b). Infants adapting to being handled instead of being securely held and understood develop "cephalic shock" syndrome (Lewis, 1983/2004) in the body/mind. They are thrown back on their own immature nervous systems to maintain balance and homeostasis, being unable to relax into their parents' embrace. Chronic muscular stiffness (especially in the neck and shoulders), CNS hyperarousal, and visceral tension are the result. Such ambient attachment trauma interferes with brain development and the functioning of biological stress systems, and contributes to dissociation as a preferred defense strategy, even if no formal abuse occurred during childhood.

When traumatic mental states become ingrained in the body/mind by repetition, they become more and more likely to re-occur (Hebb, 1949). Psychopathology at this level occurs first at the level of the body, before reaching the mind. Shock initiates a low road experience unless the patient has learned to work with the physiological overwhelm. The cortex strains to make sense of the urgent danger signals fired from the amygdala, along pathways of implicit memory. Aposhyan (2004) notes the far-reaching effects of shock experience from neglect on all the body systems of traumatized patients, including disembodiment (dissociation) and rigidity of skeletal, endocrine, muscular, and breathing structures:

> There can be agitation or frozen stillness in all the other body systems as a result of lingering shock. Generally the autonomic nervous system has to find its regulatory balance first, and then the muscles or the fluids can begin to release their shock and move back into full participation in life.... By educating clients to track their states, they can come to recognize a state of relative presence and embodiment in contrast to the static or fog of even mild shock states.
>
> (p. 254)

In a series of drawings, Keleman (1985) graphically depicts a continuum of physical adaptations to shock states which eventually result in somatic patterns affecting breathing, muscular bracing, postural rigidity and/or collapse, vitality, and muscle tone:

> These somatic patterns are processes of deep self-perception—a way of feeling and knowing the world. They are more than mechanical. They are a form of intelligence, a continuum of self-regulation.... Muscles and organs are not just contracted, they are organized into a configuration. These organizations become the way we recognize the world as well as ourselves, and in turn, they become the way the world recognizes us.
>
> (p. 75)

Group therapists are in a unique position to observe the physiological indicators of shock experience in their traumatized patients, as multiple and contradictory models of how the world works flicker across the landscape of group psychotherapy. "These models can shift rapidly outside of awareness, sometimes creating abrupt transitions in states of mind and interactions with others" (Siegel, 1999, p. 34). Shifts in voice, posture, bracing, and rigidity are regulated via implicit memory. Cognitive science suggests: "implicit processing may be particularly relevant to the quick and automatic handling of nonverbal affective cues" (Lyons-Ruth, 1999, p. 587). The superfast, supercharged early physiological warning signals of alarm, bracing the body for shock, may well initiate the transitory paranoid state shifts and low road functioning we so often encounter in group work. The paranoid states which occur during group psychotherapy are easily and frequently triggered by innocuous interactions, but since they occur primarily on a nonverbal level, neither patient nor therapist typically recognizes the phenomenon while it is occurring unless the patient blasts into an irrational rage.

Far more frequently, however, the patient will quietly "freeze," suppressing awareness and exploration of his bodily cues, and the opportunity for intervention may pass. Having spent a lifetime quietly enduring periods of primitive affect, hoping against hope to keep the crazy feelings from showing, high-functioning dissociative patients often successfully mask full-blown threat reactions unless directly asked about them, and even then frequently disavow their inner experiences.

Thoughts accompanying the threat reaction tend to be somewhat unrealistic, inaccurate, and concrete: "My body is screaming danger, danger!" Paranoid, aggressive, and withdrawn self-states may become even more rigid and inflexible with each repetition, until the therapist catches on and actively intervenes to help the patient down-regulate.

Porges (2004) has proposed the existence of a polyvagal theory of an integrated neurological social engagement system, and coined the term "neuroception" to denote how neural circuits distinguish whether situations or people are safe or dangerous. His polyvagal model encompasses a hierarchy of autonomic states: social engagement, fight/flight, or freeze.

> Faulty neuroception—that is, an inaccurate assessment of the safety or danger of a situation—might contribute to the maladaptive physiological reactivity and the expression of defensive behaviors..... When our nervous system detects safety, our metabolic demands adjust. Stress responses that are associated with fight and flight, such as increases in heart rate and cortisol mediated by the sympathetic nervous system and hypothalamic-pituitary-adrenal axis, are dampened. Similarly, a neuroception of safety keeps us from entering physiological states that are characterized by massive drops in blood pressure and heart rate, fainting, and apnea—states that would support "freezing" and "shutdown" behaviors.... Specific areas of the brain detect and evaluate features, such as body and face movements and vocalizations that contribute to an impression of safety or trustworthiness.
>
> (p. 4)

Groups clearly provide an ideal matrix for exploring interpersonal as well as intrapsychic terrors. Without being dependent on conscious awareness, the nervous system then evaluates risk in the group and regulates physiological states accordingly. A group member's ability to recognize and contain affects, ask for emotional repair, and engage in self-exploration, depends somewhat on his or her ability to activate the social engagement system, which inhibits defensive maneuvers of aggression and withdrawal, and allows the involvement of cortical functions which promote empathy, introspection, and relationship.

Aposhyan (2004) notes that both sympathetic and parasympathetic shock states may fluctuate from moment to moment or get frozen into an ongoing state over time. Such fluctuations or body/mind frozen paralysis may well contribute to instances of impasse in group psychotherapy. Repeated experiences of emotional repair facilitate the gradual development of secure attachment. Thus, enactments of terror and attachment danger followed by resolution may be critical factors in some group members' ability to eventually tolerate and process overwhelming body experiences of chronic shock and mistrust. Low road functioning, as every marital therapist knows, is typically triggered by relatively innocuous interactions. Primitive affect is less likely to be inhibited in the marital relationship than in the group, where withdrawal into invisibility is a venue of escape. As Westin put it: "I just hoped no one noticed I was feeling nuts, everything was going too fast and I just didn't trust the group to be able to handle me well."

Earned Secure Attachment

The resolution of successful psychotherapy can result in the patient and therapist/group creating an "earned secure attachment" (Pearson et al., 1994). As we have seen, issues of chronic shock and insecure or disorganized attachment often go unaddressed in therapy, with resultant impasse or therapeutic failure when therapists lack either the technical or theoretical skills to overcome the patients' resistance to experiencing the dissociated feelings inside their insecure attachment. Lewis et al. (2000), Stern (2004), Siegel (1999), Beebe and Lachmann (2002), and many others represent the breaking wave of clinicians striving to integrate attachment theory, interpersonal neurobiology, and relational perspectives. They emphasize the power of presymbolic and implicit forms of relatedness in psychotherapy, believing that the mind can update its maps of relatedness. The group therapist working with chronic shock must closely track the complex *meanings* that patients attribute to interactions, often meanings that are not readily apparent or traceable by the normal routes to unconscious communications. Therapists may even need to listen to dream language with a slightly different ear when they work with traumatized patients, scanning for encapsulation as well as conflict.

Attachment therapists tell us that psychoanalytically oriented therapists have been looking in all the wrong places to understand the enactments of preverbal primitive states that occur in certain patients, since early memories are encoded in preverbal form and not in narrative memory (Lewis, 1995; Lyons-Ruth, 1999). We have tended to look for, expect, and find the traditional psychoanalytic themes, words, symbols, and fantasies rather than listen for the physiological responses, behaviors, bodily states, and affects that are prodromal indicators of catastrophic anxiety and fear of breakdown: "Note that the system that underlies psychotherapeutic change is in the nonverbal right as opposed to the verbal left hemisphere. The right hemisphere, the biological substrate of the human unconscious, is also the locus of the emotional self" (Schore, 2003b, p. 147).

Group therapy with traumatized patients thus requires the group to monitor closely its members' bodily states, potential dissociative communications, and working models of attachment. "Interactiveness is emergent, in a constant process of potential reorganization" (Beebe & Lachmann, 2002, p. 224). Anzieu (1999) describes the development of a "group ego-skin" as a function of group-as-a-whole processes. As group members observed Marilyn and others bring fury, shattering, and longing to the table, *without meeting retaliation or distancing in the here and now*, they became more willing to take such risks themselves. Interaction—primarily confrontation, body-centered observations, affective attunement, and engagement—gradually moved into the limelight as the group's therapeutic strategies with me and one another, displacing but not altogether dislodging interpretation and the exploration of fantasies and dreams. Successful group psychotherapy with traumatized patients "may be viewed as a long-term rebuilding and restructuring of the memories and emotional responses that have been embedded in the limbic system" (Andreasen, 2001, p. 314), as the group itself grows a psychic skin capable of containment.

High-functioning DDNOS: A Workable Population

Hopper's work (2003) on failed dependency focuses upon "the difficult patient" in group therapy, presumably involving the severely characterological dissociative patient: a very different population from the Tuesday group. As illustrated in this chapter, high-functioning dissociative patients are potentially much more workable than they initially seem, lapsing into constricted role behavior and primitive functioning only during times of stress when encapsulated affects are stirred up. The key that helps unlock these patients may lie in therapeutic attunement with dissociated affects and attachment struggles. Psychoanalysts Beebe and Lachmann (2002) place nonverbal and presymbolic forms of relatedness in the foreground of work with difficult patients; the verbal, symbolic, and transference aspects of their treatment remain more in the background. Interpretation is therefore less helpful than interaction.

Marilyn, Frank, Paul, Westin, and Bernie, for example, metamorphosed from challenging patients into easy patients to understand and work with, once I understood I was dealing with second skin formations and encapsulations. Frank initially presented as a schizoid with alexithymia, which is highly associated with dissociation (Grabe et al., 2000). Yet Frank was able to access his walled-off feelings when emotional flashbacks were triggered physiologically; he treasured these moments of anguish because during them he felt alive—senses flaring, tears flowing. His access to affect was constrained by a hitherto unconscious template operating behind the scenes to shape his present, a template of absent opportunity, what Stern (2004) terms the "nonexistent past." He used to believe he had never suffered, because he had never experienced an opportunity to be listened to. Despite his exposure to intense suffering by his parents, both their suffering and his reactions were snuffed out before they could be acknowledged.

Paul looked like a tough nut to crack, with his paranoid personality, bleak cynicism, constant black humor and intermittent explosive behavior, until his vulnerable self-states became accessible in group. His tough psychic skin belied his tender heart, vulnerability to shattering, helpless fury, and hidden terror. Westin appeared to be schizoid, passive-aggressive, and narcissistic until I stumbled upon speaking to him in French. I was then able to access the fragile self that was utterly terrified of being annihilated. Another self-state predictably appeared who was desperate to find a mother. As he worked through terror and yearning, he entered many periods of compartmentalized paranoid transference which required sensitive handling. Ultimately Westin himself began to experience these feelings from the perspective of an adult, and he worked through the anaclitic depression which lay underneath his terror. Bernie initially presented as a perplexing inadequate personality with unusual strengths. His long-term analyst feared he was recalcitrant to therapy but referred him to group anyway. He had always silently struggled with three distinct emotional self-states: the brilliant, detached surgeon who was charming and successful, alongside both a cold, furious Machiavellian state who was ruthless and manipulative, and a regressive state in which he would tolerate any abuse from a woman if she just let him stay near her sometimes and please her. He could sob incoherently for hours or days if he thought one of these women was pulling away slightly or was displeased with him, insisting he must have been a "bad, bad, bad boy." Within months of diagnosis of his covert ego states, his therapeutic progress accelerated exponentially.

Unlike traditional character pathology, which typically presents as a Gordian knot requiring long years of painstaking untying before any progress is apparent, the undoing of these quietly persistent "pathological organizations" (Mitrani, 1996) pivots around a therapist's ability to teach the group and its members to recognize, identify, elicit, and resonate with the unbearable affects that were split off into defended self-states. All these patients had the motivation and introspective capacity necessary to monitor shifts in their age perspective, body sensations, and thinking patterns, which facilitated their capacity to self-soothe. Goldman (2000) presents a model for teaching patients to override amygdala-centered fear-conditioning, teaching them that shock states are modifiable although not extinguishable. "Patients develop a sense of acceptance and inevitability rather than finding themselves constantly unprepared and terrorized" (p. 707). Frank, Marilyn, Paul, Westin, and Bernie, for example, rapidly mastered the ability to notice when they were sliding down into the low road, using self-talk and what they knew about themselves to make sense of the trauma cascades reverberating throughout their body-selves and learning to recognize when they were beginning to feel "young." As a result, Frank was increasingly able to embrace his feelings, shedding the skins of empty intellectualism and formality. Paul, Westin, and Marilyn learned to stop paranoid states before shattering, replacing certainty of danger with curiosity about apprehension. Westin and Bernie were able to learn how to calm down from panic attacks, to reassure themselves about reality instead of running wild with fantasy, to stay in the present instead of regressing to the past, and to stop obsequious clinging to destructive or uninterested love objects, once they discovered the magical incantations "It's only a memory" and "Is this an adult or a child-like perspective?"

Personal Comments on a Paradigm Shift

My own group training taught me to not work harder in group than a patient does. I was thus horrified when I realized that by following this precept, I had been re-traumatizing Marilyn instead of facilitating her growth. I confused her genuine needs for attachment bonding with wishes that I pander to her. While frustration of wishes may promote growth, frustration of needs results in structural disintegration of the self (Akhtar, 1999).

Siegel's work (1999, 2003) on the nascent sense of self suggests that it is in mind-to-mind emotional resonance that we learn who we are, how to feel, and how to regulate how we feel. A therapist's inability or unwillingness to establish mind-to-mind resonance collapses the intersubjective space between patient and therapist/group and renders the patient at the mercy of the therapist/group's feelings, defenses, and projections. In this situation the terrified patient does not exist in his own right as a person to be consulted, or made amends to, but rather just as a problem to be "managed" however the therapist/group sees fit. I had "managed" Marilyn by ascribing the gross discrepancy between her emotional availability with her therapist (and other group members) and myself to hostile dependency and defensive extraction processes. Marilyn's dream helped me to become more accurately attuned to her inner world. "The first part of emotional healing is being limbically known—having someone with a keen ear catch your melodic essence" (Lewis et al., 2000, p. 170).

Bowman and Chu (2000) suggest that trauma is the fourth paradigm for understanding psychopathology, interweaving with psychodynamics, behaviorism, and neurobiology. "Until psychological trauma—especially devastating trauma occurring early in life—is incorporated into the other three paradigms of mental illness, a 'unified field theory' of mental health will elude us" (p. 10). The recent confluence of psychoanalytic cross-fertilization with fields of traumatology, dissociation, attachment theory, neuropsychoanalysis, developmental psychopathology, and interpersonal neurobiology nurtured my interest in integrative thinking.

In the months leading up to Marilyn's dream I had fortunately been teaching the concepts of chronic shock, black holes, the cumulative trauma of failed dependency, attachment trauma, encapsulation, and dissociation to other clinicians. Throughout the previous two decades I had trained extensively with psychoanalytic trauma specialists in areas of DDNOS and DID. I had taught workshops on dissociative character and dissociation in groups for many years. Yet before Marilyn's dream, I had not adapted my general group psychotherapy practice to accommodate these broader integrative perspectives unless patients reported abuse. I pay homage to Mitrani (1996, 2001), Mitrani and Mitrani (1997), and Hopper (2003) for opening my eyes to the more subtle variants of encapsulation and autistic enclaves in patients who both crave and repudiate intimacy. A well-known truism in medicine is: "If you don't at least look for it, you certainly won't find it." Fortunately, several of us collaborating in an outpatient treatment team had experience working with more florid dissociative spectrum patients, which helped prepare us to recognize the more subtle encapsulation processes evident in the Tuesday group. A caveat: the clinical or sub-clinical DDNOS patient first and foremost needs access to the secure base of an individual therapist in order to be able to endure and work through the rigors of faulty neuroception and its aftermath within the group.

"Posttraumatic growth" (Tedeschi & Calhoun, 1995) is a relatively new concept that addresses the inherent potential of suffering to catalyze spiritual, emotional, and interpersonal growth. Emerging from work with bereavement and disaster victims, their model stresses numerous opportunities for resilience provided by crises of heart and spirit: potential for improved relationships, creative destruction of constricted barriers to vitality, a greater appreciation for life, enhanced sense of personal strengths, and spiritual deepening. My experience in the Tuesday group has taught me that working through the chronic shock of cumulative attachment trauma is no less effective an incubator of growth.

Acknowledgment

This chapter has been taken from K. Adams, Falling forever: The price of chronic shock. *International Journal of Group Psychotherapy* (2006). Reprinted with the kind permission of Taylor & Francis Ltd, www.tandfontline.com on behalf of the American Group Psychotherapy Association.

References

Adams, K. (2006). Falling forever: The price of chronic shock. International Journal of Group Psychotherapy, 56(2), 127–72.

Akhtar, S. (1999). The distinction between needs and wishes: Implications for psychoanalytic theory and technique. *Journal of the American Psychoanalytic Association, 47*, 113–51.

Andreason, N. (2001). *Brave new brain.* Oxford University Press.

Anzieu, D. (1989). *The skin ego.* Yale University Press.

Anzieu, D. (1990). *Psychic envelopes.* Karnac.

Anzieu, D. (1999). The group ego-skin. *Group Analysis, 32*, 319–29.

Aposhyan, S. (2004). *Body mind psychotherapy: Principles, techniques, and practical applications.* Norton Press.

Attias, R., & Goodwin, J. (1999). *A place to begin: Images of the body in transformation.* In J. Goodwin & R. Attias (Eds.), *Splintered reflections* (pp. 39–66). Basic Books.

Balint, M. (1979). *The basic fault: Therapeutic aspects of regression.* Brunner/Mazel. (Original work published 1968).

Beebe, B., & Lachmann, F. (2002). *Infant research and adult treatment.* The Analytic Press.

Berenstein, R. (1995). *Lost boys: Reflections on psychoanalysis and counter-transference.* Norton Press.

Bick, E. (1968). The experience of the skin in early object-relations. *International Journal of Psychoanalysis, 49*, 484–6.

Blizard, R. (2003). Disorganized attachment, development of dissociative self states, and a relational approach to treatment. *Journal of Trauma and Dissociation, 4*, 27–50.

Bollas, C. (1995). *Cracking up: The work of unconscious experience.* Hill and Wang.

Bowman, E., & Chu, J. (2000). Trauma: A fourth paradigm for the third millennium. *Journal of Trauma and Dissociation, 1*(2), 1–12.

Bromberg, P. (1998). *Standing in the spaces: Clinical process, trauma, and dissociation.* The Analytic Press.

Corrigan, E. G., & Gordon, P. E. (1995). *The mind object.* Jason Aronson.

Goldman, D. S. (2000). Application of LeDoux's neurobiological findings in treating anxiety disorders. *Journal of The Academy of Psychoanalysis,* 28, 701–16.

Goodwin, J., & Attias, R. (1999a). *Conversations with the body: Psychotherapeutic approaches to body image and body ego.* In J. Goodwin & R. Attias (Eds.), *Splintered reflections* (pp. 167–82). Basic Books.

Goodwin, J., & Attias, R. (1999b). *Traumatic disruption of bodily experience and memory.* In J. Goodwin & R. Attias (Eds.), *Splintered reflections* (pp. 223–38). Basic Books.

Grabe, H., Rainermann, S., Spitzer, C., Gaensicke, M., & Freyberger, H. (2000). The relationship between dimensions of alexithymia and dissociation. *Psychotherapy & Psychosomatics,* 69, 128–31.

Grotstein, J. (1990a). Nothingness, meaninglessness, chaos, and the "black hole," Part I. *Contemporary Psychoanalysis,* 26, 257–90.

Grotstein, J. (1990b). Nothingness, meaninglessness, chaos, and the "black hole," Part II. *Contemporary Psychoanalysis,* 26, 377–407.

Hebb, D. O. (1949). *The organization of behavior: A neuropsychological theory.* Wiley.

Hesse, E., & Main, M. (1999). Second-generation effects of unresolved trauma in nonmaltreating parents: Dissociated, frightened, and threatening parental behavior. *Psychoanalytic Inquiry,* 19(4), 481–540.

Hopper, E. (2003). *Traumatic experience in the unconscious life of groups: The fourth basic assumption: Incohesion: Aggregation/massification or (ba) 1: A/M.* Jessica Kingsley Publishers.

Keleman, S. (1985). *Emotional anatomy: The structure of experience.* Center Press.

Khan, M. (1974). *The privacy of the self.* International Universities Press.

Kinston, W., & Cohen J. (1986). Primal repression: Clinical and theoretical aspects. *International Journal of Psychoanalysis,* 67, 337–55.

Kohut, H. (1971). *The analysis of the self: A systematic approach to the psychoanalytic treatment of narcissistic personality disorders.* International Universities Press.

Kohut, H. (1977). *The restoration of the self.* International Universities Press.

Kohut, H., & Wolf, E. (1978). The disorders of the self and their treatment. *International Journal of Psychoanalysis,* 59, 414–25.

Krystal, H. (1988). *Integration and self healing.* The Analytic Press.

Laing, R. D. (1959). *The divided self.* Penguin.

LeDoux, J. E. (1994). Emotion, memory, and the brain. *Scientific American,* 270(6), 50–7.

LeDoux, J. E. (1996). *The emotional brain: The mysterious underpinnings of emotional life.* Simon & Schuster.

Lewis, M. (1995). Memory and psychoanalysis: A new look at infantile amnesia and transference. *Journal of the American Academy of Child & Adolescent Psychiatry,* 34, 405–17.

Lewis, R. (1983/2004). Cephalic shock as a somatic link to the false self personality. Available at: https://www.yumpu.com/en/document/read/11428826/cephalic-shock-as-a-somatic-link-to-the-false-self-personality.

Lewis, T., Amini, F., & Lannon, R. (2000). *A general theory of love.* Random House.

Liotti, G. (2004). Trauma, dissociation, and disorganized attachment: Three strands of a single braid. *Psychotherapy: Theory, Research, Practice, Training,* 4, 472–86.

Lyons-Ruth, K. (1999). Two-person unconscious: Intersubjective dialogue, enactive relational representation, and the emergence of new forms of relational organization. *Psychoanalytic Inquiry,* 19, 576–617.

Manassis, K., Bradley, S., Goldberg, S., Hood, J., & Swinson, R. P. (1994). Attachment and teacher-reported behavior problems during the preschool and early school-age period. *Development & Psychopathology,* 8, 511–25.

McWilliams, N. (1994). *Psychoanalytic diagnosis: Understanding personality structure in the clinical process.* Guilford Press.

Migdow, J. (2003). The problem with pleasure. *Journal of Trauma and Dissociation,* 4, 5–25.

Mitrani, J. L. (1996). *A framework for the imaginary.* Jason Aronson.

Mitrani, J. L. (2001). *Ordinary people and extra-ordinary protections: A post-Kleinian approach to the treatment of primitive mental states.* Taylor and Francis.

Mitrani, J. L., & Mitrani, T. (1997). *Encounters with autistic states.* Jason Aronson.

Myers, C. (1940). *Shell shock in France 1914–18.* Cambridge University Press.

Neborsky, R. A. (2003). Clinical model for the comprehensive treatment of trauma using an affect experiencing-attachment theory approach. In M. F. Solomon & D. J. Siegel (Eds.), *Healing trauma: Attachment, mind, body and brain* (pp. 282–321). Norton.

Nijenhuis, E. R. (2004). *Somatoform dissociation: Phenomena, measurement and theoretical issues.* Norton and Co.

Nijenhuis, E. R., & van der Hart, O. (1999). Forgetting and reexperiencing trauma: From anesthesia to pain. In J. Goodwin & R. Attias (Eds.), *Splintered reflections* (pp. 39–66). Basic Books.

Ogden, T. H. (1989). *The primitive edge of experience.* Jason Aronson.

Pearson, J., Cohn, D., Cowan, P., & Cowan, C. (1994). Earned and continuous security in adult attachment: Relation to depressive symptomatology and poverty style. *Development and Psychopathology,* 6, 259–373.

Perry, B. D. (1999). The memories of states: How the brain stores and retrieves traumatic experience. In J. Goodwin & R. Attias (Eds.), *Splintered reflections* (pp. 9–38). Basic Books.

Porges, S. W. (1997). Emotion: An evolutionary by-product of the neural regulation of the autonomic nervous system, *Annals of the New York Academy of Sciences,* 807, 62–77.

Porges, S. W. (2004). Neuroception: A subconscious system for detecting threats and safety. *Zero to Three,* 32, 19–24.

Scaer, R. C. (2001). *The body bears the burden: Trauma, dissociation, and disease.* Haworth Press.

Schore, A. (2003a). *Affect regulation & the repair of the self.* Norton.

Schore, A. (2003b). *Affect dysregulation & disorders of the self.* Norton.

Schore, A. (2004). Advances in neuropsychoanalysis, attachment theory, and trauma. Research: Implications for self-psychology. *All about Psychotherapy: The Online Resource for Psychotherapy,* October 12, pp. 1–35.

Shabad, P., & Selinger, S. (1995). Bracing for disappointment and the counterphobic leap into the future. In Corrigan, E. & Gordon, P. (Eds.), *The mind object: Precocity and pathology of self-sufficiency* (pp. 209–28). Jason Aronson.

Siegel, D. J. (1999). *The developing mind.* Guilford Press.

Siegel, D. J. (2003). An interpersonal neurobiology of psychotherapy: The developing mind and the resolution of trauma. In M. F. Solomon & D. J. Siegel (Eds.), *Healing trauma: Attachment, mind, body and brain* (pp. 1–56). Norton.

Siegel, D. J., & Hartzell, M. (2003). *Parenting from the inside out: How a deeper self-understanding can help you raise children who thrive.* Jeremy P. Tarcher/Putnam.

Sinason, V. (1999). Challenged bodies, wounded body images: Richard III and Hephaestus. In J. Goodwin & R. Attias (Eds.), *Splintered reflections* (pp. 183–94). Basic Books.

Solomon, J., & George, C. (1999). The place of disorganization in attachment theory: Linking classic observations with contemporary findings. In J. Solomon & C. George (Eds.), *Attachment disorganization* (pp. 3–32). The Guilford Press.

Steele, K., van der Hart, O., & Nijenhuis, E. (2001). Dependency in the treatment of complex posttraumatic stress disorder and dissociative disorders. *Journal of Trauma and Dissociation,* 2, 79–116.

Stern, D. (2004). *The present moment.* Norton Press.

Stoeri, J. (2005). Surprise, shock and dread, and the nature of therapeutic action. *Contemporary Psychoanalysis,* 41(2), 183–202.

Symington, J. (1985). The survival function of primitive omnipotence. *International Journal of Psychoanalysis,* 66, 481–8.

Tedeschi, R., & Calhoun, L. (1995). *Trauma and transformation: Growing in the aftermath of suffering.* Sage Publications.

Tronick, E. (1989). Emotions and emotional communication in infants. *American Psychologist, 44,* 112–19.

Tronick, E., & Weinberg, M. (1997). Depressed mothers and infants: Failure to form dyadic states of consciousness. In L. Murray & P. Cooper (Eds.), *Postpartum depression and child development* (pp. 54–81). Guilford Press.

Tustin, F. (1981). *Autistic states in children.* Routledge and Kegan Paul.

Tustin, F. (1986). *Autistic barriers in neurotic patients.* Karnac Books.

Tustin, F. (1990). *The protective shell in children and adults.* Karnac Books.

Winnicott, D. W. (1974). Fear of breakdown. *International Review of PsychoAnalysis,* 1, 103–7.

Chapter 7

The Abject Self
Self-states of Relentless Despair

Sarah drags in 30 minutes late for group. She freezes outside the group perimeter, hovering anxiously as if to beseech the group's permission to enter. Arms wrapped around an enormous tote bag, she imagines herself as a hermit crab, toting her security around with her. She has been repeatedly late to group recently. The group knows she is being harassed by her boss and dares not leave the office with work unfinished. Still, her hovering is annoying. She is a seasoned group member and knows the ropes of group protocol. I bite back two competing urges: to snap at her to sit down already, and to smile in welcome. Doing neither, I ignore her, until someone else growls in exasperation: "For God's sake sit down." Sarah flinches and whines piteously that she hadn't wanted to interrupt what was obviously an important conversation. She adds that she wasn't sure whether she should come in or slip away. As she creeps into her seat, she whispers "Please don't look at me, I'm trying to be invisible." Someone quips "You couldn't have found a more effective way to bring everything to a halt than to make a big scene." Sinking more deeply into a slump, she murmurs "I was so looking forward to being here, I'm really sorry." Within a few moments, Sarah had recovered her aplomb and launched into the back-and-forth of the group process, seamlessly inserting herself into the fray. Most of the time she presents with a beguiling smile, a rapier wit, and wicked repartee, yet her alter-ego resembles a timid, confused young girl who expects to be rejected, speaks in a mumbling whisper and inspires contempt. The group has just witnessed Sarah in a moment of self-abjection, a form of diffuse, unformulated enactment of dissociated traumatic affects that can be baffling.

DOI: 10.4324/9781003262367-10

Sarah had a foot in two worlds. One part of her was able to negotiate conflicts with her siblings, colleagues, clients, and many close friends as well as within therapy settings. A second, less well-functioning side of her would emerge periodically at moments of embarrassment, yearning, and acute vulnerability. During these episodes Sarah would present in a self-state which was markedly tremulous, browbeaten and collapsed. Sarah's description of her self-states is "side-by-side" co-existence of two selves. Sarah is a high-functioning dissociative patient who can be triggered into "low-road" functioning (Siegel, 1999). When she loses her typical self-possession, she feels young, whispers, and becomes frozen in dread and uncertainty. Dissociative defenses are easily mistaken for resistance and character pathology (Adams, 2006; Hegeman & Wohl, 2000). While many such patients present with a history of abuse, others grew up under conditions of chaotic attachment and emotional neglect; recent findings from developmental psychology underscore the prevalence of subclinical dissociation in these populations (Adams, 2006; Bromberg, 2009; Liotti, 2004).

Despite the existence of an apparently strong therapeutic alliance, aspects of attachment disorganization (Solomon & George, 1999) and dissociative defenses may complicate the course of group and individual treatment. Many therapists are unaware that their groups may contain a fair number of mildly dissociative patients, since even severe dissociative defenses rarely manifest clearly until many years into treatment.

Low-road functioning is initiated by the fear center of the brain, the amygdala. According to Le Doux (2002) "…different components of the self reflect the operation of different brain systems, which can be, but are not always, in sync…allowing for many aspects of the self to co-exist" (p. 310). Therapists may frame enactments of preverbal primitive states as signs of conflict, character disorder, untreatability, and/or masochism, but if we view the enactment through the lens of traumatic attachment theory, therapeutic attention to preverbal trauma, contingent communication, attachment disorganization, and dissociation may be more helpful. Early overwhelming experiences are encoded in preverbal form as procedural memory and not in narrative memory (Siegel, 1999) and thus are likely to be enacted before they can be metabolized and explored by the conscious self.

The notion of self-states is gaining purchase in many psychotherapy circles with the confluence of perspectives from traumatic attachment theory, interpersonal neurobiology, affect regulation science, and relational and neo-Kleinian psychoanalysis. Self-states are a form of self-organization which recur over time, involve a core affect or collection of related affects, a sense of identity, "somatic sensibilities" (Chefetz & Bromberg, 2004), cognitive patterns including a view of how the world works (internal working models), and somatic patterns which affect breathing, muscular bracing, postural rigidity and/or collapse, and muscle tone (Aposhyan, 2004; Keleman, 1985).

Abject States: Not Just Sadomasochism

In her opus on the powers of horror, Kristeva (1982) delineates a realm of preverbal experience permeated by affects of meaninglessness, dread, and horror. Her constructs of abject states and self-abjection are complex amalgams of identity, attachment disorganization, affect, and enactment.

Although Kristeva's conceptualizations are no doubt highly relevant to the treatment of borderline spectrum patients, in this chapter I hope to facilitate the recognition, understanding, and management of abject self-states as they manifest in high-functioning individuals who bring this complex material into their group psychotherapy settings. Self-abjection in these individuals only superficially resembles the behavior of the masochistic character. Defining hallmarks of masochism such as self-defeating behavior, passivity and martyrdom, inability to empathize or make partial identifications (Holmes, 2009), moral masochism, denial, and idealization are largely absent in this population whose overall character structure is more depressive and dissociative than masochistic or narcissistic. Whereas the masochist suffers to gain nurture, the abject self suffers in the certain knowledge that they are beyond help.

Therapeutic technique with masochists prioritizes tactful confrontation over empathy, but effective therapeutic technique with abject self-states is more like that with depressives: "The predominantly depressive person needs above all else to learn that the therapist will not judge, reject or abandon, …and will be particularly available when he or she is suffering" (McWilliams, 1994, pp. 275–6).

Individuals like Sarah who grew up under conditions of intermittent chaos and intrusion develop attachment strategies that disorganize under stress. The younger a person is when flooded with disintegrative affects, the more likely they will fail to integrate attachment strategies (Liotti, 2004) and will manifest dissociative features. The more a young child is unable to forge a meaningful and consistent bond with his or her parents the more desperate, alienated, bereft, and *abject* they are likely to feel. Sarah is not particularly masochistic, borderline, or manipulative. She is aware of others' needs and is emotionally responsive to them. She is not plagued with abandonment anxieties nor filled with sadistic rage toward herself or others. Rather, like many others in this chapter, she regresses to a wordless domain filled with the preverbal certainty of catastrophic annihilation. The patient in an abject state writhes outside the perimeter of safety in affects of horror, isolation, and dread that are fully embodied (Chefetz & Bromberg, 2004). At such moments, no safe base exists.

When the abject self is present, the patient simultaneously pleads for connection yet abrogates intimacy; all that is life-enhancing is perceived to be in the Other, for the abject self was overwhelmed or emptied out, by active violations or terrorization early in life (Bollas, 1987). Under stress, the patient's abject self stills in apprehension and falls into silent misery, oscillating between staring with longing at the unattainable object of safety and turning away, gazing off or down. During these enactments, therapists frequently experience countertransference feelings of aversion, exasperation, helplessness, or contempt. These complementary countertransference reactions may represent the patient's projective identification of internalizations of the original rejecting caregivers. The patient's acute vulnerability and dependency may also trigger idiopathic reactions in the therapist based on the therapist's comfort with primitive material. The patient (via the abject self-state) is left holding an unbearable affect for which there is seemingly no resolution. In attachment terms, these affects represent "fright without solution" (Hesse & Main 1999, p. 484), a form of attachment disorganization characteristic of people who experienced mis-attuned, unpredictable, and frightening or frightened parenting, along with little or no emotional repair of distress. The abject enactment therefore constitutes "psychological performance art, complete with absorbing sensorial reality" (Chefetz, 2008), a performance art that powerfully conveys the patient's insecure attachment status. Therapists unaccustomed to working with dissociative processes may write off the abject enactment as masochistic character; alternatively, they may hope for the bizarre phenomenon to pass, preferring to work with the more functional selves of the patient. However, it may be more useful to explore this phenomenon as a communication of something important, in order to set a context for linkages between the various self-states of the patient, as well as between group members. Group therapists especially are in a unique position to support the thawing and opening of frozen self-states. By proxy, one person's breakthrough can become a breakthrough for the whole group.

Abject States: A Neural Network

Abject states are not easy to sit with. "The presence of the 'abject' causes us to flinch away, recoil and reject; it is the black hole, the abyss, the place in which all meaning collapses" (Adams, 2006). In the grip of abject feelings, one feels unworthy, unlovable, and in utter despair about the situation ever changing. Implicit memories of helplessness, dread, horror, and rejection are activated neurologically and communicated in posture, voice, and words. Abjection is a powerful neural network combining cognitive and behavioral components, sensory images of past experience, recollection of strong aversive emotions, and over-arousal (Folensbee, 2008).

Self-abjection is an interpersonal communication, an enactment of impossible need. Whereas projective identification can partially control unbearable affects by placing them into someone else, self-abjection conveys and preserves unbearable affects in complex enactments without achieving relief. Self-abjection represents a simultaneous enactment of need, rejection, horror, impossibility, and worthlessness that is closer to notions about the basic fault, hostile dependency, and the black hole than to pure object hunger.

The underlying world view of abject self-states is based upon the realization that one's being was formed in the face of the impossible, the unnatural, the unthinkable and the unspeakable. When abjection is embodied within the self as an identity equivalent, "the impossible constitutes its very being" (Kristeva, 1982).

Abjection of the self repels the other as ardently, and adamantly, as it simultaneously seeks proximity and connection; the abject individual defines himself by his certainty of unbridgeable space between himself and an unattainable object. During enactments the object of attachment is perceived only as a movement of rejection/dejection through the self, "like the wind through trees…the intangible ghost of a profoundly familiar [rejecting] other who inhabits the self and becomes indistinguishable from it" (Bollas, 1999). Past blurs with present as helpless yearning and embodied recoil from old rejections oscillate in a rhythm of doom. Implicit memories of abject, desperately insecure attachment are unanchored in time and lived out in the body, along with early working models of how life works that predict catastrophic rejection.

When Sarah crept uncertainly into group, she revealed abjection more powerfully than she could have in words. At core, Sarah has always described herself as a lost soul, metaphorically cast down upon a barren tundra, besieged by a blizzard, convinced that all hope of life being different is illusory. She experiences life as a series of one unendurable shock after another, echoes of a chaotic, frightening childhood. She has struggled from childhood with the worry: "What if there is nothing except the frying pan and the fire?" Part of her longs to sink silently into the snow's frozen embrace, to give up the futility of struggling for hope and vitality; yet another side of her is a vibrant artist and powerful professional who clings to life with ferocious tenacity and feels in harmony with the world when she is painting, befriending neighborhood children, practicing her profession, and gardening. Like many of my patients, Sarah slips in and out of abject states.

Abjection, Boundaries, and the Body-self

Abjection damages not only the identity-self but also the body-self. Children who grow up under conditions of neglect, abuse, attachment chaos, medical challenges and/or sexual assault not only develop a skewed sense of self, but their very experience with their bodies is compromised from the outset. How can they come to value visceral and kinesthetic aliveness when the body is a permanent repository of raw vulnerability, when the body has survived on toxic nourishment, a

veritable garbage dump (Eigen, 1996) for psychic and physical predation? Unspeakable terror involves the dissolution of the very boundaries of the self, the debridement of core self from psychic skin (Anzieu,
1989). "It is as if the skin, a fragile container, no longer guaranteed the
integrity of one's 'own and clean self' but, scraped or transparent, invisible or taut, gave way before the dejection of its contents" (Kristeva,
1982, p. 53). Kristeva elaborates how the abject person comes to reject
his body: "[The abject] presents himself with his own body and ego as
the most precious non-objects; they are no longer seen in their own
right, but forfeited, abject" (p. 5). These patients rarely feel good about
their physicality and are not truly embodied; their minds have become
the only refuge they can depend upon (Corrigan, 1995).

Intrusive Medical Procedures and Peritraumatic Dissociation

Chronic medical procedures can isolate children from their parents
and peer group and tax their nervous system with overwhelming pain
and helplessness. Jill was born with a hole in her brain that twisted
and compromised her left foot and leg (see Chapter 3 for more of Jill's
story). She had to endure ten brutal surgeries throughout her adolescence on orthopedic units where she was inundated with the constant
screams of other panicked youngsters in pain. Almost no parental
visitation was allowed, and Jill was often on display in the teaching
hospital as a fascinating case of pathology, which she found humili-
ating. Her parents were stoic intellectuals who encouraged toughness.
Her adolescence was difficult; she could not run, play, and dance as
others did.

She felt always that her face was pressed to a glass divider between
herself and people who knew nothing of deformity or handicap.
When discussions turned to sexuality and physicality, she put up the
same glass wall between herself and the rest of us by cringing and
complaining about how we "normals" had gotten the better deal in life.
She hated having a body at all; what pleasure had it ever brought her?

In one session Jill revealed that she had been having dreams about
a self-state called "Yuk" who pronounced that Jill was mousy, wimpy,
totally lacking in pizzazz and mostly dead. A series of self-portraits
emerged in art therapy, with handwritten notes indicating that Yuk
thought Jill disgusting and weak for having been a crybaby in the

hospital. The group embraced the Yuk side of Jill and urged her to share strengths with Jill instead of berating Jill for being human; everyone felt different in some ways. As the group and Jill/Yuk worked the abject issue together with compassion, Jill began to realize that she had gifts that others did not. She began to connect through laughter instead of simply through tears and empathizing with others' suffering. She transformed over a 2-year period into a lovely woman full of warmth and wit. No longer did she whine about how deformed she was. As the Yuk self-state began to integrate, Jill developed the confidence to date, leave group and finally fulfill a cherished dream of adopting a baby from China.

Bollas (1999) argues that turmoil intrinsic to transferential suffering *is* the presence of the object, and I agree that self-abjection preserves original abandoning/horrifying objects.

Yet he further asserts that suffering patients are resistant to treatment because quiescence leaves behind an intolerable void. My clinical perspective privileges implicit memory and dissociation over resistance, and intersubjective attunement/affect regulation over interpretation. I believe that the quiescence following attunement to the affective distress in abject states can constitute successful affect regulation, strengthening the attachment bond while dissociated unformulated experience (Stern, 2003) is processed. The abject self-state needs a treatment situation that is "dense with the feeling of safety" (Badenoch, 2008, p. xvii).

Encased in Deadness

Psychic death is the shadow of abjection, haunting many individuals who have wrestled with horror. Psychic deadness presents clinically across a wide spectrum, ranging from characterological listlessness and anomie (Eigen, 1996) to the dissociated dead selves of individuals who have splintered under the pressure of unbearable childhood experience.

In her core, the trauma survivor remains solitary in the moment of her own extinction. No one knew her in the moment when she died without dying: no one knows her now, in her lived memory of annihilation. This place where she cannot be known is one of catastrophic loneliness…it is an area of deadness strangely infused with a yearning for life...Death has possessed her in its impenetrable solitude. But life makes her desire to be known in that solitude... (Grand, 2000, p. 4).

Boulanger (2007) introduces another dimension of the dead self: the collapsed self. Adult-onset trauma survivors, and children like Jill who endured repeated exposures to terror after they developed a sense of self, experience dissolution of the baseline sense of self, the psycho-biological substrate that one normally takes for granted. The universe on which the self depends is obliterated, fractured into "before" and "after." Whereas catastrophic psychic trauma in early childhood usually results in the dead self being cloaked and sequestered in shards of "Not-Me" dissociated self-states (Chefetz & Bromberg, 2004) leaving the rest of the personality relatively free from knowledge of trauma, in adult-onset trauma (and traumatized adolescents like Jill) it is the "Not-Me" living self that is dissociated from the parts of the self that are suffused in deadness. The self collapses rather than fractures. Memories of a non- traumatized self become blurry and unreachable. It is never clear that the trauma has been survived until the full impact of psychic annihilation has been witnessed and turned into narrative, by assembling all the bits and pieces of self-experience and giving them meaning.

It is "...the death that happened but was not experienced" (Winnicott, 1974, p. 106).

Dead Voices in the Group: Leigh

An earnest, vulnerable, and resentful young man named Jacob joined the group. Leigh, a previously stable and committed member, careened into crisis upon his entry. Leigh was startled by the intensity of her panic. Whereas group had previously been her safe space, now group felt ruined and dangerous. She felt she could no longer tolerate staying in the group because Jacob was about the same age as her young adult daughter, who had terrorized Leigh several years ago with bipolar rages. The mother/daughter rift had largely healed, but Leigh felt as if the group atmosphere was as poisoned by the new group member as her home environment had been by her daughter. She was furious with the group's therapists for their empathic failure in not anticipating this development. Horrified by Leigh's intense reaction to him, the new member offered to leave the group and go elsewhere for his therapy;

the group challenged him to explore his own brushes with terror. Leigh offered to quit in his stead. The therapists consistently intercepted projections and interpreted that the group, as a whole, was ready to deal with fight/flight, paranoia, and annihilation anxiety.

The night that Leigh processed her paranoid reaction to the new group member, James (about to become a father) instinctively recognized Leigh's abject terror and paranoia as parts of himself. Shaking, he asked for help in putting what he felt in his body into words. "How deep can we go, and still get back?" he asked. "I think I'm feeling the abyss for all of us. I'm at the bottom." He described feeling terrified, nauseous, and on the verge of throwing up.

When I asked him "what was in the throw-up" (Griffin, 2008, personal communication) he said: "You are, and all the violence of my life and the terror and abandonment and hopes and despair and your damn vacations and the paranoia and love and hatred that we feel in here…the abject stuff too, I want to puke it all out before my daughter comes. I am shaking with the violence of this."

The group deepened over the next few weeks as the maw of the pit that James and Leigh had opened up was metabolized. Although Leigh continued to maintain that she might have to leave because she "could not work in this group anymore," her threats to leave felt specious and paradoxical, for she was more present than ever before. She brought in sculptures and paintings she had done of the traumatic years with her daughter, her reactions to Jacob, terror, and paranoia. James also brought in abject art. The group worked with the art as they would a dream. One night Leigh announced it was her last group and burst into tears of grief. We were all speechless: her departure didn't seem real, or possible. By the next session she was back, announcing that she had returned to group because she realized she was caught up in a profound enactment. Group as she knew it had to die in order for her to be able to live. She was not coming in as the same member who had left; she was a different Leigh, she insisted.

Over the next few months, we were able to piece together the fragments of this enactment. Leigh had grown up in a terrifying religious environment of hellfire and damnation. Despite the presence of several traumatized self-states, she had developed into a confident, relatively put together woman with deep bonds to her husband, children, and community. She had struggled off and on with major depression. As a teenager, Leigh's beloved daughter had spun out of control in a 3-year rampage of snarling contempt, malevolence, and physical violence, all of which occurred when Leigh's husband was not at home. He sided with the daughter and blamed Leigh's depression. Leigh felt that her chemistry had been irrevocably altered during these years, not into depression (she knew depression well), but into a dissociative, numb deadness instigated by her husband's denial and her daughter's violence. In individual sessions and group, she was frustrated with my attempts to link her adulthood trauma to her terrible childhood; I was proving to her that I did not truly understand her reality. In the face of her daughter's assaults, and emotionally abandoned by her spouse, she had actually experienced psychic death of the hopeful, loving, and confident mother-self: This disaggregated self experiences a "chronic sense of paralysis, numbness, disruption of the sense of time, and a feeling of rupture with the self who existed before the crisis" (Boulanger, 2007, p. 15). Recalling Boulanger's book, I suddenly understood that I was dealing with a collapsed adult self, not a dissociated self-state from childhood. Although she would not yet disclose what we were working on to the group, for several weeks a very different Leigh presented in group: her face took on a waxy, grayish pallor; her demeanor was wooden and unresponsive, and she appeared to be deeply dissociated. She reported amnesia for several group sessions. She was terrified to tell the group about her "dead self" because she was sure they would think her to be crazy. Another group member told Leigh that her face had been looking so waxen and gray that she looked like a corpse. Leigh finally took a deep breath and shared about her dead self-state. She couldn't breathe since Jacob had first walked into the room, she felt irrationally traumatized by his very presence. Group felt like it had died, and she had died, but at last she was grieving the deaths.

To Leigh's amazement seven other group members immediately joined her in a dead-self subgroup. James had been locked in a closet by his preschool teacher when his stay-at-home mother had returned to work; family lore has it that he became remote and withdrawn after this preschool year. He grew up in the inner city of a violent neighborhood and was the only surviving member of a close network of high school friends who had died violently one by one. Leigh's work galvanized him into creating a series of writings and paintings about his dead selves. Randall, a cleric, had lost a huge part of himself when his son nearly died from a serous suicide attempt, leaving a note blaming his Dad. Grace Anne, a rape survivor, joined in with memories of life after catastrophe. Isabelle, whose father would collapse into diabetic rages, wondered if she had ever felt anything but dead. Jacob, the new group member who had triggered Leigh, identified two dead self-states: one, a terrified little boy whom his parents never understood or related to emotionally; and another, the sexually abused little boy whom no one believed, because his abuser was the beloved star quarterback of the high school. Alister had turned to martial arts to restore vitality after his drunken father repeatedly tried to kill him and had died inside after he sexually abused his own little brother. Lisa, whose childhood was blotted out by a loveless silence, felt that she had been dead since birth.

It should be noted that for many years this particular group had earned from me the weary moniker of being the ultra-boring, "dead" *nice group*. The membership was selected on the basis of their relative discomfort with intensity, difficulty with self-expression, high level of functioning in their lives, the presence of neurotic conflicts, and a willingness to learn about feelings. The dissociated layers of deadness and abject terror catalyzed a deepening process that enlivened the group process. I have since learned to listen carefully for themes of dead states.

Death by Starvation: Mariah

Like acute shock, the chronic shock (Adams, 2006) of failed dependency and emotional neglect can create encapsulations of deadness and annihilation anxiety. One woman's dream reported nonchalantly in a different group opened my eyes to the prevalence of dissociative self-states in a composed, avoidant, high-functioning patient (see Chapter 6):

> A botanical garden had a rare and beautiful species of tree, lush with multicolored flowers and delicious fruit. The tree was slowly dying, however; unbeknownst to the caretakers, the ground beneath

the apparently healthy tree was frozen. The roots beneath the tree were rotting, starving, and desperate for nurturing attention.

(Adams, 2006, pp. 128–9)

This dream heralded a shift in my work with this particular group. Not only did this patient have a starving, dying baby self that had been almost entirely dissociated, but so did many of the other high-functioning patients in this group. However, at the time I completely missed the reference to the dead self in this dream; it took the "nice group" to teach me to listen for deadness. Recurrent dreams and dream series sometimes bear useful clues to underlying states of emotional starvation and abject self-states, as the story of Mariah will illustrate.

Despite her liveliness and vitality under other circumstances, Mariah had wept wordlessly and silently in the group since her entry. Mariah had always felt desperate and alone. A history of early childhood deprivation and terror was activated most recently by the death of her cat just before she entered group. Her bonding figure had been a purring cat, as her mother had had intermittent psychotic states and was emotionally rejecting and chaotic. As Mariah listened to the "dead self" subgroup, she finally began to understand about the dead part of herself; her face began to animate for the first time. She suddenly remembered a piece of history that she hadn't thought about in years: she had stopped speaking for a year as a toddler when her mother went away to a psychiatric facility. Mariah was left in the care of abusive grandparents for several years. Her vitality had withered on the vine, until the family cat began to share her crib with her. Of course, she was now decimated since the death of her 20-year-old cat; her psychic skin (Anzieu, 1989) had vanished along with him. Although her dead self did not vanish with this realization, she was able to make room for this part of herself without *becoming her*, or enacting her, any longer, and had compassion for the shocked silence of the toddler within. This is a recurring dream series from Mariah that illustrates the prominence of her dead self-states:

In an early version of the dream, I keep turtles in a terrarium. No matter how hard I try, the turtles turn black, and I find them dead. I feed them the wrong food or too much raw meat and the water turns poisonous and murky, and they shrivel up and die. In another version of the dream, I reach into the china cabinet only to find a shriveled up dying baby on the plate. It is suffering so much, I can hardly stand to touch it or even look at it. I pick it up in horror and it looks at me, chastising me with its eyes, turns black and dies.... I am in an aquarium filled with giant sea urchins heedless of my existence. I am a little fish and try desperately to stay out of the sea urchins' way. No matter where I turn, there are more giant sea urchins bobbing about. There is no safe place.

Self-abjection: A Barrier Experience

Abject affects are so difficult to tolerate that they are often encased in encapsulations such as roles that interfere with intimacy. Roles are autistic islands of body/mind that partially insulate us from unbearable affects while communicating these affects to others. Self-abjection is a "barrier experience" (Agazarian, 1997) that creates an impermeable boundary between self and other, as well as between the true self and the adapted self. "It is the role relationship with oneself inside the barrier experience that is the major source of human suffering" (p. 294). Inside a barrier experience one is pretty much trapped until one learns to question the tyranny of the role-induced beliefs. Suffering feels like *the* reality, *the* fate that others are too dense to understand, but actually when functioning from inside a barrier experience, one is cut off from any sense of destiny, from self-discovery and from becoming known by others. The spontaneous, true self is encapsulated away from the conscious self. Shame, outsider, cynicism, paranoia, and omnipotence are common roles that defend against the helplessness, shattering, and terror triggered by emotional vulnerability.

Relentless Despair: Barrier to Relatedness

Abjection is an unbearable preverbal state in which only need exists along with an active sense of being "jettisoned, repelled, and repellant" (Kristeva, 1982, p. 1). Condensing yearning and rejection, abjection is embodied in cringing postures and enactments of *ambitendence*: beseeching and disintegrating; desperation and recoil; raging against and pleading for understanding; worthlessness and demand. To feel abject is to plunge relentlessly into the horror of the black hole, of meaninglessness, of non-existence: "an awesome force of powerlessness, of defect, of nothingness, of 'zero-ness' expressed, not just as a static emptiness but as an implosive, centripetal pull into the void" (Grotstein, 1990, p. 257). The black hole of abjection embodies "relentless despair" about the possibility of being helped or soothed. Since abject experience tends to be a closed loop, reiterative and autonomous from actual positive experiences (Green, 1999), the challenge becomes timing and creation of a pathway inside. Therapists must weave their way through the maze of alienation and despair.

Alienation and Estrangement

Psychotherapy narratives featuring themes of suffering horror com-municate powerfully the nature of traumatized existence. The per-petuation of abject states may stem in part from the inevitable gulf that spans the difference between the traumatized and the normal. Children who grow up under conditions of neglect, abuse, or bereave-ment have an uncanny sense of how they are different from peers who have loving families.

> [T]he essence of psychological trauma…[is] a catastrophic loss of innocence that permanently alters one's sense of being-in-the-world. [Trauma] exposes the inescapable contingency of exist-ence on a universe that is random and unpredictable and in which no safety or continuity of being can be assured. Trauma thereby exposes the "unbearable embeddedness of being".… It is in this sense that the worlds of traumatized persons are fundamentally incommensurable with those of others, the deep chasm in which an anguished sense of estrangement and solitude takes form.
>
> (Stolorow, 1999, p. 467)

The misery intrinsic to roles of abjection relates to feeling different and untouchable. Group therapy can be a powerful mediator of the chasm of separateness between the abject self and the normal self, but the therapist must facilitate the linkage between self-states. Group treatment protocols abound for survivors of disasters (Spitz et al., 2006), who can turn to each other for help in developing a sense of meaning. However, the private catastrophe of childhood deprivation, abuse, or attachment chaos is largely suffered in despairing isolation. Early in life, the personal meaning of abject experience is established in implicit (procedural) memory as essential truth, an internal working model of how things are (Badenoch, 2008): "I am utterly, wretchedly alone. This is the way things are, were meant to be, and will be forever more."

Fate versus Destiny

Abject individuals feel "fated" to be denied the joys of being human that others take for granted; hence, when positive moments do occur, they may flinch away instead of embracing them. Fatedness (Bollas, 1991) comprises projections of past experience into the future, manifestations of relentless despair and fear of breakdown (Winnicott, 1974). The fatedness of abject individuals keeps them from using the connections they have with others to build a self and a life. Destiny (Bollas, 1991), on the other hand, entails developing a vision of whom one might ultimately become, along with pursuing an active strategy for moving toward this end. Self-abjection entails an enactment of fatedness and doom, an interpersonal role of relentless despair. Hopper (2003) believes that such roles serve to provide the traumatized self with an identity within a field of chaos and turmoil. While no doubt each persistent maladaptation serves some survival function, I believe that self-abjection is first and foremost a complex preverbal communication of "the unthought known": a mood or physiology in implicit memory that we know intimately but cannot think about, or have not yet thought about (Bollas, 1987). Isabelle struggled to recognize or share thoughts and feelings spontaneously; she experienced a formidable blankness that amputated any sense of internal experience.

Her mother had had a traumatic childhood and was depressed much of Isabelle's life. Isabelle's father was subject to diabetic rages when his blood sugar dropped. Isabelle would hide under the table as he screamed. Before entering group, she had extensive neurological workups to rule out petit mal seizures or other brain abnormalities because she had difficulty forming emotional memories. She couldn't recount or even remember most of her life experiences. She felt utterly inept at life and would tearfully break into frozen panic whenever she tried to talk in group. She was convinced that her future will deliver only more of the same and that she would continue to fall further and further behind her peers in creating any vision for herself. She couldn't imagine what she might like to do over a weekend, much less what career path to pursue. She felt like a hamster on a wheel, trying madly to get somewhere but ending up at the beginning.

Isabelle likened her panicky self-consciousness to that of a speaker hearing his own voice reverberate on a microphone; as she listened to herself speak, her ideas began to dissolve and her words to lose significance, becoming random sounds devoid of meaning. Ogden (1989) describes anxiety states bordering on panic when the symbolic and binding power of language becomes dismantled, a state which leads to a sense of disconnection from other people who know how to share with each other in a meaningful system of words. Isabelle was convinced she was boring and a total drag to listen to and had no idea how to respond to others' affects except to offer hollow advice. She didn't feel she deserved to be loved or even liked since her insides were so empty of vitality. Traditional analytic therapy made her feel completely hopeless; she couldn't even do therapy "right." For the first few years, she experienced group as a great divide between normal people and herself. In our individual sessions I was unusually active and self-disclosing. We laughed a lot, and she began to look forward to her sessions instead of dreading them. Early "homework" was to find three opportunities to say anything at all in each group. Slowly she began to experience moments of spontaneity that did not dissolve into meaninglessness, and to make connections between past and present. Her group validated Isabelle whenever she spoke from bodily experience instead of robotically from her mind. Instead of flinching away from bodily cues, she began to get excited when she noticed she might be feeling something.

Over the years I have observed the power of even a spark of the destiny drive to light up the darkness of abjection. Usually the trigger is some unexpected exposure to positive affect, a dimension of neural circuitry that is sadly underdeveloped in this population. Positive experiences have incredible power to awaken latent internal strengths. Sometimes the spark is kindled by a spontaneous musing on the possibility of innate potential that was smothered by indifferent or absent parenting: "I wonder what I would have been like had I been raised by different parents?" One woman with a history of severe abuse had her life turned upside down as she happened to gaze in the newborn nursery at a hospital while visiting a friend and was filled with awe. She realized that once, long ago, she had been innocent and full of potential like those babies. I have seen the acquisition of a kitten or puppy melt the heart of grim old codgers who were waiting to die. The matrix of group therapy provides multiple opportunities for threads of destiny to interweave with fatedness to alter the tapestry of life experiences and choices.

Incoherence of Narrative

Incoherence of narrative, the holes in the story of one's life, is one indicator of disorganized attachment and dissociative states. The narratives of individuals who struggle with abjection and relentless despair are replete with the tangles and confusion of unrelieved traumatization and chronic shock (Adams, 2006). These holes in narrative discourse and consensual meaning-making can waylay the therapy, creating a spiral of confused negativity (as occurred in the following example). After group one night Sarah waylaid me in my waiting room to bring up the issue of her bill again. It had been a long day and I just wanted to get home and relax. She had bugged my office staff repeatedly about wanting them to write out in longhand the diagnostic and medical service delivery codes on her bills. I didn't understand the purpose of this and showed her that the codes were printed on the superbills, as were the diagnoses. She started to cry and said she would write them herself, but it was illegal to do so. I rationally replied "Ok, bring them in; we'll do it for you," in the "patient" tone I usually reserve for young children and the very impaired. As I struggled to understand what was going on, I told her I could tell she was frustrated with me, and I just wanted to fix everything the way she wanted; what was I not understanding? She cried harder, saying that it had been like this all her life: she couldn't make people understand what she needed and had been stupid for even trying. Finally, a light bulb went off for me: group statements were not printed on superbills, like other therapy sessions, but on my accounting system, which for some reason doesn't include CPT codes or diagnoses. Nobody else I saw in combined treatment bothered with sending the group accounting statements for insurance reimbursement. I asked her if I had understood her correctly yet, and she tiredly nodded at me saying that she had been trying for a month to get this done so that she could pay me what she owed me, and then hurried out of my office. We were later to discover that her elementary school experience had been a nightmare of mis-attuned communications like this.

Abject enactments are a way to "show" rather than "tell" about experiences with rejection, neglect, and profound deprivation. Indeed, the "telling" about abject experience is often incomprehensible because of cognitive interference, flashbacks, and over-reliance on metaphor. Metaphor allows complex threads of nonverbal experience to be woven together and offers a road map to inner experience that is inscribed in a personal language. Yet if it is mixed in with chaotic narrative discourse deriving from a lifetime of trauma and disorganized attachment, metaphor can be difficult to follow (van der Kolk, 1987).

Sarah would often break down in frustration when other group members indicated that they were struggling to understand her. Listening to her sharing in group was a bit like winding one's way through a complicated maze; eventually one was bound to reach the exit, but it was difficult to sort blind alley from direct path. She would start in one place and end up in another, her words either captivating or confusing the listener, depending on their tolerance for right brain communications. Her words were eloquent with visual images and metaphors, always shared with earnest vulnerability and purpose, often laden with dialogue and scenes from classical books and movies. "I think in pictures…I can't connect them until I tell you all the pictures." When group members expressed their confusion about what exactly she was trying to talk about, Sarah would flinch and pull away, collapsed into an alienated humiliation that is all too familiar to her from her school days. "If emotional charges cause the return and re-enactment of scenes, the [traumatized] child is pulled toward predominantly visual and less developed and interactive structures of thought…. Time sequencing is difficult because of the concentration on the here-and-now" (van der Kolk, 1987, p. 99). Eventually Sarah learned to "get to the point" or to at least "translate" the metaphors for us.

The Abject Self in Life Metaphors

Although metaphor can sometimes be as difficult to follow as poetry, it can also capture and convey the essence of a dilemma in a way that straight discourse might evade. "I long for a time when clinicians routinely consider the potential for the existence of unspoken words, images, sensations, and more, that are the unwanted property of people rendered speechless by inescapable painful experience" (Chefetz, 2008, p. 38). Life metaphors, which condense the thematic narratives of a life into poetic symbolism or concretize visceral implicit memory, poignantly articulate nonverbal experience. Life metaphors abound in personal narratives but could easily be overlooked if the therapist is not alert. Metaphors describing abject experience typically involve a level of preverbal fear, alienation, and/or deprivation for which there is no coherent language available (Chefetz, 2008). Some life metaphors are quite straightforward: Marilyn talked of loving to read books and watch movies about survival after shipwrecks or other catastrophes, like Robinson Crusoe. Other life metaphors are difficult to decipher at first. Because of the gaps and tangles extant in incoherent narrative, metaphorically rich language can appear psychotic or grossly disorganized when it actually may signify abrupt changes in self-states and/or the underlying presence of dissociative processes (Chefetz, 2008).

Mariah experienced frantic anxiety states that tended to alienate her peers. She used to make up stories about herself in an attempt to coerce empathy from others, such as describing a time she nearly died in a house fire. In group she came to understand her compulsive lying as abject enactments, attempts to bridge the gap between herself and others, to convey her lifelong suffering and horror. Even if the stories were not factually accurate, the underlying affects of desperation, terror, and horror conveyed in these metaphoric stories aptly captured the nature of Mariah's emotional existence. Her life metaphors reveal traumatic attachment:

> I am blindfolded, stumbling through a cactus forest. I am stabbed by needles no matter where I turn. ...I am in the ocean, choking on water and pummeled by waves, terrified I am going to drown. I can't catch my breath. Then, I find myself collapsed on a beach. I cling to the warmth and solidity of the beach, digging my fingers into

the sand to reassure myself I can stay put. But then the waves come and drag me out into the water again. …Birds are flapping around and screams are trapped in my head. …I was making chicken soup and was overcome by horror when the backbone of the chicken disintegrated in my hands; what was holding me together, would I disintegrate like that? …When my husband and I fight, everything just keeps getting worse, we're in a particle accelerator chamber going faster and faster until we are smashed like atoms and then I hear glass break inside my head and we shatter into shards.

The Power of "We"

What keeps people mired in abjection is the utter isolation endemic to lifelong fragmentation and annihilation anxiety. Many individuals with backgrounds of deprivation, failed dependency, and attachment chaos often have little sense of being part of a "we" for at least the first 12 or 13 years of life. These youngsters struggle to metabolize overwhelming experience for themselves in isolation, intuiting the futility of trying to raise themselves. They are forced to develop a brittle, precocious appearance of self-reliance because of premature awareness of their separateness and excessive vulnerability. Their misery is "their" problem to solve. Even siblings in such families have such an experience of drowning in the muck, they climb upon each other's backs simply to survive. In adolescence, youngsters may turn to a peer group or romantic relationship to stabilize themselves, but invariably these relationships spiral into failure as abjection, scapegoating, disorganized attachment, and desperation intercede. If they can successfully rely on their intellect to get by, they at least can thrive in academic and work settings; they become high-functioning dissociative individuals who look like they have life figured out because they make a good income (Adams, 2006). Relationally, these individuals may be a disaster. Raising their own children to have secure attachment is a major challenge. By the time they arrive in our offices, they have endured many cycles of hope and collapse; they are worn out, and they wear us out.

The most powerful interventions a therapist can offer are intersubjective compassion and contingent communication. The transformation of "you have a problem" into "we have a problem to figure out together" is a profound difference in perspective that promotes attachment, affect regulation, and neural integration. Overwhelming pain in early childhood becomes encapsulated within an individual's implicit body memories (procedural memory) and cannot be worked through without affective resonance from a therapist who can tolerate immersion in primitive experience. When we are called upon to witness an unbearable experience, we sometimes put up a wall to protect ourselves a bit from the rawness of horror by using experience-distant language, describing from an outside perspective (Kohut, 1971, 1978), instead of using experience-near, intersubjective language (resonating from the world view of the patient). The consequence is that our most vulnerable patients may feel more abject and alone. With patients who experienced little attunement or interactive repair in childhood, it is vital for them to discover that "someone is available who is capable and desirous of knowing what it feels like to be him or her" (Stern, 1985, p. 266). With chronically traumatized individuals, the core curative factor in therapy is the gradual facilitation of earned secure attachment provided by a sense of safety, a holding environment, and being "seen" and "met" (Schore, 2003; Siegel, 1999).

Nonverbal Attunement

Soothing an abject patient is not unlike soothing a distressed infant: "the baby in the patient" (Mitrani, 2001) needs our nonverbal acknowledgement of, and attunement with, his distress. Words alone will simply not be effective. We are destined to fail repeatedly in our attempts to relieve our patients' distress, until we accept it as "really real," and feel it from the inside out. It is helpful to approach abjection nonverbally at first, with especial attention paid to distancing maneuvers on the part of the therapist. On a good day I attempt to monitor my tone of voice, posture, gestures, and facial expressions, trying not to back away despite my patients' earnest efforts to create a circle of hell meant uniquely for them alone. Engaging eye contact with a person in an abject state is crucial, as it breaks up the isolation intrinsic to the enactment. Shame literally begins to dissolve if the individual encased in shame looks slowly around the room and permits emotional connection with other group members. I talk about self-abjection and abject affects with my groups, describing how it feels and looks until invariably several group members join the discussion with personal examples. Therapeutic soothing of abject states is not by nature pre-emptive nor enabling, but contingent communication.

Really Getting It

It has not been my experience that interpretation is particularly helpful to many group patients in abject states. "As a primary factor in psychic change, interpretation is limited in effectiveness to pathologies arising from the verbal phase related to explicit memories, with no effect in the pre-verbal phase where implicit memories are to be found" (Andrade, 2005, p. 677). A mis-timed verbal interpretation (left brain intervention) risks creating attachment distress (Schore, 2007) and/or disintegration (Knox, 2008), whereas attuned emotional engagement (right brain intervention) promotes self-reflection and integration. Interpretation during turbulent and painful enactments of abjection is often an attempt by the therapist to dissociate away from affect, ground himself, and resist the pull toward the primitive (Bromberg, 2006).

Patients in abject states don't simply *want* to be understood, they *need* to be met and understood. While frustration of wishes may promote growth, frustration of real needs results in structural disintegration of the self (Akhtar, 1999). In abject enactments, patient and therapist are stirred up at the same psychic level: both are invited to endure the terror of annihilation. When our work begins to slide into the abyss despite our best efforts, we may fail patients in three primary ways (Van Sweden, 1995): dropping them, withdrawing from them, or trying to get them to stop suffering. "If a group therapist does not develop oneself with regard to his or her personality, the members of that group will only in a very limited way be able to broaden their identity" (Richarz, 2008, p. 158).

When we offer our reality of a problem, treating "messes as mere potholes" (Bromberg, 2006) that the therapy must bump across (as I did with Sarah and our billing "mess"), we ignore the abyss that the patient is falling into. Sarah's screams at me masked the desperation and shame that were being dissociated by both of us in the interaction.

Understanding that the mess is an abyss and not simply a pothole requires us allowing the patient's abjection to enter into our psychic reality, to become *"really real"* (Bromberg, 2006; original emphasis) instead of just "real for the patient." Trying to talk "about" or stop what is happening only makes the nightmare worse. Being able to take on a trial identification with the abject patient is an essential step in being able to lead him out of the labyrinth: "There is an obligation to know intimately your own unique resonating pain in the quest to make the other's pain coherent, livable...This is a relational matrix woven from threads of intense pain..." (Chefetz, 2008, pp. 18–19). Yet, the temptation to withdraw, to jettison, to reject the abject patient is strong, as Richarz (2008) notes in his exploration of enactments in group: "I did not want to meet myself in her suffering" (p. 146).

Interruptions in the Rhythm of Safety

Interruptions in the rhythm of safety between patient and therapist sometimes cross the threshold between surprise and shock, the harbinger of mutual traumatization (Bromberg, 2006). In these situations, Winnicott's fear of breakdown (1974) is operative: we dread a terrifying future that has already occurred to us many years before. Implicit memory has no time stamp: the sense is of something happening *now*, with no awareness that the past has been triggered (Badenoch, 2008). The feel of a looming treatment crisis echoes that of any attachment ruptures from early childhood. The cycle of rupture, repair, and the inevitable attachment distress that accompanies a treatment crisis bring powerful signals to the therapist's soma that are helpful to listen to and acknowledge. For example, I knew my interaction with Sarah over the bills had made me feel a bit crazy. I realized something was wrong with what I was doing, but I couldn't figure out what was happening. In our next group I asked Sarah what was going on inside her on that night we had the struggle about bills. She said she felt like she was drowning, going under for the third time, right in front of me, and that I didn't even notice or care. It reminded her of being sent home from first grade with a demand from a teacher about needing a check for school pictures: "Just tell your mother she needs to write a check first, before I can send them home with you" and then encountering the crazy-making of her mother saying, "You tell that teacher I'm not paying for pictures until I see them." Back and forth between them she trudged, a ping-pong ball of chaotic confusion. As she cried about how hard it had been to make me understand what she needed, I was able to acknowledge how deeply my not understanding had traumatized her. No longer was I treating her abyss as a little pothole. The group responded by offering up other ways in which I had failed to understand them. Affective repair was underway.

Subgroups: The "We" in the Group

Group therapy offers significant hope for individuals struggling with abject affects if they can work the feelings alongside several others who are doing the same thing. Empathic attunement from a therapist is necessary but not sufficient, because the abject patient may misconstrue empathy as pity. When peers join in the maelstrom with their own version of abjection, then the darkness of the abyss automatically lights up with solace. One patient likens this to being linked by a belay rope to another mountain climber who can stop the plummet should one person lose his balance. Working within a subgroup (Agazarian, 1997) allows for a deepening of the level of intimacy around an issue without one group member becoming the identified patient doing work for the entire group. It also allows room for group members who feel different and are not trapped in a defensive role (perhaps they are feeling hopeful, or in a good mood, for example) to form their own subgroup, rather than being highjacked by suffering. Working an issue alongside others doing the same provides a sense of perspective. Subgrouping allows the barrier experience to be dismantled by the undeniable fact of joint ownership of a troubling affect state. As the perceptual field is broadened, fear is slowly supplanted by curiosity and study of the phenomena in others. When other group members also acknowledge cynicism, despair, shame, deadness, or paranoia, the unbearable aloneness of underlying abjection is abated.

As group members recognize themselves in the abject communications of others, they can by turn balance, confront, and support each other. Randall and Leigh were adamant about reminding each other of their considerable strengths, especially when one or the other of them collapsed into a misery of self-recrimination over parenting difficulties. Sarah and Paul often supported each other during abject meltdowns. Sarah started off the group in tears of wonder one evening, reporting that Paul had murmured to her in the parking lot after group the week before: "Let's agree to approach next week with courage, ok?" These simple words had changed her life. Not only had no one ever offered her the perspective of *"let's"* before, but no one had ever suggested that she live in courage. "My friends urge me to be more self-confident, but I can't find a way to live in a world of confidence. The word means nothing to me. Living in courage, though: *courage* is something I can and will do." As several other group members resonated to the concepts of "let's" and "living in courage," *the power of we* gained momentum.

Tracking Hope: Hallmarks of Change

"One reason that therapeutic growth takes as long as it does is that the mind's self- state organization is linked to the brain's organization of neural networks" (Bromberg 2009, p. 352). As long as the *same* groups of neurons continue to fire and wire together in unchanged fashion (as in abject states), it is difficult for other groups of neurons to wire into the neural network to allow new self-experiences to integrate into the self-as-a-whole (Bromberg, 2009). Because so many interactions in group involve safe surprise and novelty (like Paul's comment to Sarah), group therapy offers many opportunities for inspiration, self-observation, and skills acquisition. New skills such as self-soothing can support the destiny drive and facilitate identification with one's own growth potential.

Somatic Markers and Self-soothing

Patients struggling with unbearable affects have learned to dissociate from their bodily experience; they have not experienced sufficient soothing to be able to calm themselves down when feelings surge. "In the dissociative mind, what is remembered…is a somatically lived experience of ripped flesh and disemboweled self-esteem ready for instant replay" (Cheftez, 2008, p. 24). An important part of their therapy work is learning how to self-soothe. In combination with explorations and group discussions about the nature of self-soothing, the notions of fear of breakdown and implicit memory have been transformative. Self-attack, a response to early shame about dependency, is ritualized in abject states. When I introduce the notion of self-compassion to my groups, it meets with derision and incredulity. Yet the interception of self-attack is an important early step in the transformation of abject states into mourning. As somatic experience is the birthplace of affective awareness, affects frequently present first as physiological states. Learning to notice and ask about physiological states helps the therapist and group work with abject affects. Somatic markers are bodily feelings that normally accompany our representations of the safety or danger of a social situation. In other words, feelings *mark* response options to our felt sense of what is happening around us (Damasio, 1999). Most importantly, patients need to learn to *mark* positive as well as negative experiences as significant. Most self-soothing takes place in the context of remembered positive experiences that have been marked and noticed as calmative: laughter with a friend, appointment television, the rhythm of a walk, the purr of a cat, the soft fur of a beloved dog, immersion in a movie, the burble of a brook or aquarium, the comical play of pets, the hum of a sewing machine, music, the smells and textures of a bookstore and its denizens, etc.

Asking group members about bodily experience teaches the group to track somatic cues about what they may be experiencing. By becoming more self-aware, hypervigilance and enactments can be replaced by self-reflection and curiosity. A paranoid patient may observe that things feel like they are going too fast again, or that she feels surrounded by enemies, and reminds herself not to freak out; her terror is from the past. A panicky patient may share that he has an urge to leave but may delay the impulse while telling himself that exploration will help. A patient frozen in an abject state may notice that she covered her mouth and turned away just as she asked for connection. A patient in the midst of a shame attack may stop the attack mid-thought and ask for help instead. As the observing self learns to notice when self-abjection has just occurred, abjection begins to shift away from an ego-syntonic mechanism of communication, a way-of-being-in-the-world that feels entirely normal and familiar. Instead, patients begin to notice something "off" in the way they feel or think and link their thoughts and somatic feelings with a familiar role. A shame-ridden patient may observe that her tears are forming a wall to keep others out again. An "outsider" patient may ask for help in bringing herself into the group instead of stoically enduring alienation and blankness. Suffering can then be shared and explored, "talked about," instead of being endured and enacted.

I find it particularly useful to comment on subtle shifts the patient is making that might be outside their awareness. The work is so pains-taking and difficult, every little step forward is a victory; I think in terms of years, not months, for changes to be integrated.

Patients will protest that they still feel the same misery and there-fore couldn't have changed at all. No matter where we go, there we are; we can't outrun our shadows. Light at the end of the tunnel is imperceptible to us because it's a long, twisty tunnel; it is normal to despair at its length and darkness. Psychic growth occurs at a snail's pace. We need to envision our patients' future selves until they can actualize bits of their true destiny. In our feedback, we spotlight hope and perseverance; the patient is part of a "we" that is paying attention. James used to chafe in silent annoyance with Isabelle, telling his individual therapist that Isabelle reminded him of a blank canvas with holes torn throughout. He refused to talk with Isabelle about these feelings in group because he sensed they would devastate her. As Isabelle became more alive, James finally was able to tell her about the canvas metaphor. As he noticed swaths of vibrant color replacing the empty holes, he observed multiple layers of depth developing within her and was moved by what he saw. This feedback was the spark that catalyzed Isabelle's renewed commitment to growth. She might suspect my feedback of being motivated by positive bias, but she intuited that James was nothing if not bluntly honest. If he saw her changing for the positive, then it was the truth.

A watershed of critical mass in the growth process occurs when the patient notices himself saying or doing something constructive that he never would have said or done at one time. Raine, an entrenched skeptic about therapy, caught herself saying to a friend: "Just breathe through the pain, it will pass, and you will be the better for it." Leigh noticed herself enjoying Jacob instead of fearing him. Isabelle laughs more and has begun to open to her sexuality. Although the music of suffering may seem the same, the lyrics are actually different. We, and they, have actually arrived at a different place in the spiral that is growth. "So we sit, no longer only healer and healing, but two souls on one journey, each facing the Void, each alone and together" (Steele, 1991, p. 14).

Acknowledgment

The chapter has been taken from K. Adams, The abject self: Self-states of relentless despair. *International Journal of Group Psychotherapy* (2011). Copyright © 2011. Reprinted with the kind permission of Taylor & Francis Ltd, www.tandfonline.com on behalf of the American Group Psychotherapy Association.

References

Adams, K. (2006). Falling forever: The price of chronic shock. *International Journal of Group Psychotherapy,* 56(2), 127–72.

Adams, K. (2011). The abject self: Self-states of relentless despair. International Journal of Group Psychotherapy, *56*(2), 333–64.

Agazarian, Y. (1997). *Systems centered therapy for groups.* Guilford.

Akhtar, S. (1999). The distinction between needs and wishes: Implications for psychoanalytic theory and technique. *Journal of the American Psychoanalysis Association,* 47, 113– 51.

Andrade, V. M. (2005). Affect and the therapeutic action of psychoanalysis. *International Journal of Psychoanalysis,* 86, 677–97.

Anzieu, D. (1989). *The skin ego.* Yale University Press.

Aposhyan, S. (2004). *Body mind psychotherapy: Principles, techniques, and practical applications.* Norton Press.

Badenoch, B. (2008). *Being a brain-wise therapist: A practical guide to inter-personal neurobiology.* Norton Press.

Bollas, C. (1987). *The shadow of the object.* Columbia University Press.

Bollas, C. (1991). *Forces of destiny.* Free Association Books.

Bollas, C. (1999). *The mystery of things.* Routledge.

Boulanger, G. (2007). *Wounded by reality: Understanding and treating adult-onset trauma.* Analytic Press.

Bromberg, P. M. (2006). *Awakening the dreamer: Clinical journeys.* Analytic Press.

Bromberg, P. M. (2009). Truth, human relatedness, and the analytic process. *International Journal of Psychoanalysis,* 90, 347–61.

Chefetz, R. A., & Bromberg, P. M. (2004). Talking with "me" and "not-me": A dialogue. *Contemporary Psychoanalysis,* 40, 409–64.

Chefetz, R. (2008). *Nolens volens* out of darkness: From the depersonal to the "really" personal. *Contemporary Psychoanalysis,* 44(1), 18–39.

Corrigan, E. G., & Gordon, P. E. (1995). *The mind object.* Jason Aronson.

Damasio, A. R. (1999). *The feeling of what happens.* Harcourt-Brace & Company.

Eigen, M. (1996). *Psychic deadness.* Jason Aronson.

Folensbee, R. (2008). The brain in psychotherapy: A framework. *Texas Psychologist,* Winter, 17–21.

Grand, S. (2000). *The reproduction of evil.* Analytic Press.

Green, A. (1999). *The work of the negative.* Free Association Books.

Grotstein, J. (1990). Nothingness, meaninglessness, chaos, and the "black hole." I, *Contemporary Psychoanalysis,* 26(2), 257–90.

Hegeman, E., & Wohl, A. (2000). Management of trauma-related affect, defenses and dissociative states. In R. Klein & V. Schermer (Eds.), *Group psychotherapy for psychological trauma* (pp. 64–88). Guilford.

Hesse, E., & Main, M. (1999). Second-generation effects of unresolved trauma in nonmaltreating parents: Dissociated, frightened, and threatening parental behavior, *Psychoanalytic Inquiry,* 19(4), 481–540.

Holmes, L. (2009). The technique of partial identification: Waking up to the world. *International Journal of Group Psychotherapy,* 59(2), 253–66.

Hopper, E. (2003). *Traumatic experience in the unconscious life of groups.* Jessica Kingsley Publishers.

Keleman, S. (1985). *Emotional anatomy: The structure of experience.* Center Press.

Knox, J. (2008). Response to "Report from borderland." *Journal of Analytical Psychology,* 53, 31–6.

Kohut, H. (1971). *Analysis of the self.* International Universities Press.

Kohut, H., & Wolf, E. (1978). The disorders of the self and their treatment. *International Journal of Psychoanalysis,* 59, 414–25.

Kristeva, J. (1982). *The powers of horror: An essay on abjection.* Columbia University Press.

Le Doux, J. E. (2002). *The synaptic self.* Viking.

Liotti, G. (2004). Trauma, dissociation and disorganized attachment: Three strands of a single braid. *Psychotherapy: Theory, Research, Practice and Training,* 14(4), 472–86.

McWilliams, N. (1994). *Psychoanalytic diagnosis.* Guilford.

Mitrani, J. L. (2001). *Ordinary people and extra-ordinary protections: A Post-Kleinian approach to the treatment of primitive mental states.* Taylor and Francis.

Ogden, T. H. (1989). *The primitive edge of experience.* Jason Aronson.

Richarz, B. (2008). Group processes and the therapist's subjectivity: Interactive transference in analytical group psychotherapy. *International Journal of Group Psychotherapy,* 58(2), 141–60.

Schore, A. (2007). Review of *Awakening the dreamer: Clinical journeys* by Philip M. Bromberg. *Psychoanalytic Dialogues,* 17(5), 753–67.

Schore, A. (2003). *Affect regulation & the repair of the self.* W. W. Norton & Company.

Siegel, D. J. (1999). *The developing mind: How our relationships and the brain interact to shape who we are.* Guilford Press.

Solomon, J., & George, C. (Eds.). (1999). *Attachment disorganization*. Guilford.

Spitz, H., Danieli, Y., Schein, L., & Burlingame, G. (Eds.). (2006). *Psychological effects of catastrophic disasters: Group approaches in treatment*. Haworth.

Steele, K. (1991). Sitting with the shattered soul. *Treating Abuse Today*, March/April, pp. 12–15.

Stern, D. N. (1985). *The interpersonal world of the infant*. Basic Books.

Stern, D. B. (2003). *Unformulated experience: From dissociation to imagination in Psychoanalysis*. Analytic Press.

Stolorow, R. D. (1999). The phenomenology of trauma and the absolutisms of everyday life. A personal journey. *Psychoanalytic Psychology, 16*, 464–8.

van der Kolk, B. A. (1987). *Psychological trauma*. American Psychiatric Press.

van Sweden, R. (1995). *Regression to dependence: A second opportunity for ego integration and developmental progression*. Jason Aronson.

Winnicott, D. W. (1974). Fear of breakdown, *International Review of Psycho-Analysis, 1*, 103–7.

Index

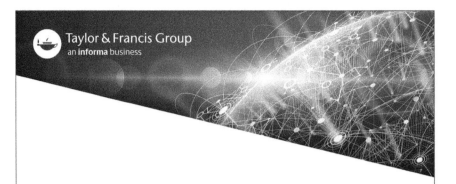

Lightning Source UK Ltd.
Milton Keynes UK
UKHW022048010323
417894UK00005B/14